IMAGES
of America

VILANO AND THE NORTH BEACHES

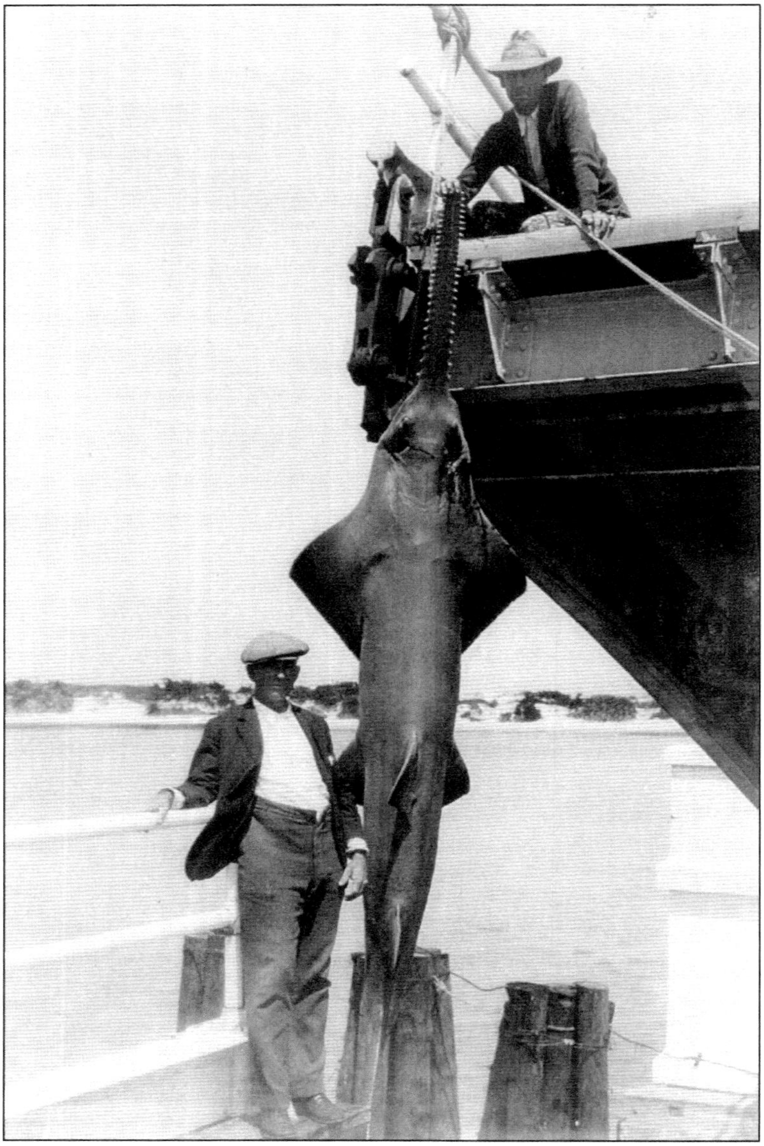

Isolated from the mainland, residents of Vilano and the North Beaches thrived at using any available resource. The first bridge connecting Vilano to downtown St. Augustine was constructed in 1927. It was subsequently replaced by newer structures, the last built in 1995. Here, Daniel Webster Borum, father of Mary Borum Usina, after whom the newest bridge is named, displays a huge sawfish hoisted by the drawbridge and a friend. (Courtesy of Elizabeth and Frank D. Usina.)

ON THE COVER: This grand entertainment and recreation mecca was built by New York philanthropist August Heckscher. He opened the Mediterranean-style facility at Vilano Beach in 1927. His St. Augustine & Atlantic Company also completed the Vilano Toll Bridge. Over the years, many locals and tourists used the bridge to drive their automobiles from St. Augustine to this oceanfront casino for social events. (Courtesy of St. Augustine Historical Society.)

IMAGES
of America

Vilano and the North Beaches

Vivian C. Browning, Sallie L. O'Hara, and John T. Pilecki
with Vilano Beach Main Street

ARCADIA
PUBLISHING

ISBN 978-1-4671-1435-6

Published by Arcadia Publishing
Charleston, South Carolina

Printed in the United States of America

Library of Congress Control Number: 2015932397

For all general information, please contact Arcadia Publishing:
Telephone 843-853-2070
Fax 843-853-0044
E-mail sales@arcadiapublishing.com
For customer service and orders:
Toll-Free 1-888-313-2665

Visit us on the Internet at www.arcadiapublishing.com

This book is dedicated to founders of Vilano and the North Beaches for their pioneer spirit, which lives on today.

Contents

ACKNOWLEDGMENTS

Many individuals were instrumental in assisting the Main Street leaders in creating this book, and we are grateful for their willingness to share treasured family photographs. Many of these photographs document the untold local history of the first settlements on the island. This book would not have been possible without a committed effort by all of our supporters.

With the help of a core group of Vilano Main Street volunteers, Main Street president Vivian C. Browning, MEd, along with program manager Sallie L. O'Hara and John T. Pilecki, spent many hours talking with residents and families and collecting long-forgotten photographs. Unlike in prior publications, new images of intimate and closely connected coastal communities emerged from the time of Ponce de León's landing until the present day. If we have overlooked anyone, please forgive the omission. We wish to thank the Vilano Main Street Board of Directors, and we especially recognize long-standing community activists and contributors Sacha Martin, Mary Lou McEver, Tom Barry, Elaine and Jim Dilbeck, Jacqueline Johns, Dr. Barrie Jo Price, Dr. Anna McFadden, and members of the North Shores Improvement Association.

The authors wish to express appreciation for the generous outpourings of stories and images from historians, fishermen, photographers, and longtime residents, including the following: the St. Augustine Historical Society, the Beaches Museum and History Park, Cynthia Barrancotto, Jimmy and Marilyn Beach, Philip Bernstein, Beth Rogero Bowen, Mary Louise Usina Brown, Brendan Burke, Susan Burke, Terry and Maria Burke, Jane Clifford, Jackie and Nadine Connahay, Walter Daniels, Karen Harvey, Henry Hird, Dawn Jones, Joan Kramer, Irene Kaufman, Cecelie Lavinghouse, Mel Longo, Bunny and C.J. Manucy, Art McGinnis, Terran McGinnis, Thomas Parham, Glen "Bo" Pitts, Carole Prior, Tom Rahner, Mark and Cindy Scott, Frank and Susan Timmons, Judy Tripi, Jackie Ward, Phillip Whitty, and Sue Williams.

Many of the images from the recent past are from Sacha Martin, editor/archivist for the *North Shores News* for North Shore Improvement Association and Vilano Beach Main Street. A substantial amount of turn-of-the-century photographs are from Elizabeth and Frank D. Usina, whose family dates to the earliest settlement era in the 1900s. Their ongoing contributions to the community are unsurpassed to this day.

INTRODUCTION

Vilano and the North Beaches have been the backdrop to the history of the nation's oldest town founded by Europeans—St. Augustine, Florida. For hundreds of years, this barrier island remained a buffer for the town against pirate attacks and various takeover attempts. The peninsula had natural protective features and was surrounded by water and marsh for fishing and hunting by indigenous peoples and early settlers.

Ponce de León of Spain came ashore just north of this area and founded Florida in 1513. The explorers of this period documented their travels with maps and ships' logs. These records led Pedro Menendez back to this area to permanently settle what is now St. Augustine, just south and within view of these north beaches. From the early 1500s through permanent settlement, this area was subject to Spanish rule, which lasted up to 1764, when the British took over. During the early British period, plantations were established in the northern area (the Guana), reflecting the way of life in the British colonies to the north. Archeological research in the area has confirmed these early but temporary efforts at farming along the coast. During this time, the American Revolution was being fought; however, these coastal areas remained loyal to the Crown. After the Second Spanish Period, all of Florida became an American territory in 1821. Florida became the 27th state admitted to the union, in 1845.

During the Civil War, Florida joined the Confederate States of America, then rejoined the United States after the war. The first permanent settlement of this area came three decades after the war, in 1890, with the founding of North Beach. After Henry Flagler brought railroad lines to St. Augustine, a company from Macon, Georgia, brought a railroad line from across the river to these beaches. It connected to the main north-south line in St. Augustine. North Beach was the closest beach for tourists visiting the grand Flagler hotels in St. Augustine. The new community included a beach pavilion with a pool. A bathhouse allowed tourists arriving in formal attire to change into their modest woolen swimsuits. This company also offered vacant lots for sale. The pavilion was destroyed in a fire in 1895, and the development venture was abandoned shortly thereafter.

Frank Andreu and Catherine "Kate" Usina moved to North Beach in 1900, into a home left behind by the unsuccessful railroad project. With hard work and perseverance, this first pioneer family started businesses serving tourists and locals oysters and fish caught in the North River, and operated a tour boat, the *Victory I*, and horse-drawn trolley to bring tourists and locals from St. Augustine to the beach. Their restaurant and tour-boat businesses, started more than 100 years ago, thrive today under the leadership of descendants of the original Usina family.

In the early 1900s, another pioneer family, Paul and Helen Capo, established a tour boat and horse-drawn trolley south of the North Beach community, along the North River and the ocean to what became Surfside Beach. In 1904, the Capos moved to land south of North Beach along North River. They built a dock on the river in the area of what is now Surfside Avenue, formerly Capo Avenue. This family also ferried tourists and locals from the bayfront in St. Augustine to the oceanfront on the east side of the property in their boat, the *Pauline II*. During their years here, they platted the area as North Beach City in 1914. The plat shows a pavilion, hotel, horse trolley rail line, and bathhouse at the beach. This land was sold to the Mario brothers, who re-platted it as Surfside subdivision in 1926.

In 1939, the North Shores Improvement Association, Inc., a civic group, was founded and held its meetings in Surfside. This group and its community center, built in the 1950s, as well as the surrounding recreational park and fire station in Surfside, continue today as integral parts of Vilano and the North Beaches. Today, Surfside is the site of many permanent homes, and a portion of Surfside is included in the Vilano Beach Town Center. The earliest plans for the area that became Vilano Beach started as a result of the Fountain of Youth, opening to tourists across the bay in 1901. The site included plans for the Fountain of Youth Hotel. The owners of this site also owned the oceanfront land across the bay at what was to become Vilano Beach. These owners started a causeway from Magnolia Avenue and began building a toll bridge across the North River to the beach. They sold the land and partially finished causeway and bridge in 1924. The bridge was purchased and completed in 1927 by the company that founded Vilano Beach.

The turning point in the history of this area was the building of the coastal highway and the first bridge into St. Augustine in 1927. This road, which runs the length of Florida's east coast, brought automobile travelers from near and far to Vilano and the North Beaches. Vilano Beach was founded by the August Heckscher Company of New York City. It was located on the Atlantic oceanfront, along the newly built Vilano Road to the base of the new drawbridge into St. Augustine.

Vilano is the only community on this peninsula originally designed as a town. The official plat recorded in St. Johns County records shows locations for businesses and residences along Vilano Road, with service alleys and a wide boulevard like small towns in the Northeast. From the time the Vilano Beach Casino was built in 1927 to attract development, through the Depression and World War II, until today, Vilano Beach has had a colorful history of business owners providing services, restaurants, and accommodations to residents and tourists.

For more than 100 years, Vilano and the North Beaches have mirrored the growth of other beachside communities along the coast of Florida. While keeping its small beach-town feel, the uniqueness of this area is its closeness and shared history with the oldest town of European origin in the United States, St. Augustine.

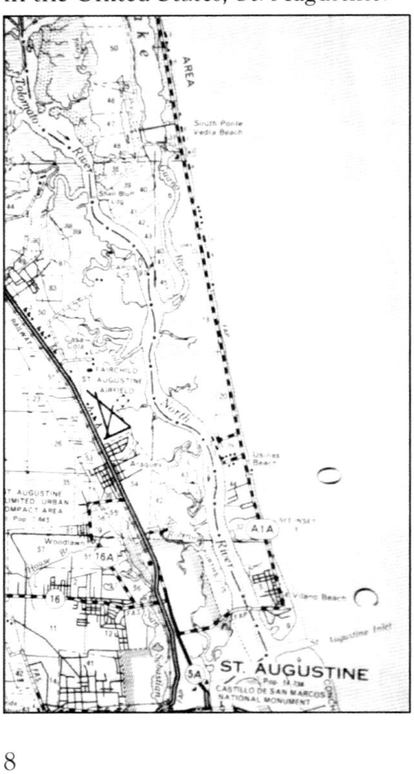

This 1962 Florida road map shows the coastal communities of Vilano Beach, Usina Beach, and South Ponte Vedra. Vilano and the North Beaches are within two miles of the city of St. Augustine. Pioneer settlers viewed history from across the bay and served as guardians of the inlet into historic St. Augustine. (Flagler College Archives.)

One

The Early Years

In 1513, Ponce de León sited land at latitude 30 degrees, 8 minutes north in Northeast Florida at Guana Preserve in South Ponte Vedra. The landing left the new discovery unexplored until Pedro Menendez arrived with Spanish settlers in 1565 to establish the first settlement.

In the early 1700s, there was a British attempt to capture the city. A fort built in 1698 provided shelter for residents as the city burned. In 1764, the British returned by treaty, as British-held Cuba was exchanged for Spanish St. Augustine, leaving the British to govern.

The British Crown assigned James Grant as governor. He was given 1,400 acres where the North River and Guana River meet, four miles northeast of St. Augustine. Grant's Villa Plantation used African slaves to clear the land for lucrative indigo farming. He provided each slave family a house. As the North River land was worked out and depleted in nutrients, rice was planted. Other plantations began to appear and prosper.

The Revolutionary War resulted in a British exodus, creating the Second Spanish Period. The Villa Plantation barely survived. In nearby New Smyrna, Grant's overseer learned of Minorcan and other European farming prowess on the part of indentured slaves. Then 500 Minorcans accepted an invitation to receive acreage at the Villa to farm and share earnings. Their resulting walking journey is of historic importance to the North Beach lands they claimed in the summer of 1777.

The Spanish overseers issued a headright (grant) providing 100 acres to the head of a family and 50 to each family member. Joseph Arnau accepted the grant and created White Oyster Bay Plantation. Several other families accepted, and soon there was a North River Settlement with 130 people (1797 census). With Arnau's death, the land passed to three generations.

As Florida moved toward statehood in the 1800s, Fort Mose provided refuge for runaway slaves. The Civil War found St. Augustine amid another transition. The city's history of cultural reception and change made it a destination for plantation owners as well as for freed and escaping slaves. The North River–Guana Peninsula was once again a point of departure for change.

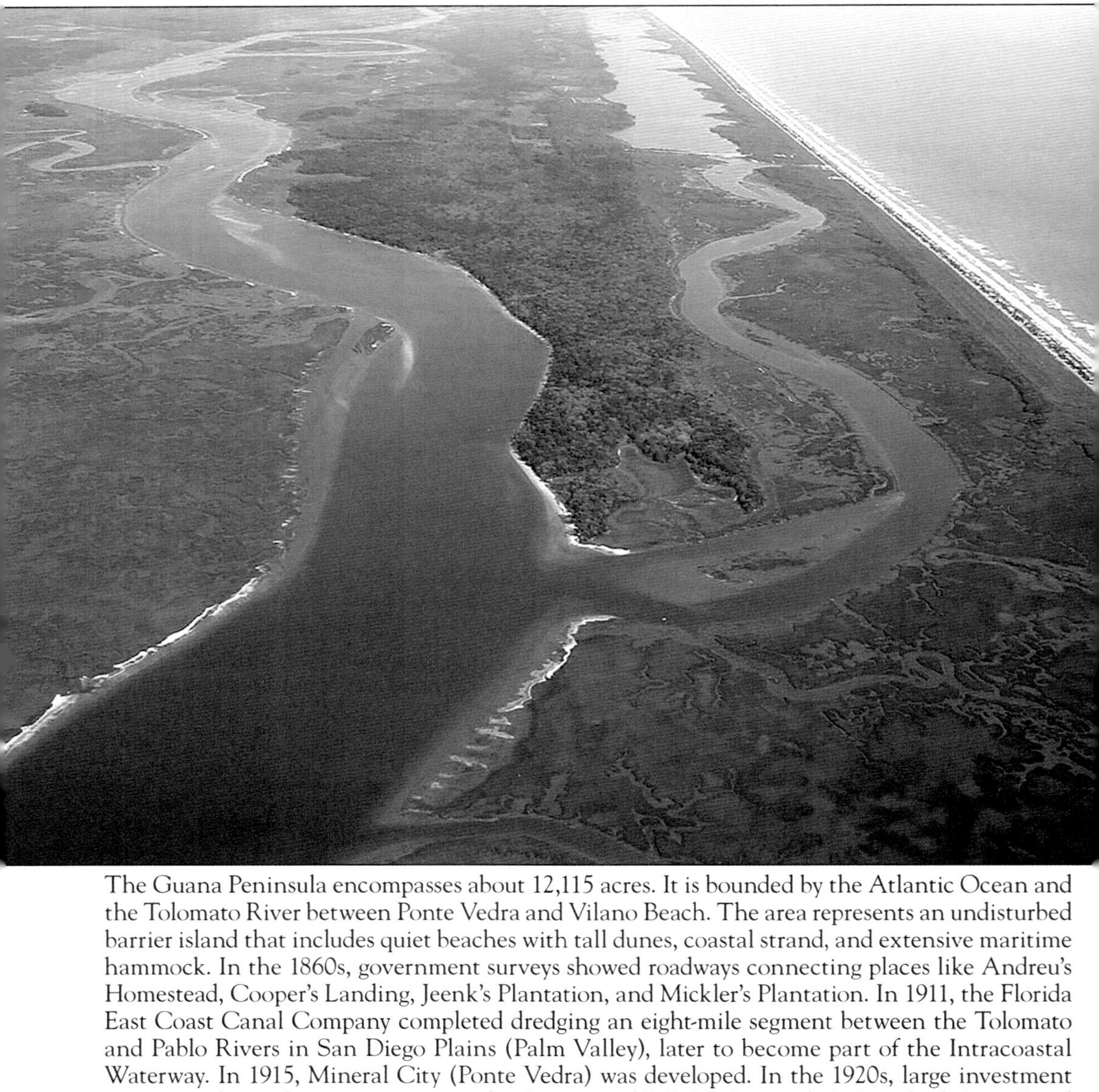

The Guana Peninsula encompasses about 12,115 acres. It is bounded by the Atlantic Ocean and the Tolomato River between Ponte Vedra and Vilano Beach. The area represents an undisturbed barrier island that includes quiet beaches with tall dunes, coastal strand, and extensive maritime hammock. In the 1860s, government surveys showed roadways connecting places like Andreu's Homestead, Cooper's Landing, Jeenk's Plantation, and Mickler's Plantation. In 1911, the Florida East Coast Canal Company completed dredging an eight-mile segment between the Tolomato and Pablo Rivers in San Diego Plains (Palm Valley), later to become part of the Intracoastal Waterway. In 1915, Mineral City (Ponte Vedra) was developed. In the 1920s, large investment companies began buying property in the Guana, and B.B. McCormack & Sons built State Road A1A, which connected communities. Construction of the Guana River Dam (1957–1961) enhanced the habitat. In 1984, the State of Florida purchased the property as a wildlife management area. In 1999, the Guana Tolomato Matanzas National Estuarine Research Reserve (GTM NERR) was designated. It is managed by the state in partnership with the National Oceanic and Atmospheric Administration. (Courtesy of Tom Barry.)

At noon on April 2, 1513, Ponce de León's navigator took a reading of 30 degrees, 8 minutes (the only known reading) before coming ashore to claim the land for Spain to La Florida. A statue, marker, and nature overlook now mark the location in the GTM Research Reserve. Residents annually celebrate the landing with reenactments. In this rendering, de León's ship, *El Espíritu de Santiago*, waits offshore. (Courtesy of the St. Augustine Historical Society.)

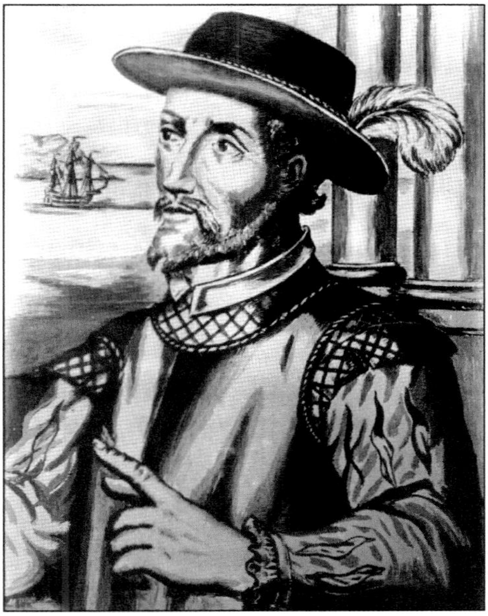

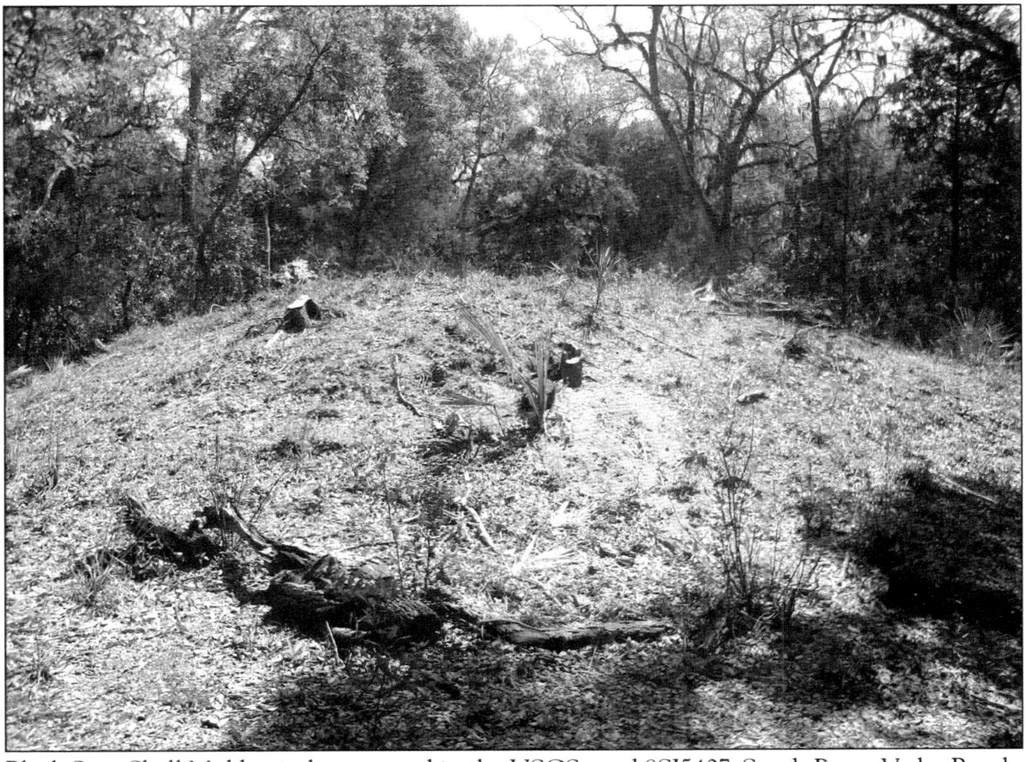

Black Soot Shell Midden is documented in the USGS quad 8SJ5407, South Fonte Vedra Beach, the approximate location of the later Grant's Villa. Middens are dump sites of materials revealing past human activity. There are several archaeological shell middens and mounds in this coastal area, providing insight into the life of the Guana River cultures in the days prior to the arrival of the Spanish. (Courtesy of Tom Barry.)

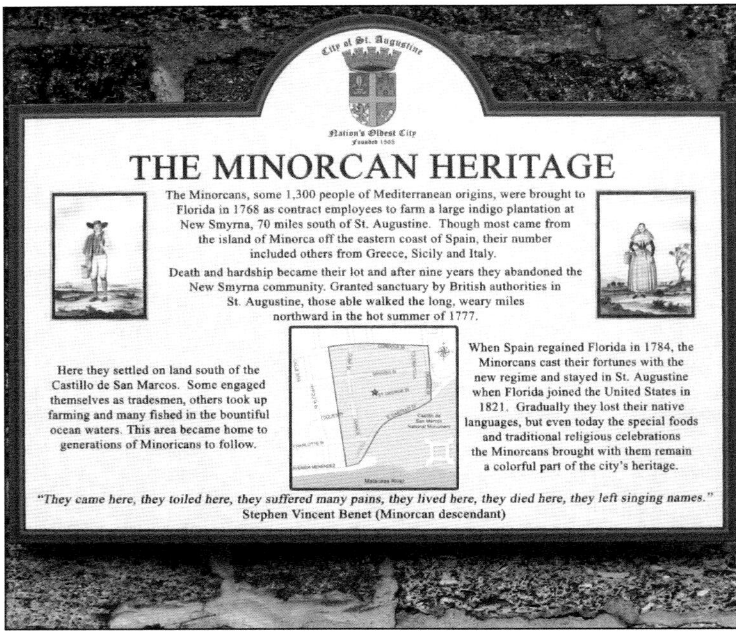

The Minorcans were brought to Florida in 1768 as contracted laborers to farm a large indigo plantation in New Smyrna, 70 miles south of St. Augustine. Author Stephen Vincent Benet's forefathers were among those who settled in St. Augustine and, later, its farming environs, including Governor Grant's Villa Plantation. The north part of the city was sparsely populated until the Minorcans arrived. (Courtesy of the City of St. Augustine.)

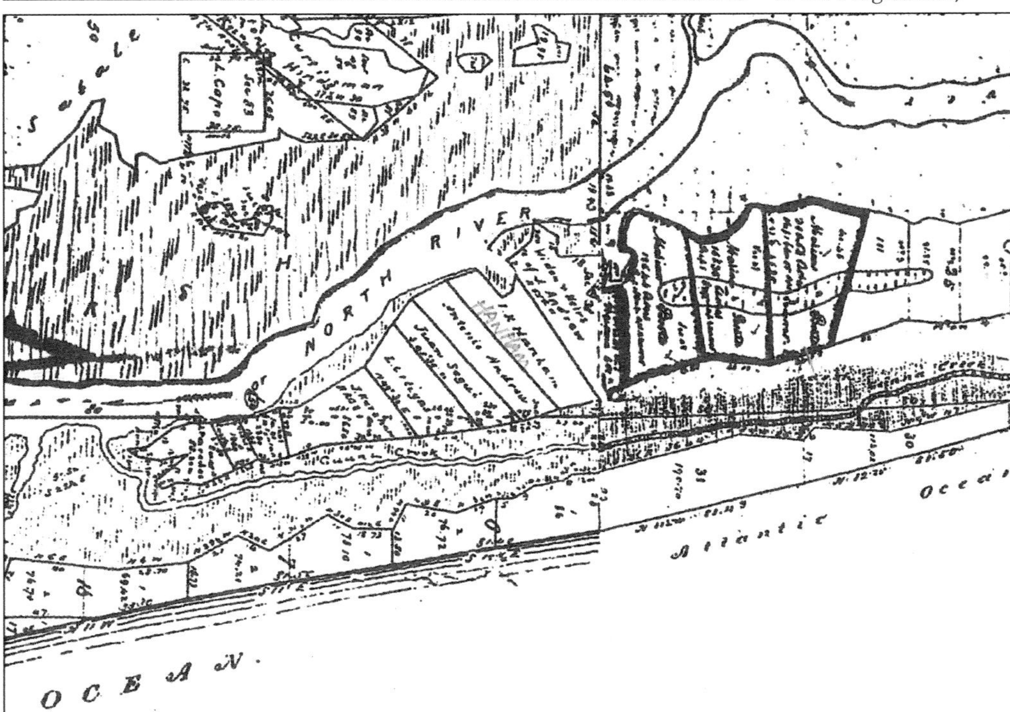

English colonies continued to harass the Spanish. Gen. James Olgethorpe laid siege to San Augustin and captured the Spanish Fort Diego, in present-day Palm Valley. The British later acquired Florida by treaty, and British subjects invested in lands for farming. The anti-American governor James Grant lost his holdings after the British departed. Headrights (grants) were awarded to Minorcan settlers along the North River. (Courtesy of Tom Barry.)

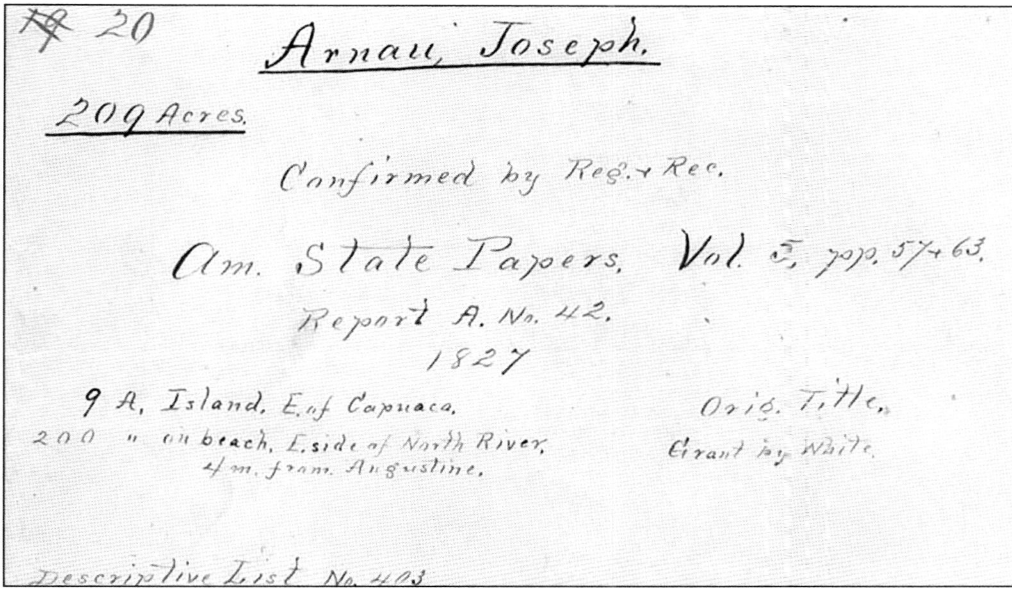
#20
Arnau, Joseph.
209 Acres.
Confirmed by Reg. & Rec.
Am. State Papers, Vol. 5, pp. 57 & 63.
Report A. No. 42.
1827
9 A, Island, E. of Capuaca. Orig. Title,
200 " on beach, E. side of North River, Grant by White.
4 m. from Augustine.
Descriptive List No. 403

In 1784, Spanish king Carlos III decreed that British landowners could keep title to their land if they swore allegiance to Spain and converted to Catholicism. Most British subjects departed, and the Guana River area was settled by Minorcan farmers. Joseph Arnau's 209-acre Spanish land grant is located four miles north of St. Augustine, on the east side of the North River. The grant was confirmed by Congress in 1827. (Courtesy of Florida Memory.)

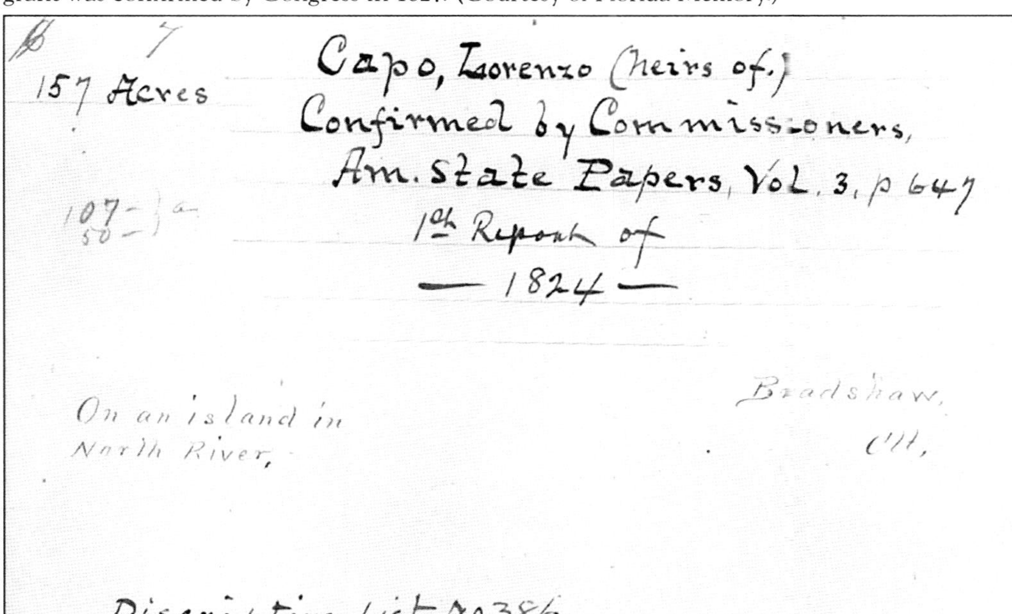
7
157 Acres
Capo, Lorenzo (heirs of.)
Confirmed by Commissioners,
Am. State Papers, Vol. 3, p 647
1st Report of
— 1824 —
On an island in North River,
Bradshaw, Cll,
Discriptive List No 386.

Family names, such as Andreu, Arnau, Canova, Capo, Genovar, Masters, Pacetti, Perpal, Ponce, Reyes and Usina, reflect the legacy of Minorcans, who struggled for survival. They were known as "a distinct community retaining their natural features, language, religion and manners, yet honest, simple and laborious in their occupations as fishermen and farmers." Lorenzo Capo's 15-acre land grant is "on an island in North River." (Courtesy of Florida Memory.)

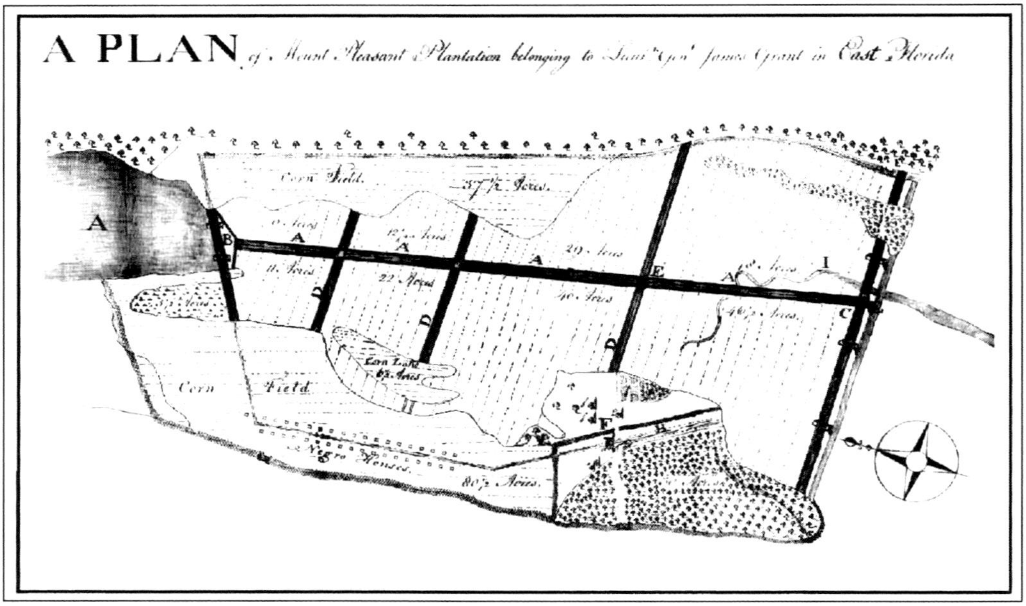

This 1780 land map features Mount Pleasant Plantation, where Gov. James Grant grew rice using extensive irrigation systems. He built two dams by 1782, and profits exceeded expectations. A dam currently still exists at the Guana Tolomato Matanzas National Estuarine Research Reserve, near the Educational Center. (Courtesy of Tom Barry.)

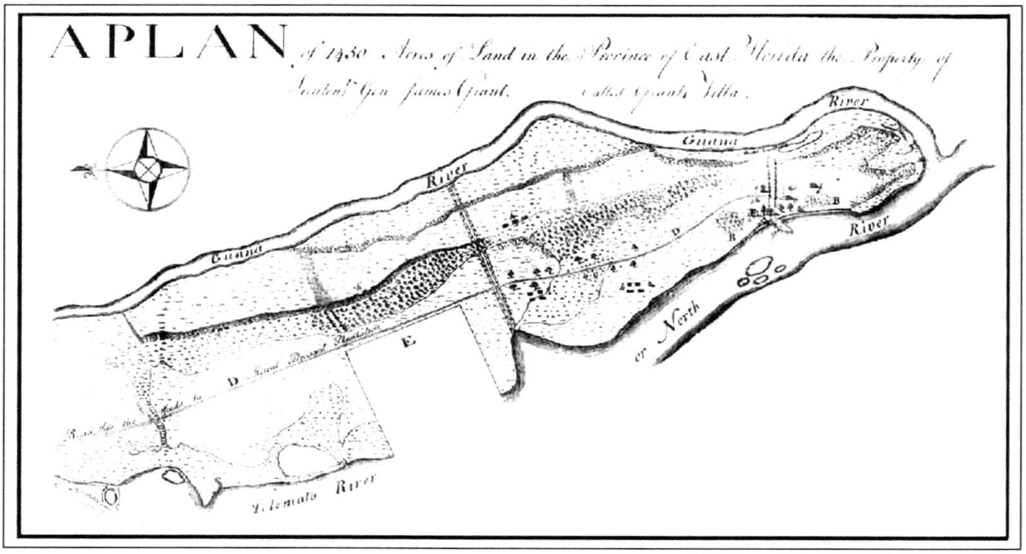

This 1768 map identifies Grant's Villa Plantation, a prosperous farming area bounded by the Tolomato and Guana Rivers. By 1777, all the indigo fields were exhausted and land was converted to provision crops and naval stores, such as lumber, pitch, and turpentine. Former indentured laborers from Minorca worked the land. (Courtesy of Tom Barry.)

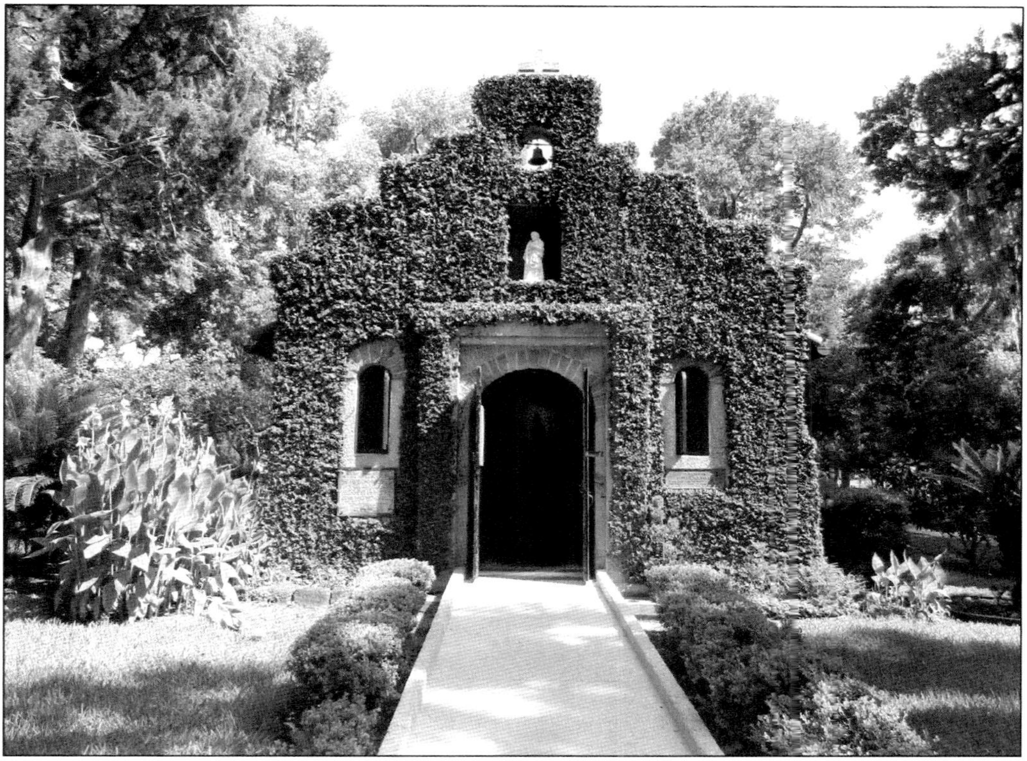

The current chapel of the Mission de Nombre de Dios is a reconstruction, representing many prior buildings destroyed by fire over the centuries. Catholic services were a high priority from 1565 to 1595. Missions employed a system of moving goods and people using Native American labor. In the early 1600s, Franciscan missions, including the Nuestra Senora de Guadalupe de Tolomato, appeared in the Guana River area. (Courtesy of Tom Barry.)

Pre-Columbian Archaic and St. Johns Period middens are also located at Wright's Landing. This 49-acre tract also produced Spanish barrel artifacts from later times. Native American population is estimated at 25,000 on the Florida Peninsula prior to the arrival of the Spanish. By the end of the Second Spanish Period in 1821, the Native American population was pushed out or taken as slaves. (Courtesy of Florida Memory.)

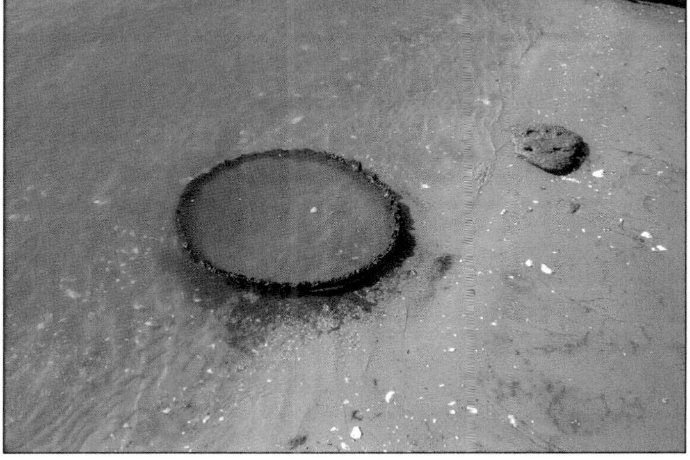

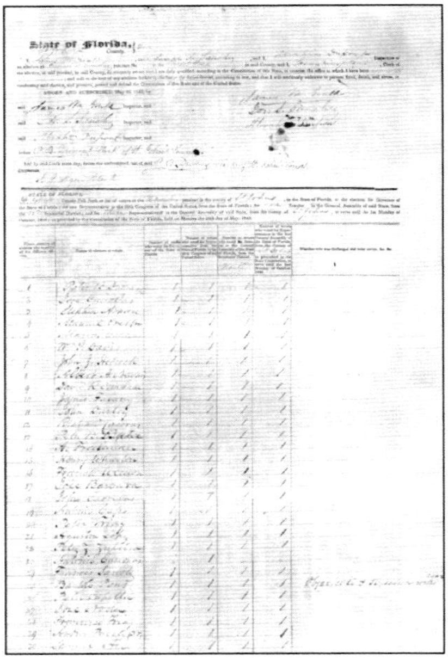
State of Florida,

Florida became a US territory in 1821 and a state in 1845. There were eight registered voters in the "North River Precinct-House of Edwin T. Jenckes." In the 1860s, the Dorr coastal survey map shows a roadway beginning at Shell Bluff and heading north. Among identified places are Andreu's homestead, Cooper's Landing, Jeenk's Plantation, and Mickler's Plantation. (Courtesy of Florida Memory.)

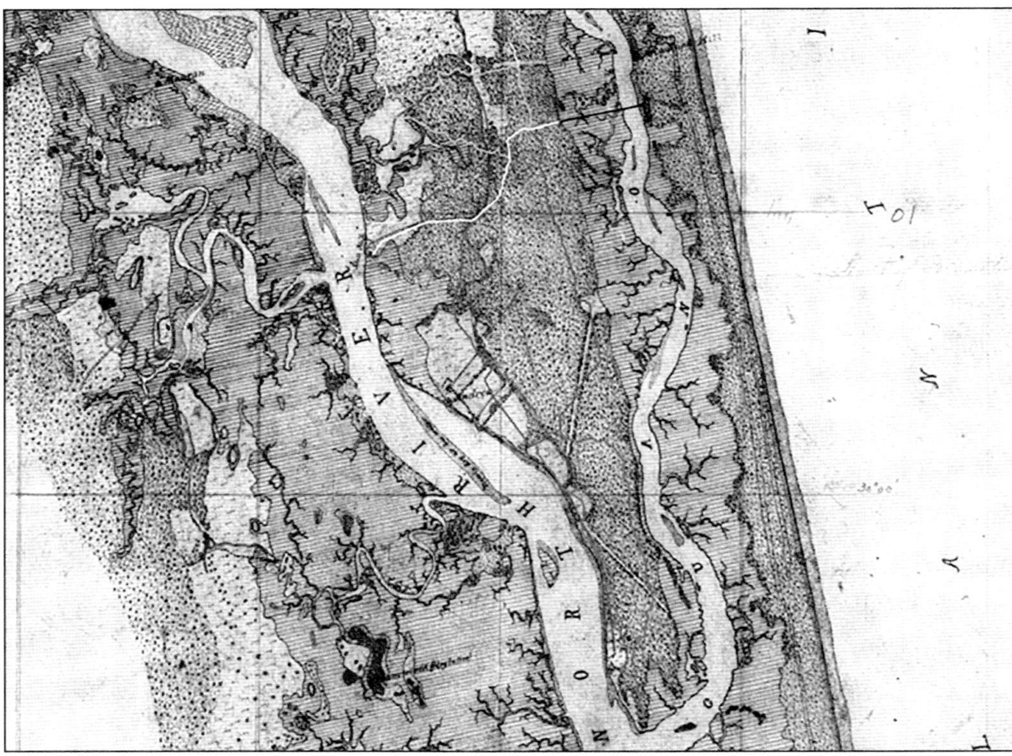

Governor Grant established large plantation tracts at the fertile area where the Guana and Tolomato Rivers merge. Subsequent Minorcan landowners worked the emerging farmlands, yielding bountiful crops for the nearby city of St. Augustine. This 1860s Dorr coastal survey map details terrain and waterways, which still retain their pristine state at the GTM Research Reserve today. (Courtesy of Tom Barry.)

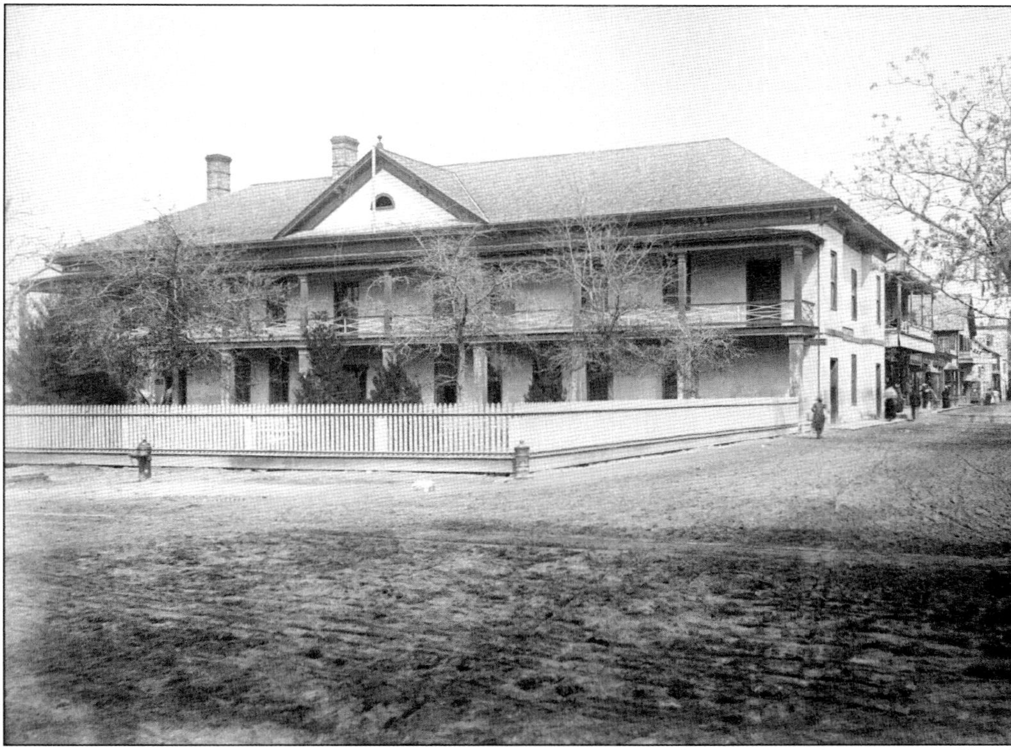

The Government House in St. Augustine has been used by Spanish, British, and American officials since 1604. It was destroyed in 1702 and renovated in 1759 by the British governor James Grant. Upon his departure, his Spanish successor remodeled it again. Americans have used the building for civil offices. This 1886 photograph depicts a large building, then called the "Courthouse," for the soon-to-be growing city. (Courtesy of the St. Augustine Historical Society.)

EST. 1565

St AUGUSTINE™

CELEBRATING 450 YEARS

Don Pedro Menendez arrived with European settlers in 1565, fifty-two years after Ponce de León claimed La Florida for Spain. The oldest continuously settled town founded by Europeans in the United States, the City of St. Augustine celebrates its 450th anniversary on September 8, 2015. Much of its history is rooted in the development of coastal communities across the bay. (Courtesy of the City of St. Augustine.)

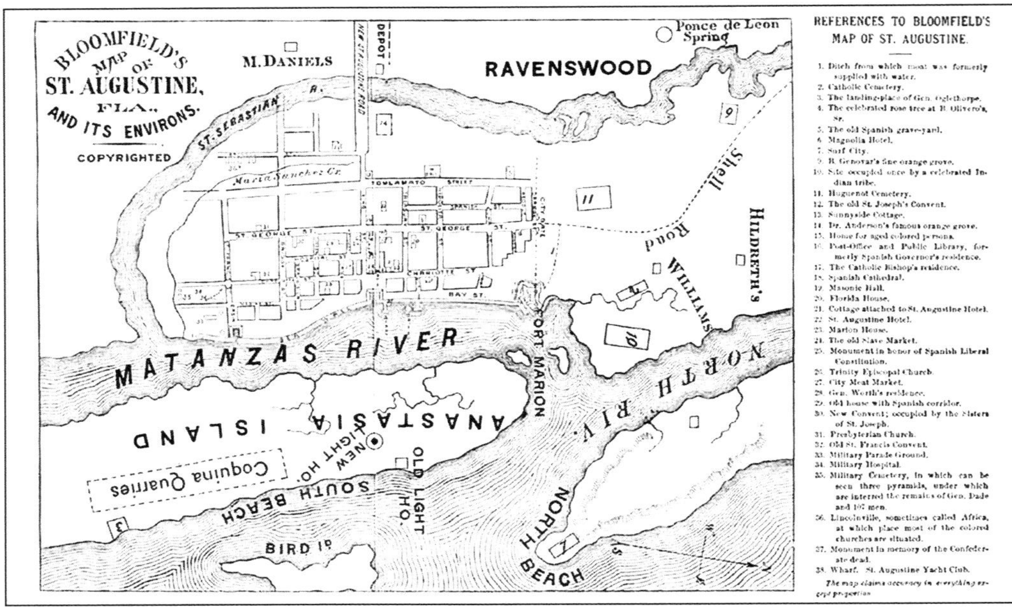

This 1884 Bloomfield's map of "St. Augustine, Fla., and its Environs" depicts the barrier island and North Beach in the lower right corner. Vilano Beach, then called North Beach, is within two miles of St. Augustine. Pioneer settlers served as guardians of the inlet into historic St. Augustine. Surf City is identified as no. 7 on the reference chart. (Courtesy of Henry Hird.)

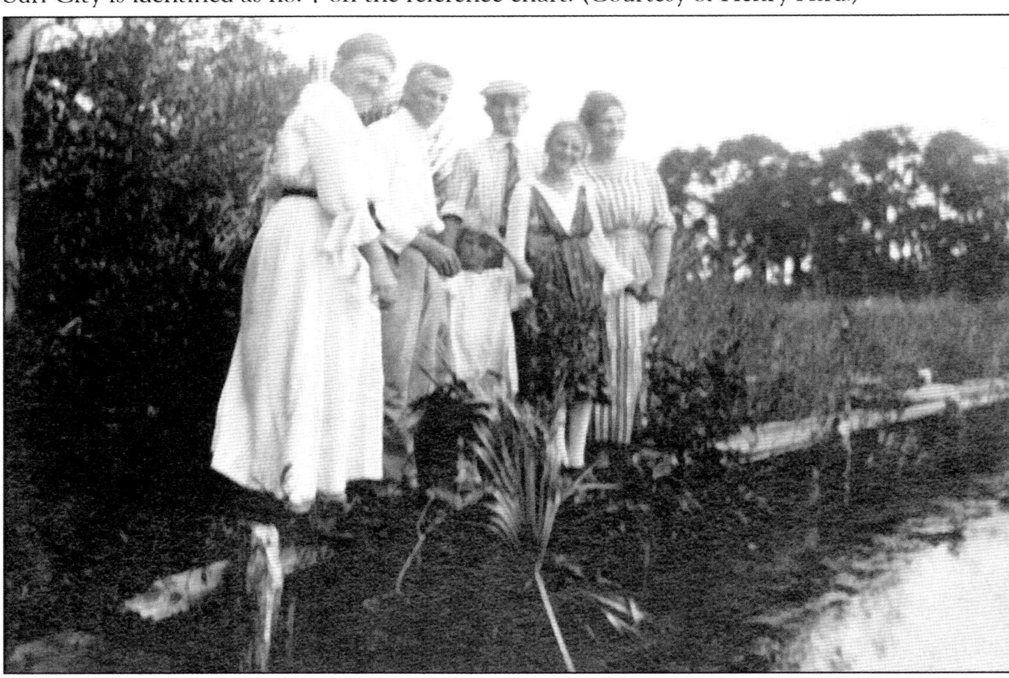

The Guana Lake, where rice was grown centuries earlier, became an oddity of nature among tourists visiting Mineral City (Ponte Vedra) in the late 1800s. Long dresses worn by ladies of the time were not conducive to watery adventures along the lakeside and marshes. (Courtesy of Beaches Museum and History Park.)

Two

North Beach—First Permanent Settlement

Established in 1890 by the North Beach Land & Railway Company, North Beach is the story of the Usina family. Catherine "Kate" and Frank A. Usina arrived and settled in the community in 1900. This development, which had since failed, was originally a Spanish land grant owned by Aldophus Pacetti, who continued to own a portion of the lots.

This pioneer family became adept at using the North River as their main food source, catching fish and oysters, which they prepared so well that Henry Flagler brought his guests ashore for the oysters Kate Usina roasted on the shore. This encouraged the family to establish a ferryboat business to bring tourists from St. Augustine to enjoy the beach and their seafood and garden-fresh meals. They used a horse-drawn trolley to deliver their paying customers to the oceanfront.

Over the years, and mainly after 1926, when the second official plat of North Beach was recorded, the Usina family began to buy larger tracts of land to operate their businesses and to sell individual lots. The recession in 1929 and the building of Highway A1A, including the automobile bridge into St. Augustine, brought more full-time residents to this community. Locals raised their children in this natural setting, and St. Augustine residents spent summers at this nearby beach.

Francis E. (son of founders Frank A. and Catherine) and Mary Borum Usina, followed by their sons and daughter—John F. "Jack," Frank D., and Mary Louise—and their descendants, have provided leadership and continuous businesses in North Beach for more than a century. A key business, their North Beach Utilities, has provided water and sewer service to many homes and businesses throughout the beaches, including Vilano Beach. This service laid the foundation for area growth. They have also operated a campground for decades, and their tour boat, now the *Victory III*, and Aunt Kate's Restaurant and the Reef Restaurant have continued for generations. With neighborhood restaurants and a campground, North Beach is the largest residential community in Vilano and the North Beaches.

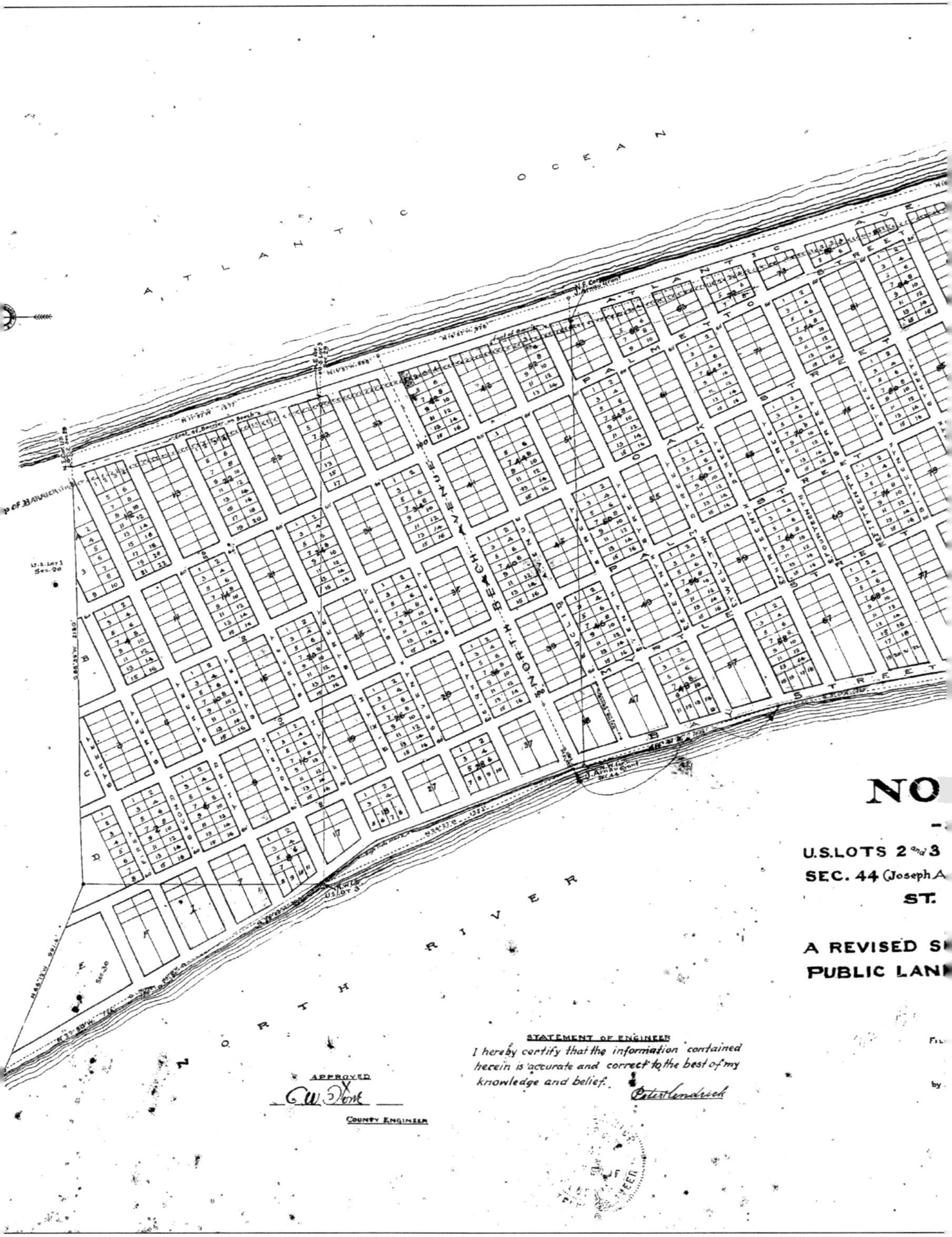
ATLANTIC OCEAN
NORTH RIVER
ATLANTIC AVE
PALMETTO STREET
OAK STREET
MYRTLE STREET
BAY STREET
NORTH BEACH AVENUE
U.S.LOTS 2 and 3
STATEMENT OF ENGINEER
I hereby certify that the information contained herein is accurate and correct to the best of my knowledge and belief.
APPROVED
COUNTY ENGINEER

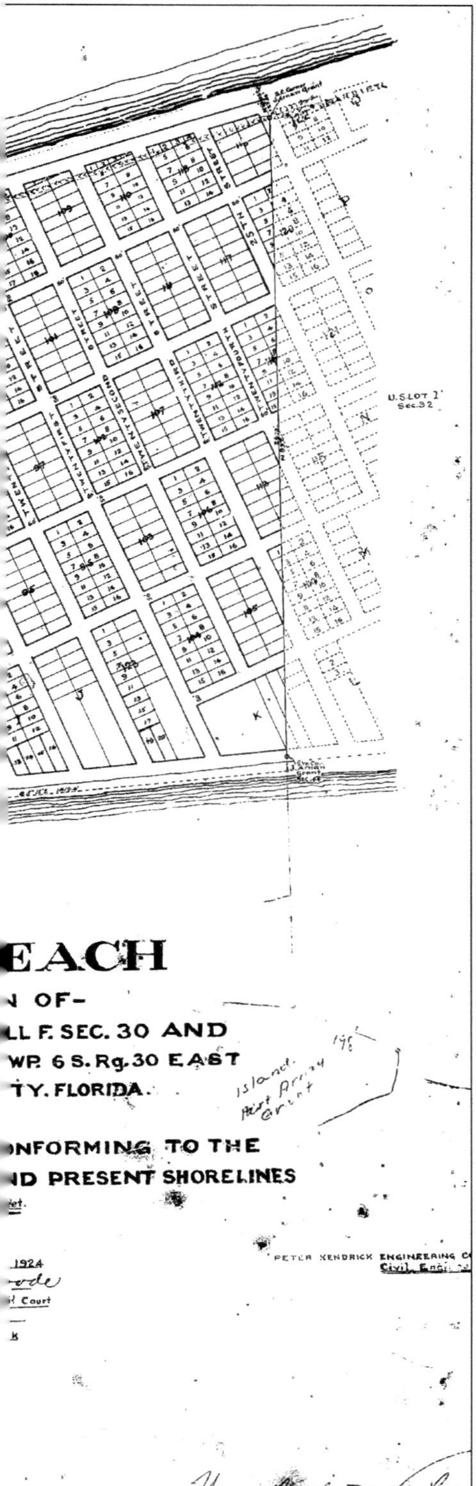

The first North Beach subdivision, platted in 1890, was the first plat recorded in this area. Adolphus Pacetti separated his landholdings in 1890, anticipating great profits from North Beach lot sales. The 1926 plat map references Sec. 44 of Joseph Arnau's Grant. In the 1920s, State Road A1A, then called Ocean Highway, was built along the oceanfront of this plat, connecting it to Ponte Vedra Beach and Jacksonville Beach to the north and St. Augustine to the south. Bay Street along the river was never built and is now incorporated into the riverfront home lots as private property. The businesses added within this plat over the years include the North Beach Camp Resort and store established in the 1960s, the Reef Restaurant, Aunt Kate's Restaurant, and Cap's Restaurant. (Courtesy of St. Johns County.)

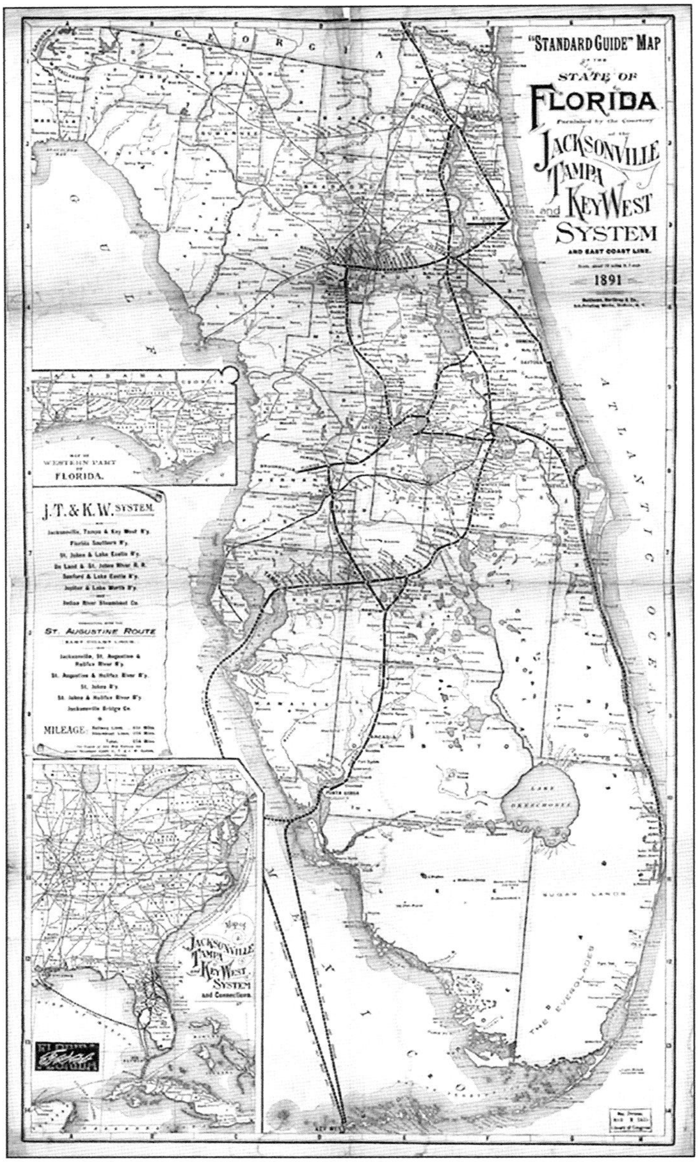

The 1891 *"Standard Guide" Map of the State of Florida, Jacksonville, Tampa, and Key West System* shows the St. Augustine Route and connections in the state. In 1890, the narrow-gauge railway lines opened the gates for settlement along the coast. In 1895, Henry Flagler began building the Ponce de León Hotel and realized that the key to developing Florida was a solid transportation system. He consequently purchased the narrow-gauge (three feet) Jacksonville, St. Augustine & Halifax River Railway on December 31, 1885. He also discovered that a major problem facing existing railway systems was that each operated on a different gauge system, making interconnection impossible. He converted his purchased network of rail lines to standard gauge (four feet, eight and a half inches) in 1890. The connecting line to North Beach was changed to standard gauge and incorporated in 1892. (Courtesy of Henry Hird.)

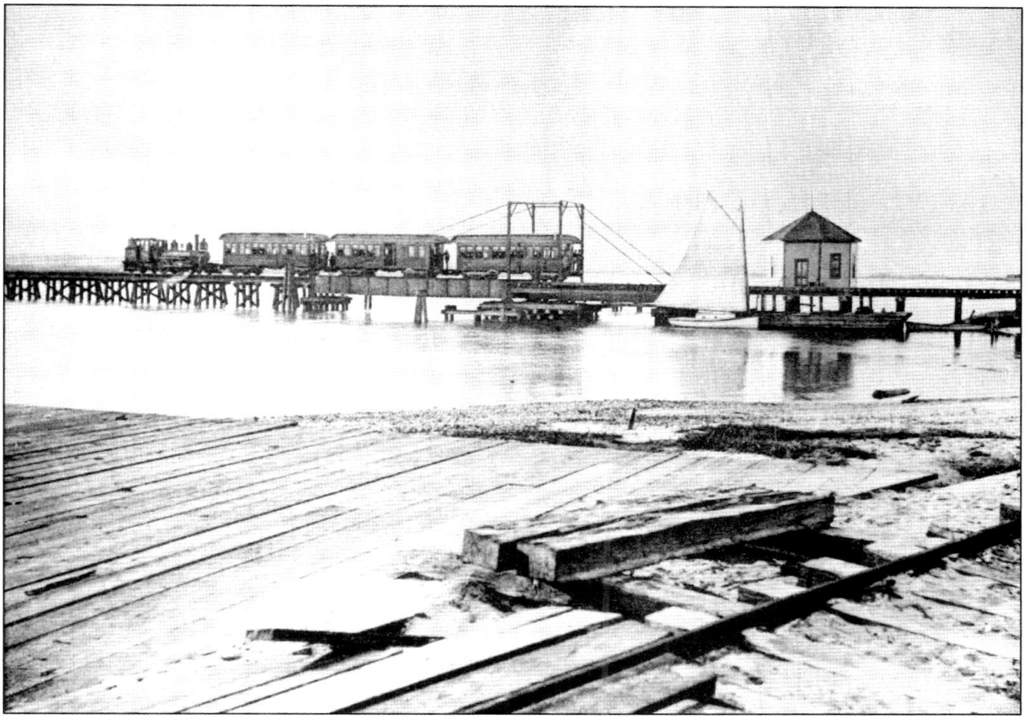

In 1890, following a real estate arrangement between Adolphus Pacetti and a Georgia firm, known as St. Augustine and North Beach Railway Company, a bridge was constructed to bring visitors and residents to North Beach. On the mainland, the bridge would connect with the existing Jacksonville, St. Augustine & Halifax railway line. The bridge had a swing draw on the east end. (Courtesy of Elizabeth and Frank D. Usina.)

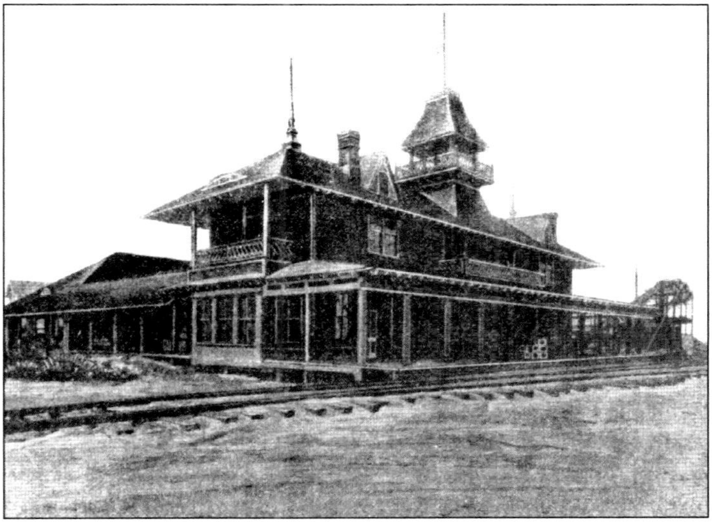

The railway station connecting the mainland to North Beach was constructed overlooking the Atlantic Ocean at the site of today's Reef Restaurant. The structure featured a 56-room bathhouse, bowling alley, pavilions with tropical gardens, a toboggan chute, fountain, and livery stable. Fire swept the Oceanfront Pavilion in 1895, resulting in heavy losses for the investors. (Courtesy of Elizabeth and Frank D. Usina.)

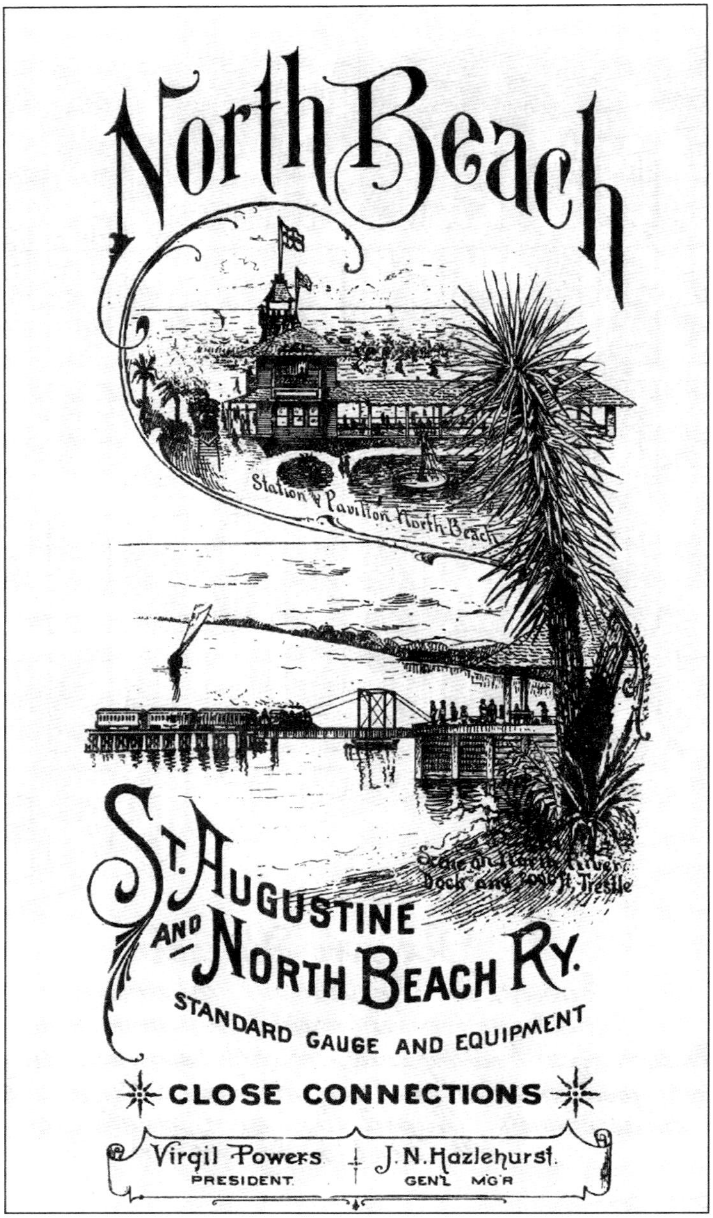

An advertisement for the St. Augustine & North Beach Railway and "St. Augustine's New Suburb" features the station pavilion at North Beach as a "standard gauge" train crosses the North River. The ticket shows the image of the pavilion at the ocean and the bridge. The North Beach subdivision was platted in 1890 with a railroad line built across the river from St. Augustine to the ocean. The rail line began on March 4, 1890. Tourists from the grand hotels in St. Augustine flocked to the beaches using the railway as the quickest access to the coast at North River. The railway continued until it was overshadowed by automobiles and newly built roads and bridges in the late 1920s. Early alternate modes of transportation included tour boats. (Courtesy of Elizabeth and Frank D. Usina.)

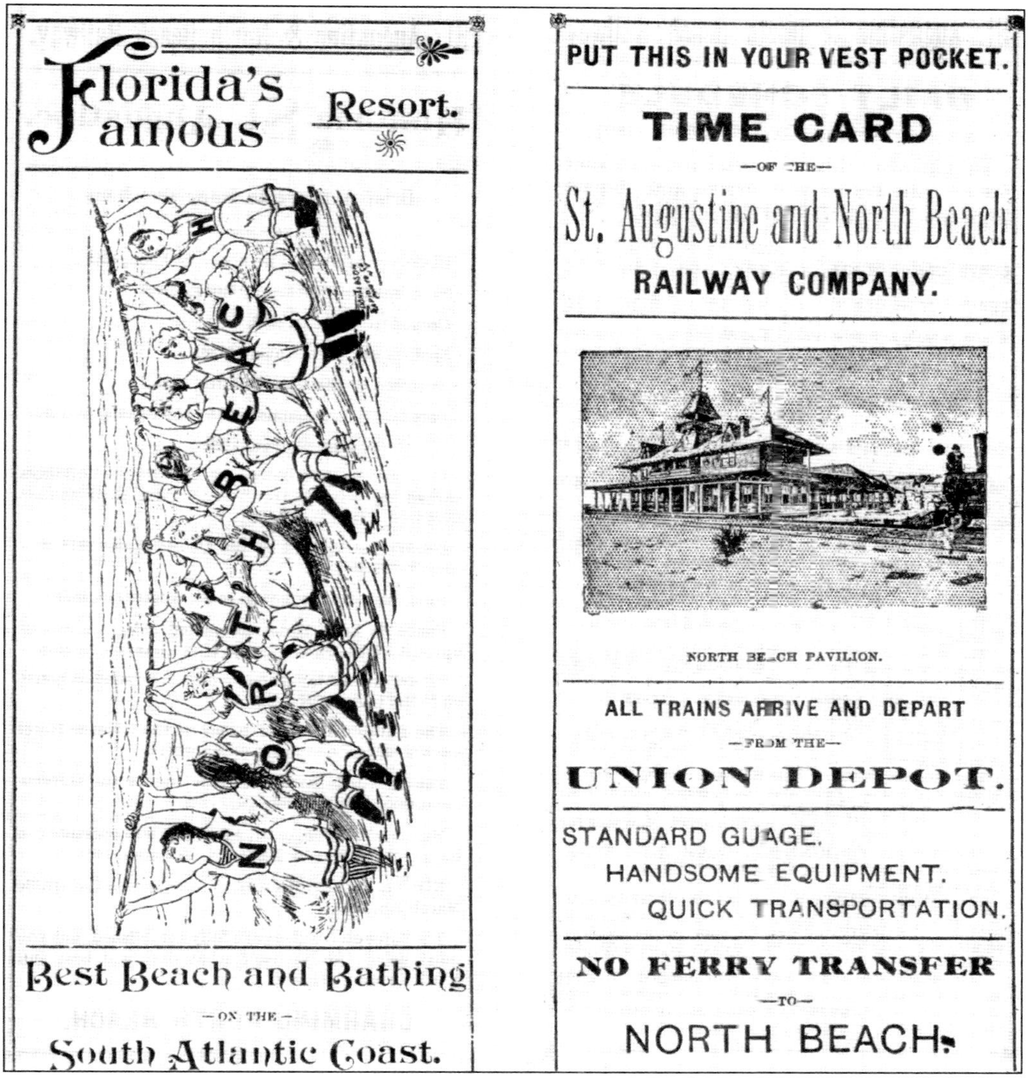

This "time card" for the St. Augustine and North Beach Railway Company provides instructions for passengers: "Put this in your vest pocket. No ferry transfer to North Beach." Between 1890 and 1927, the limited access to North Beach was by boat. Passengers first boarded at the depot in Davenport Park on San Marco and later used the Union Depot on Malaga Street. Many visitors came to St. Augustine for its sunny weather, beautiful beaches, and popular resorts. Touted for the "Best Beach and Bathing on the South Atlantic Coast," North Beach, Surfside Beach, and Vilano Beach were dotted with coastal resorts and casinos during this 40-year tourism era. At this time, the hospitality industry blossomed to include restaurants, lodging, and attractions. To accommodate the growing workforce, residential communities began sprouting up in the county. A good transportation network was essential for them as well as for tourists. (Courtesy of Elizabeth and Frank D. Usina.)

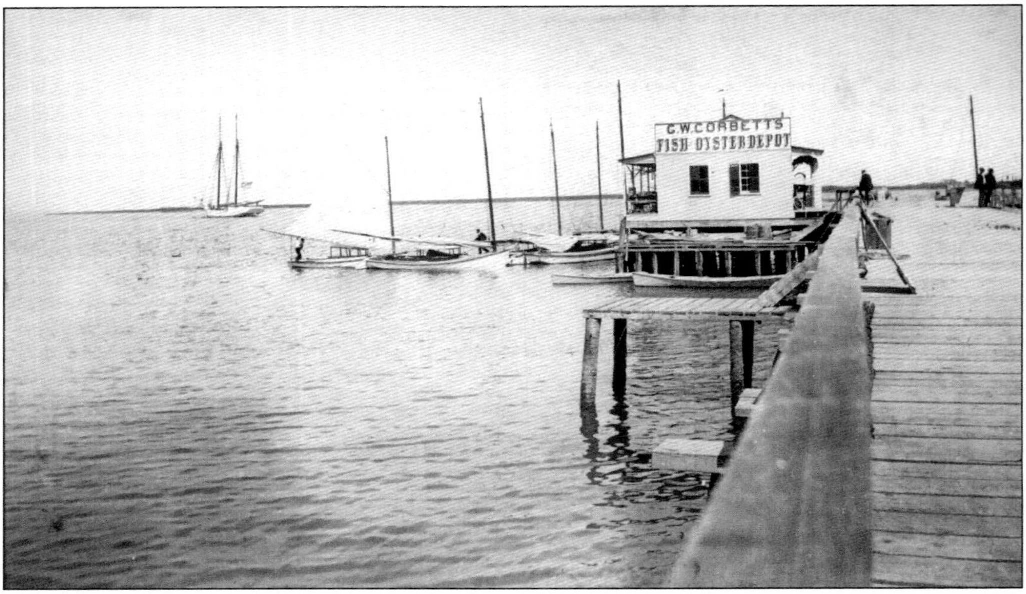

Capt. T.F. Corbett ran a steam launch, *Ida,* from bayfront St. Augustine to North Beach in 1893. After the railway lines opened, tourism expanded. Seafood, especially fresh oysters, was a favorite for all. There was no bridge connecting downtown to the North Beach area before 1927. (Courtesy of the St. Augustine Historical Society.)

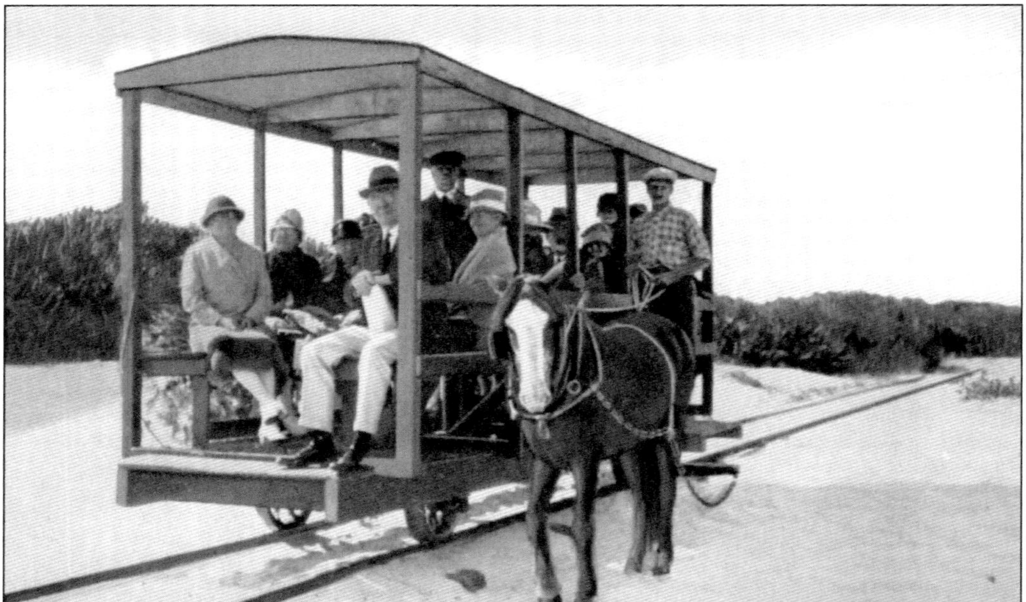

In the early 1900s, horse-drawn trolleys carried visitors from the river to the ocean. The trolley met the Usinas' boat, *Victory I,* used for river crossings from St. Augustine. In the 1890s, the St. Augustine and North Beach Railway Company brought visitors by rail across the river to a huge pavilion on the ocean. The use of old railway tracks helped horses to pull trolleys filled with passengers. (Courtesy of Elizabeth and Frank D. Usina.)

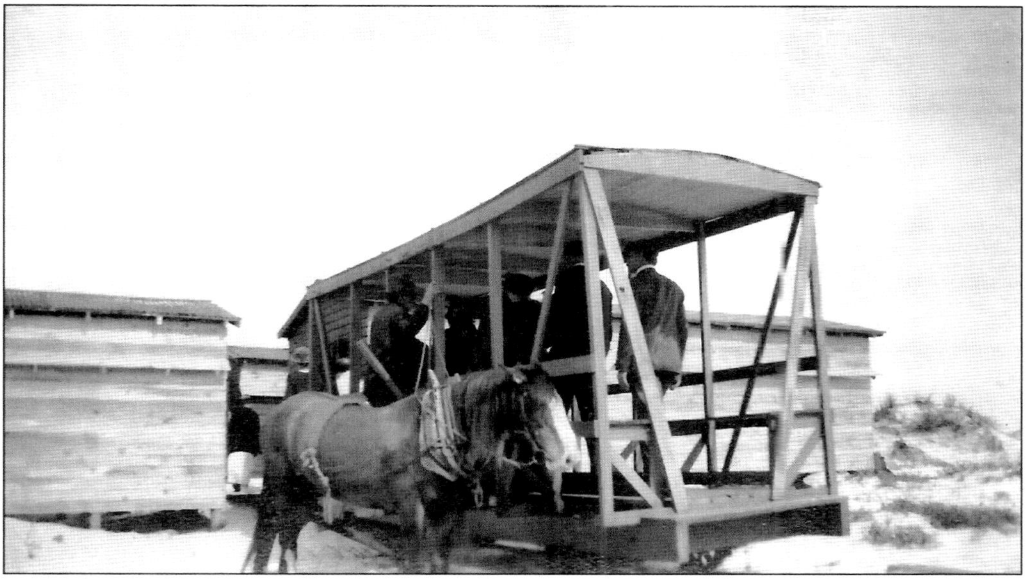

Horse-drawn trolleys were unique to remote North Beach. Robert Ripley reported them as the only ones in the United States. Operating from 1890 to the early 1930s, the trolleys were built to carry passengers from the river to the oceanfront, about a third of a mile over sand dunes. Horses were hitched to the side of the trolley. (Courtesy of Karen Harvey.)

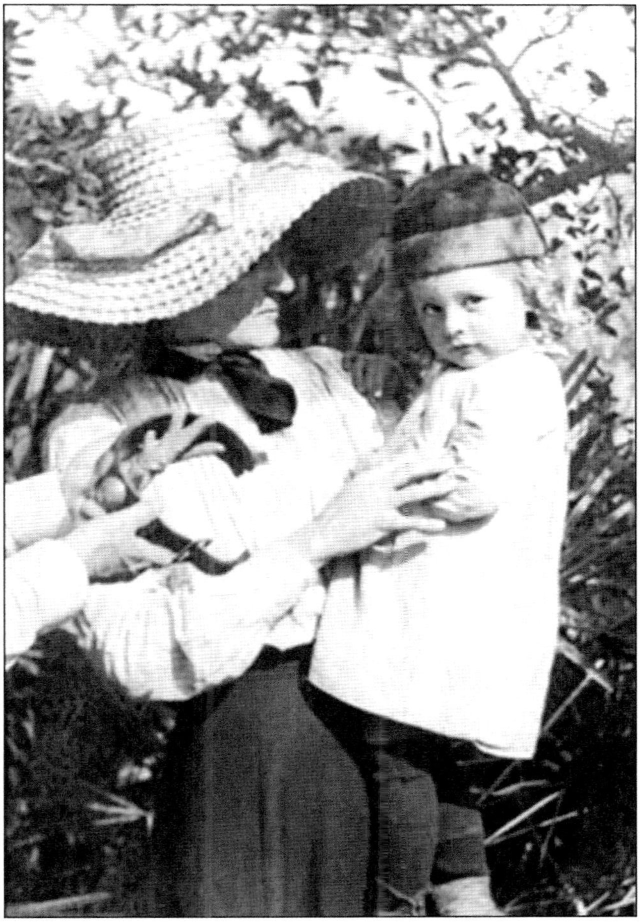

Floppy-hatted Catherine "Kate" Usina holds young Francis E. Usina, age four, at North Beach in 1904. Francis was the only child of Frank Andreu and Kate Usina. Francis grew up learning the ways of fishermen with a strong Minorcan heritage and passed that learning on to the next generation. (Courtesy of Elizabeth and Frank D. Usina.)

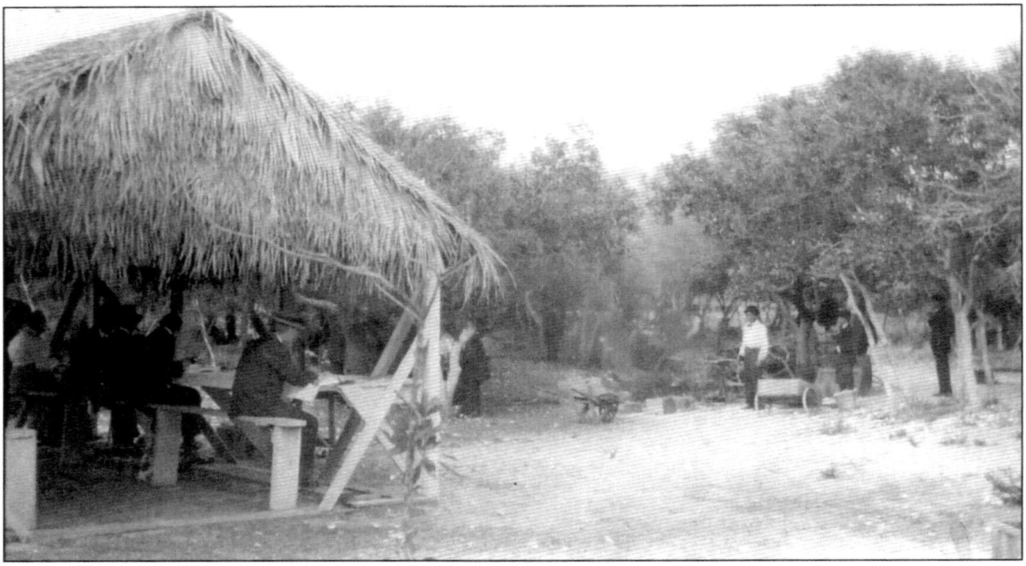

Henry Flagler loved to share Florida's favorite foods with his guests during their sailing outings. Frank Andreu Usina (right), dressed in a white shirt, serves oysters to visitors at North Beach. The Usina Beach Oyster Shed was located where Aunt Kate's Restaurant is today. This 1920s photograph reflects the use of palmetto fronds as construction materials. (Courtesy of Elizabeth and Frank D. Usina.)

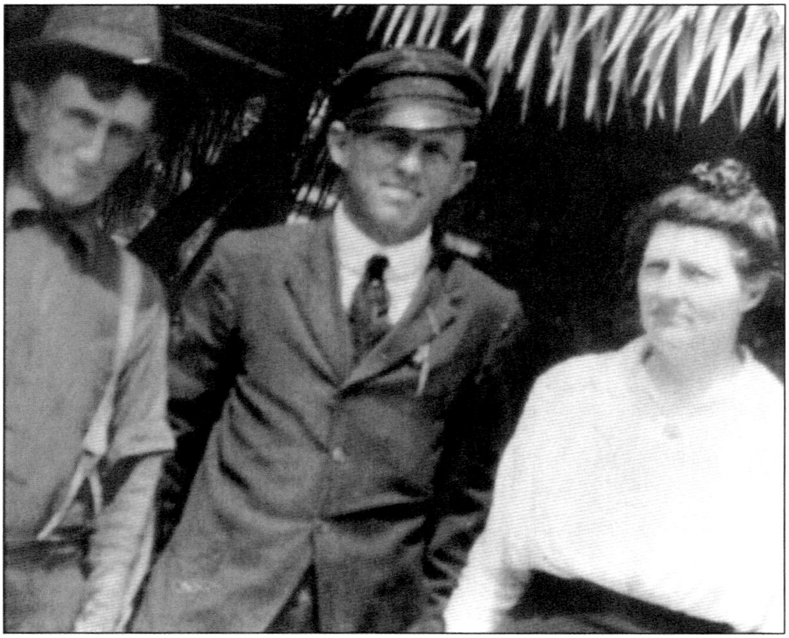

Frank A. (left), Francis E. (center), and Kate Usina pose by their palmetto-thatched pavilion. They enjoyed the company of neighbors as well as tourists, sharing local recipes for Minorcan dishes. In later years, the family remained in the restaurant business, still entertaining and sharing recipes. (Courtesy of Elizabeth and Frank D. Usina.)

Shown here are, from left to right, Mary Louise Evans Ponce, Frank Andreu, Kate Usina, and an unidentified friend at the thatched Usina's Pavilion at North Beach. Not only the tourists liked local Usina oysters—so did Minorcan neighbors. The Ponce family is one of the oldest Minorcan families in St. Augustine. The families still hold celebrations in which they reenact events in their ancestors' lives. (Courtesy of Elizabeth and Frank D. Usina.)

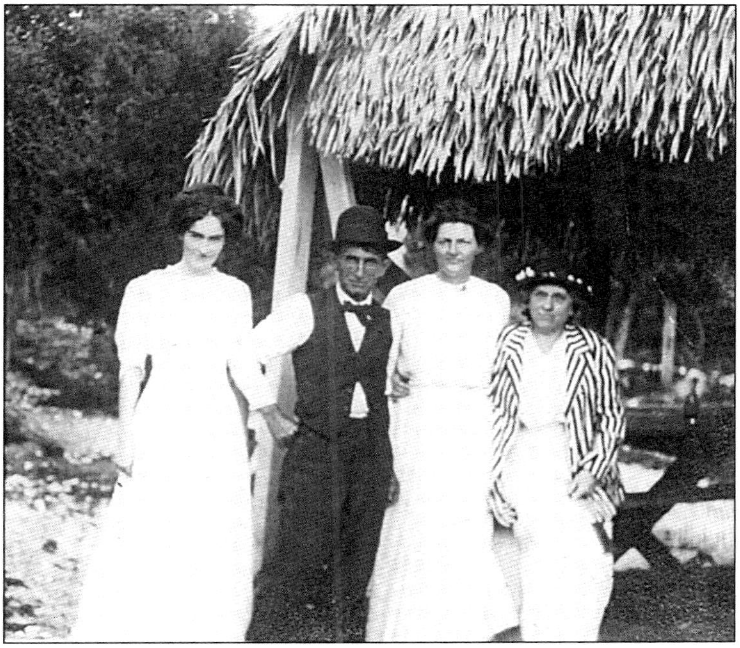

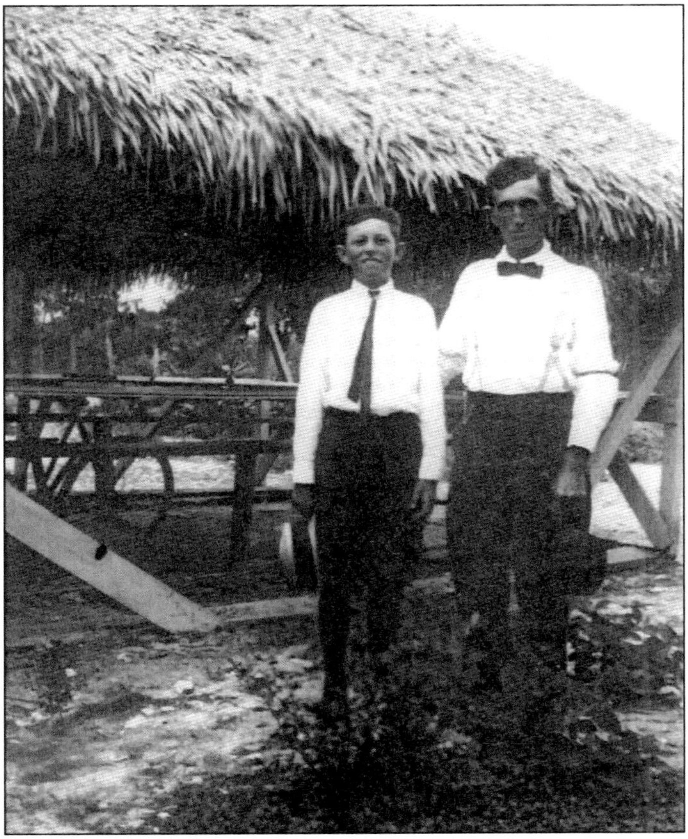

Young Francis E. and Frank A. Usina stand "all dressed up" in front of the Usina Oyster Shed at North Beach. The open-air pavilion was a popular gathering spot for both locals and tourists. To this day, North Beach residents and others gather at the same area to have oyster roasts to raise money for charitable causes. (Courtesy of Elizabeth and Frank D. Usina.)

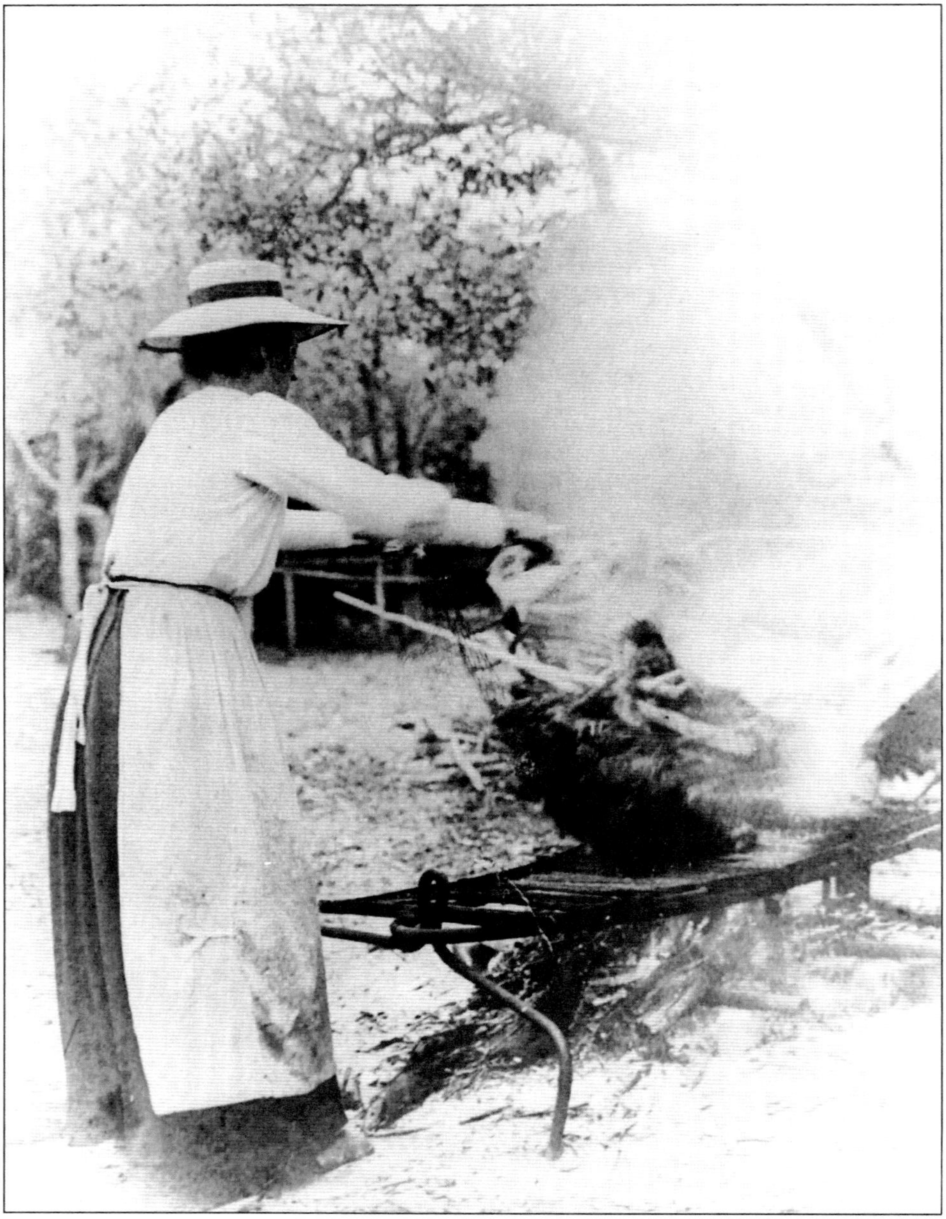

Catherine "Kate" Usina's methods for roasting involved collecting fresh oysters from the river, putting them on a wire screen over a low fire, and carefully handling the hot shells that popped open easily after a little roasting. Outdoor palmetto sheds allowed guests to dine in comfort close to the "kitchen." The restaurant business of the Usinas has endured for more than a century. A fire destroyed the old Usina's Pavilion, then known as Oscar's, in the early 2000s. In 2009, Aunt Kate's Restaurant opened to continue the family traditions. The restaurant is home to dozens of old family photographs depicting life and times along the North River as the Usina family grew and prospered over the decades. Annually, the family supports the oyster roasts for charities, bringing back the memories of Kate Usina and company enjoying freshly shucked oysters under the Florida skies. (Courtesy of Elizabeth and Frank D. Usina.)

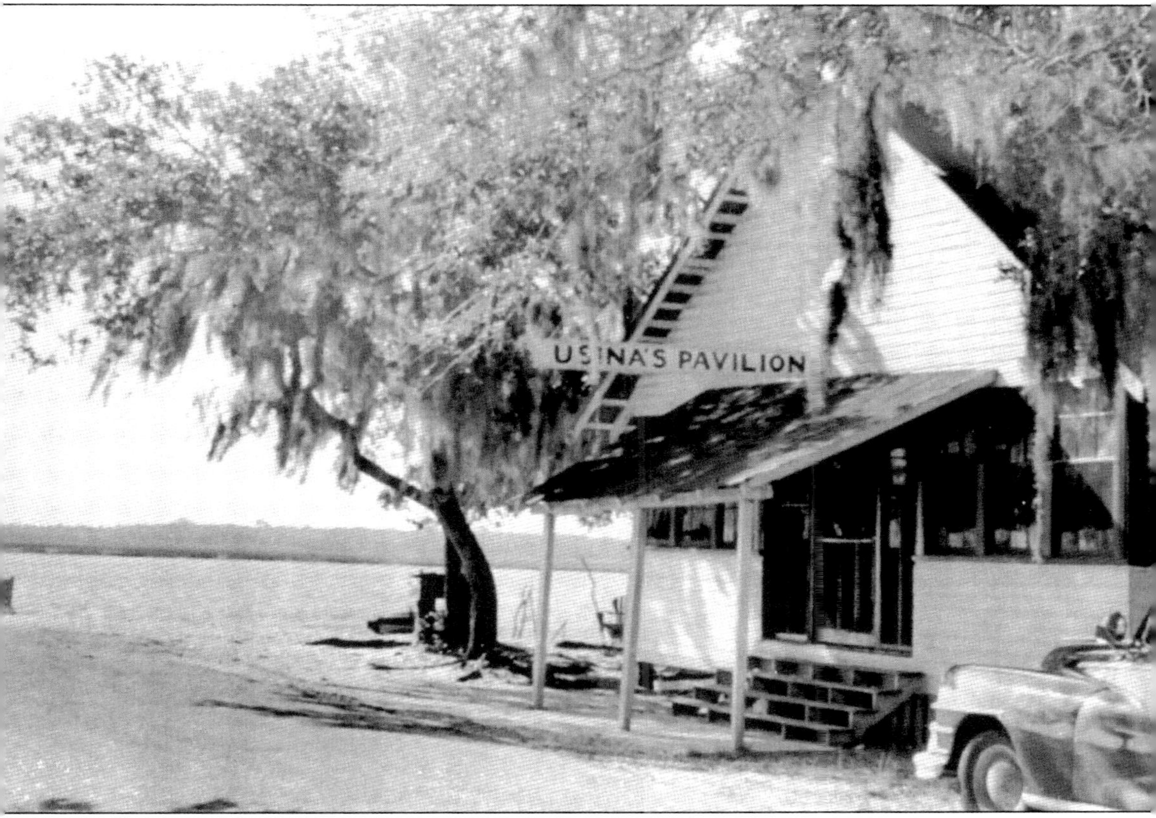

In 1909, the Usinas purchased the *Victory* as their business was expanding. Shortly afterward, the permanent building for their new pavilion was erected by an old-fashioned barn raising. The site of Usina's Pavilion housed many businesses, and in 2009, it became the site of Aunt Kate's Restaurant. The *Victory I* was a favorite attraction for Flagler Hotel visitors venturing out to the beaches from downtown St. Augustine. Tickets were sold on the bayfront. The *Victory I* was in service until 1918, when it was replaced by the *Victory II*. It handled quite a lot of passengers (locals and tourists), who dined at the North River Pavilion. When the *Victory II* was replaced in 1988 by the *Victory III*, parts of the older vessel were used in the construction of the new Aunt Kate's Restaurant. So the *Victory* lives on. (Courtesy of Elizabeth and Frank D. Usina.)

HOW TO CATCH FISH

FIRST, TAKE TWO BRICKS — BE SURE THEY ARE BRICKS THAT WILL FLOAT. PURCHASE NICE BIG SHRIMP FROM US. PUT 3 SHRIMP ON THE FLOATING BRICKS AND SPRINKLE WITH RED PEPPER. THE FISH COME UP AND START EATING THE SHRIMP, AT THE SAME TIME INHALING THE RED PEPPER, THEREBY CAUSING THE FISH TO SNEEZE. THE FISH DRAWS HIS HEAD BACK TO SNEEZE AND THEN DASHES HIS BRAINS OUT ON THE BRICK. GET A ROWBOAT FROM US AND PICK UP THE FISH. ASK US. WE KNOW.

(OVER)

Fishing was a favorite pastime of coastal residents, as was luring in tourists in great abundance. This 1920s advertisement for Usina's North Beach Fishing Camp notes its many amenities, including instructions on "How to Catch Fish." The size of the fish were smaller than in the tales of the fishing trip. (Courtesy of Elizabeth and Frank D. Usina.)

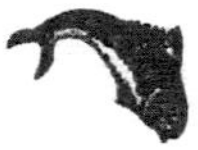

GO FISHING

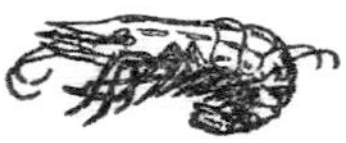

AT USINA'S NORTH BEACH FISHING CAMP

LOCATED ON NORTH RIVER IN THE HEART OF FLORIDA'S BEST FISHING — 4 MILES NORTH OF ST. AUGUSTINE ON BEACH RD. A1A, OR 24 MI. SOUTH OF JACKSONVILLE BEACH.

BOATS — MOTORS — LIVE AND DEAD SHRIMP — COTTAGES
POLES AND LINES FOR RENT
SANDWICHES — FREE SHADY PICNIC GROUNDS — COLD DRINKS

FRANCIS E. USINA — TELEPHONE 824-1806

BOX 301 (OVER) ST. AUGUSTINE, FLORIDA

For sure, some Northerners may have needed fishing instructions, but it is unclear how many actually followed them—humor and all. If anyone knew about fishing, it was the Usinas. All members of the family were expert fishermen and fisherwomen and were excellent at preparing a variety of seafood dishes. (Courtesy of Elizabeth and Frank D. Usina.)

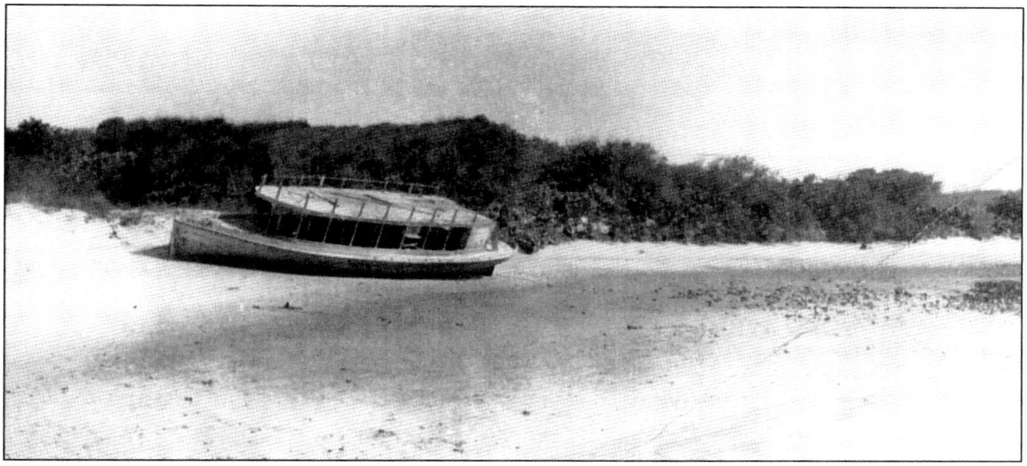

Frank A. Usina acquired his first boat in 1909, when he bought and raised the sunken vessel. The repaired 45-foot *Victory I* subsequently carried passengers to North Beach on a regular basis until it was replaced by *Victory II* in 1918. Docks were used at the west end of Euclid Avenue for passenger boarding. (Courtesy of Elizabeth and Frank D. Usina.)

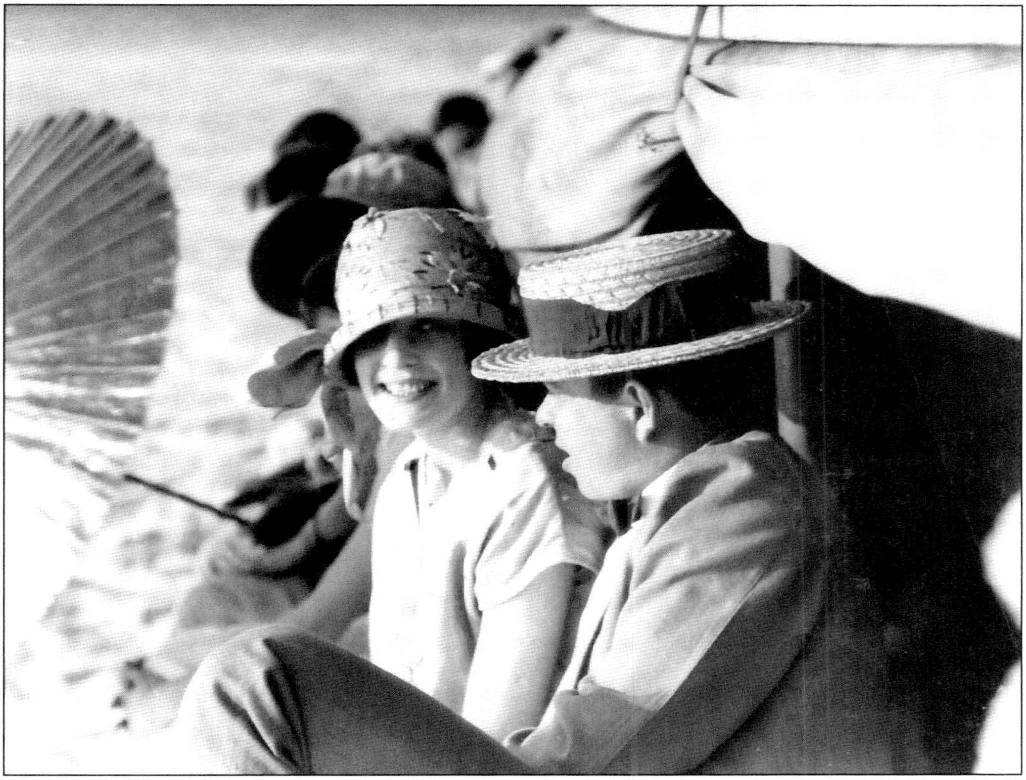

Victor Rahner and his future wife, Clara, enjoy an outing along the North River aboard *Victory II* in the early 1920s. Everyone enjoyed the rides on the riverboats. Before a regular ferry service was started, travelers used private sailboats and other marine craft to reach the North Beach. The Rahners later became neighbors of the Usinas, whose property was two miles to the north. (Courtesy of Tom Rahner.)

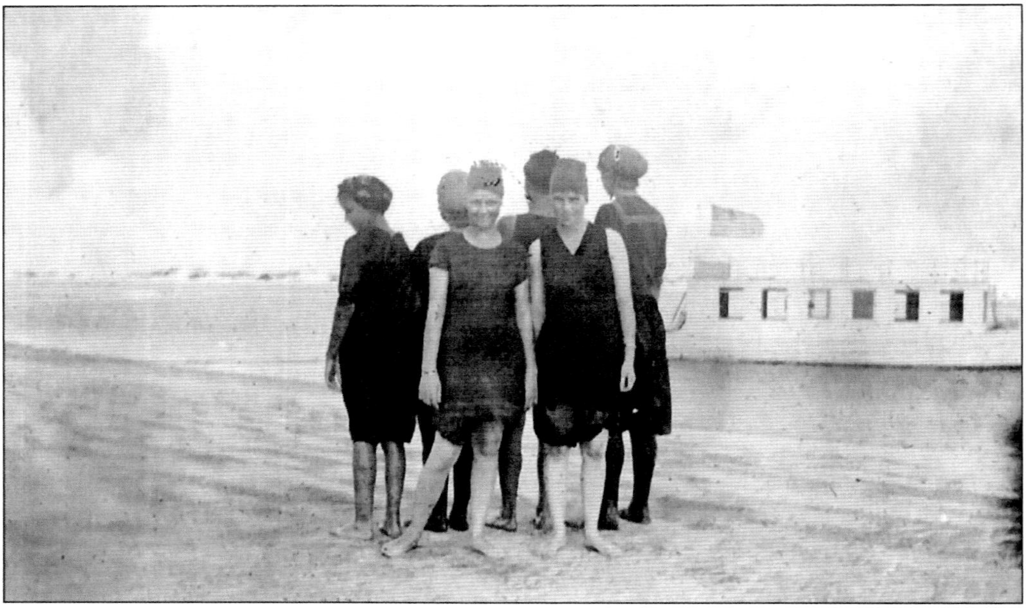

St. Augustine visitors loved to ferry across the bay to the beach. Bathing was popular, as seen here in front of *Victory I*, waiting in the distance. *Victory I* ran on Thursdays and Sundays, leaving Corbett's Dock on the St. Augustine bayfront at 10:00 a.m. and 2:00 p.m., with return trips at noon and 5:00 p.m. (Courtesy of Tom Rahner.)

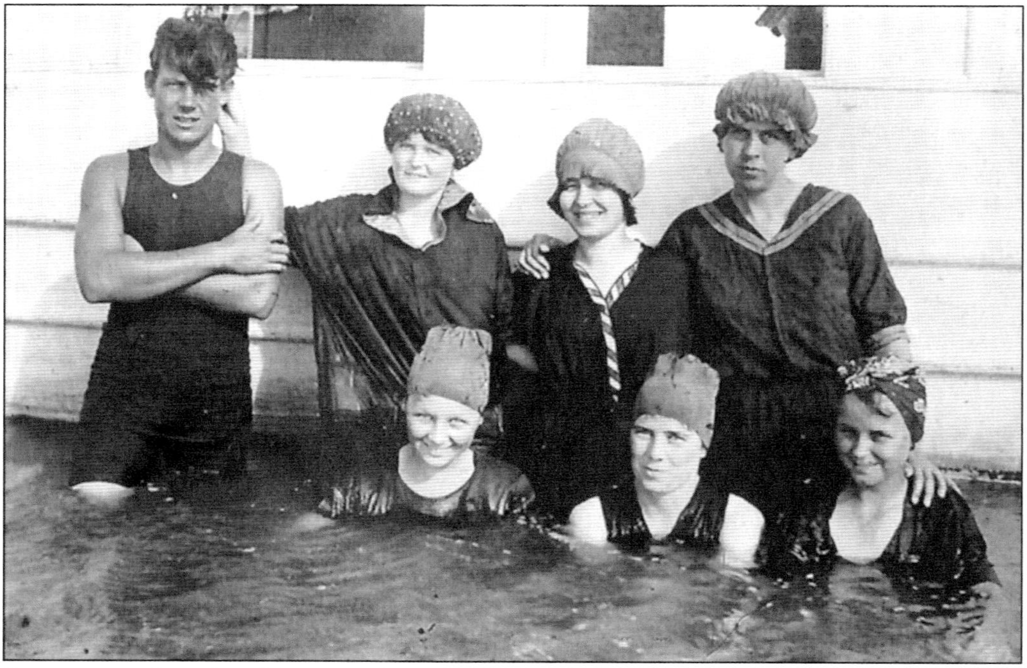

Swimmers strike a fanciful pose in front of *Victory I*. Bathing caps in the early 1900s were made of rubber, as synthetics were not developed until the late 1930s. Bathers of old knew to cover up from the Florida sun's rays, not for health concerns but because of the style. (Courtesy of Tom Rahner.)

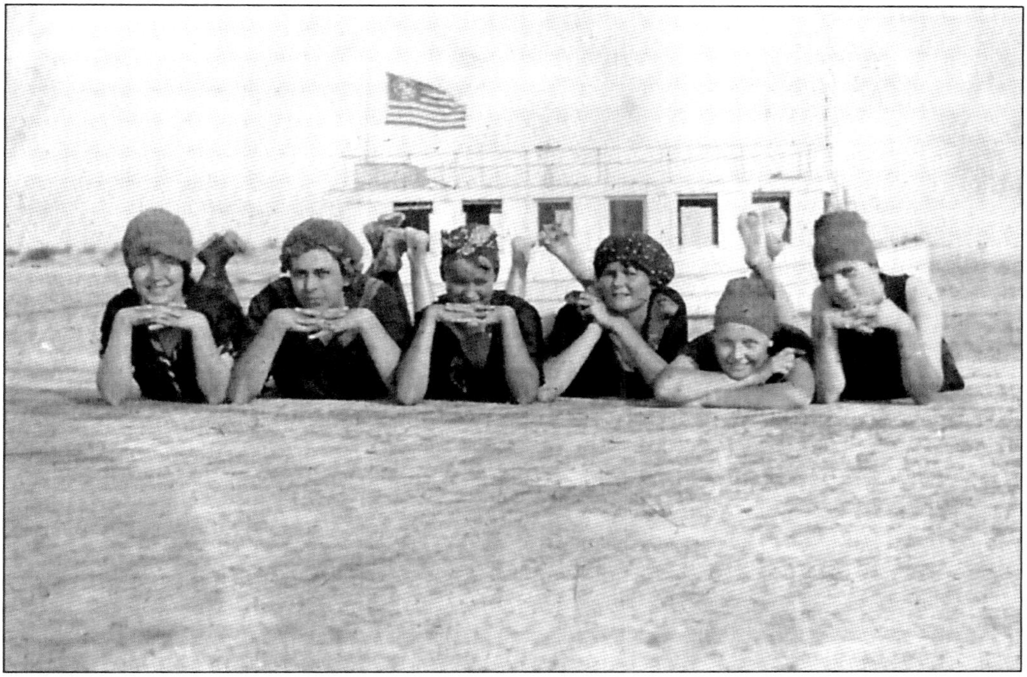

Victor Rahner Sr., a budding photographer in the 1920s, practiced his new profession by capturing these swimmers on the beach in front of the *Victory I*. Northern visitors loved the adventures in the surf at North Beach. Other boats were available along the river, but *Victory I* was the most popular. (Courtesy of Tom Rahner.)

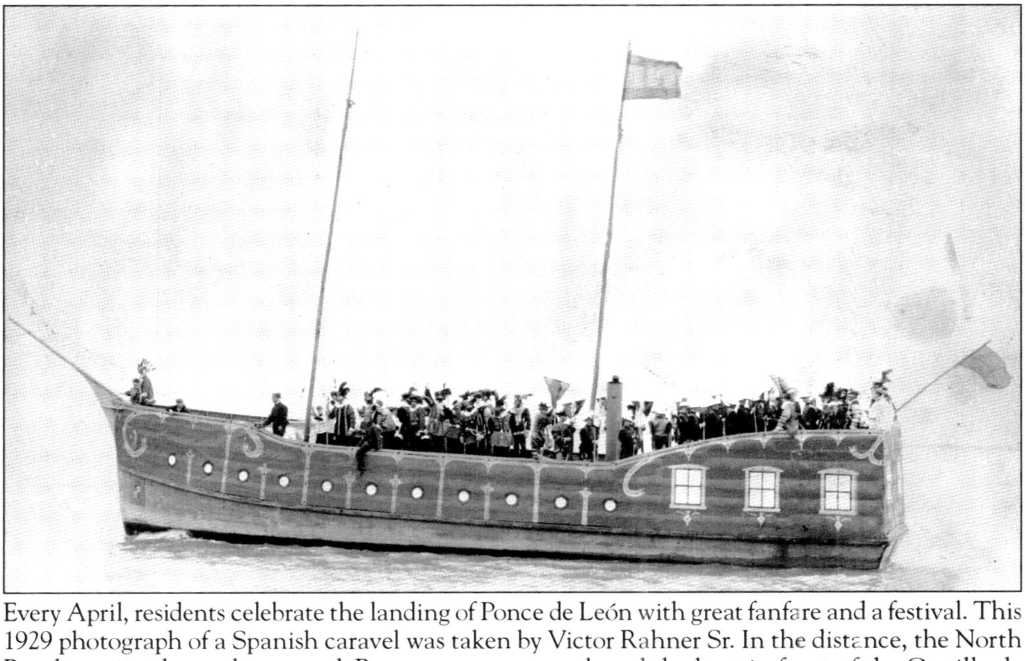

Every April, residents celebrate the landing of Ponce de León with great fanfare and a festival. This 1929 photograph of a Spanish caravel was taken by Victor Rahner Sr. In the distance, the North Beach peninsula can be spotted. Reenactors are seen aboard the boat in front of the Castillo de San Marcos. (Courtesy of Florida Memory.)

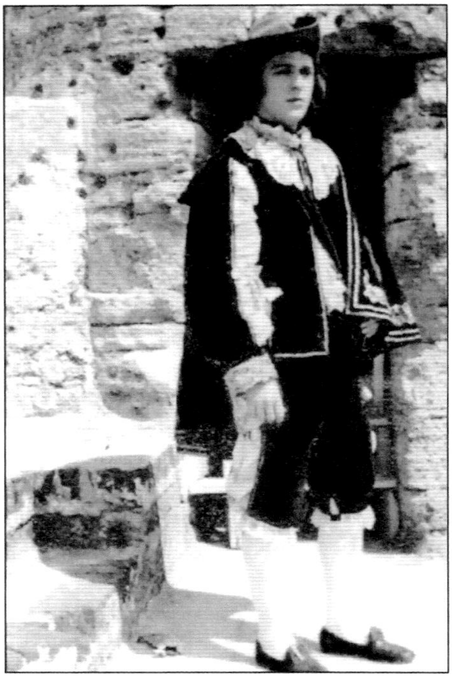

Henry Coopman Kernan poses as a Spanish settler in the 1929 Ponce de León Celebration. Costumed reenactments are common today. Kernan, also known as "Rebe," was a native of the area and resident of North Beach at Euclid Avenue. Somewhat of a character, he worked for the Usinas over the years along with Leon Carrera, first mate of *Victory II*. (Courtesy of Tom Rahner.)

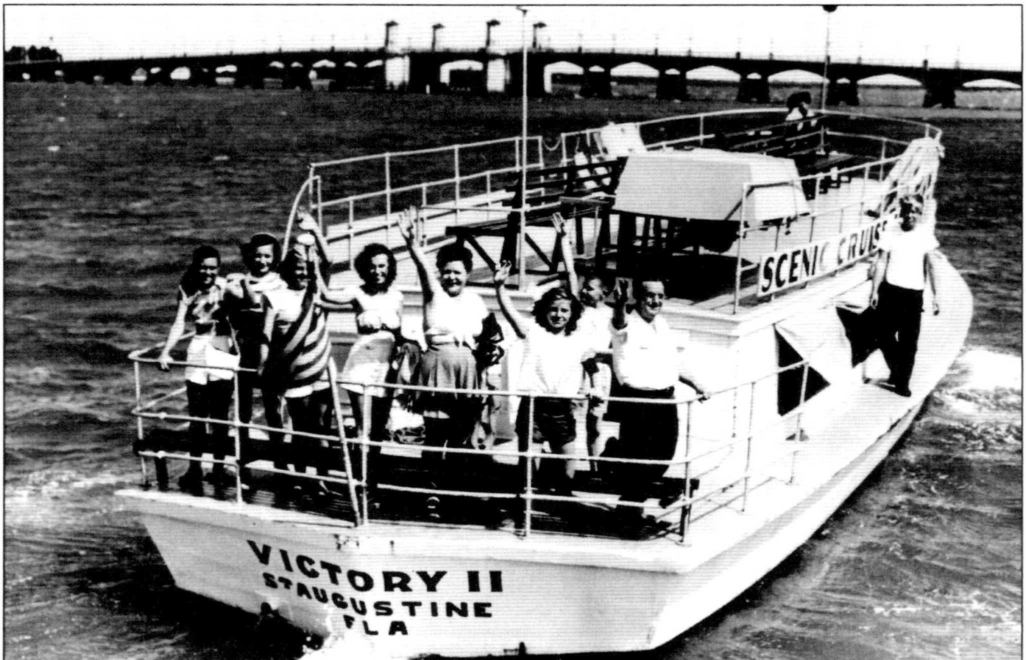

Victory I was replaced by *Victory II* in 1918. The family business outgrew the original vessel and commissioned local boatbuilder Warren Sanchez to create a vessel 54 feet, 4 inches long and 16 feet, 3 inches wide. In 1928, the single-screw engine was replaced by a standard marine direct-drive engine with a 28-inch propeller. This vessel stayed in service until replaced by *Victory III* in November 1988. (Courtesy of Elizabeth and Frank D. Usina.)

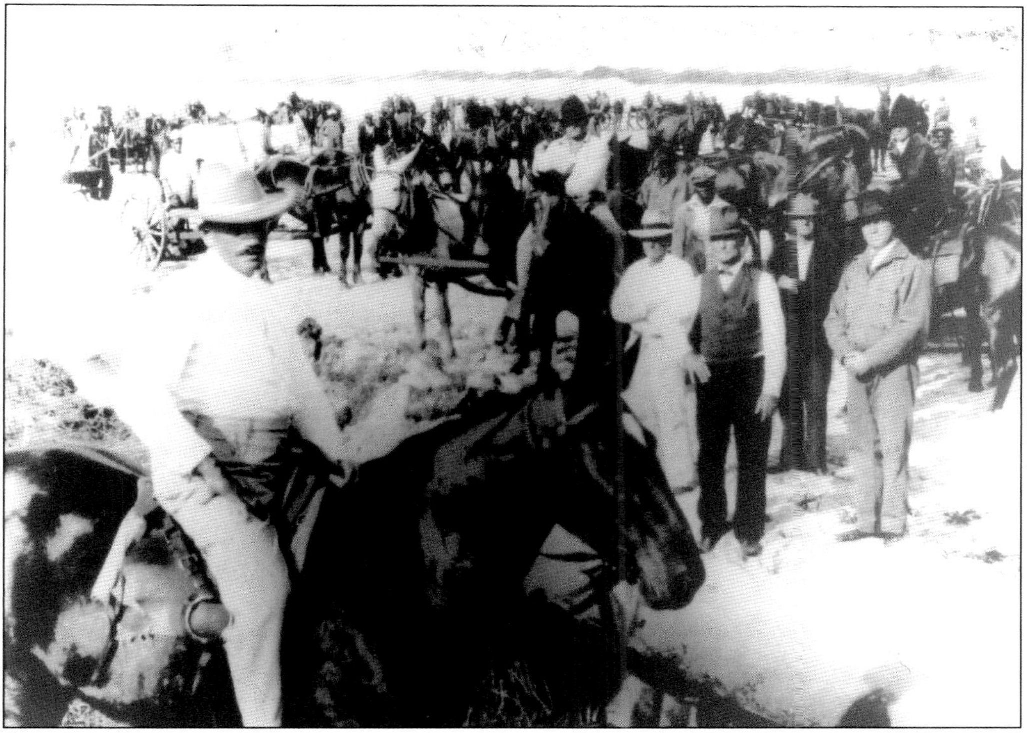

In 1926, B.B. McCormick & Sons was hired to complete roadwork to develop a coastal highway connecting Ponte Vedra to Vilano Beach. Construction crews used mules and slip pans on what is now Highway A1A. The project was completed in a year. (Courtesy of Beaches Museum and History Park.)

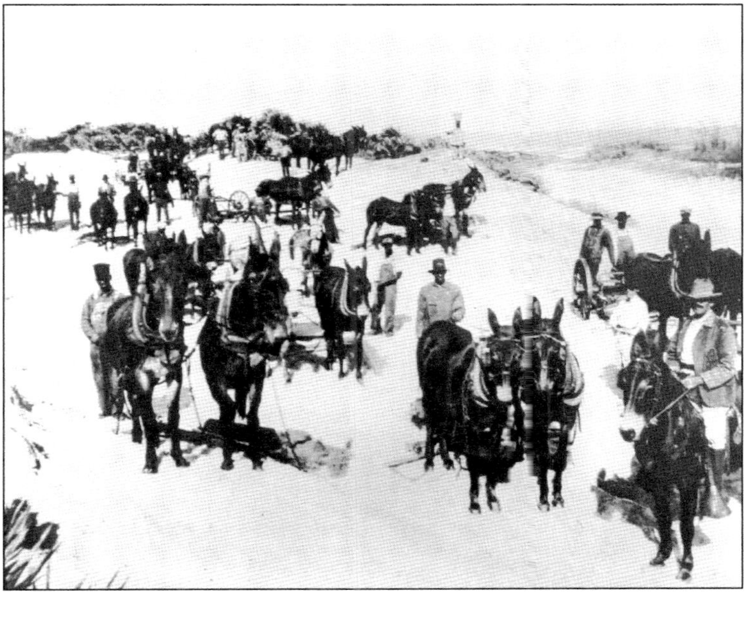

The 1920s saw completion of roads along the coast, the most significant being Ocean Highway, now State Road A1A. Mules were used to pull slip pans for the roadbed, which was lined with oyster shells and later overlaid with asphalt. Wells were constructed to water the mules. Grub hoes requiring much manpower were used to dig out coastal scrub plants. (Courtesy of Beaches Museum and History Park.)

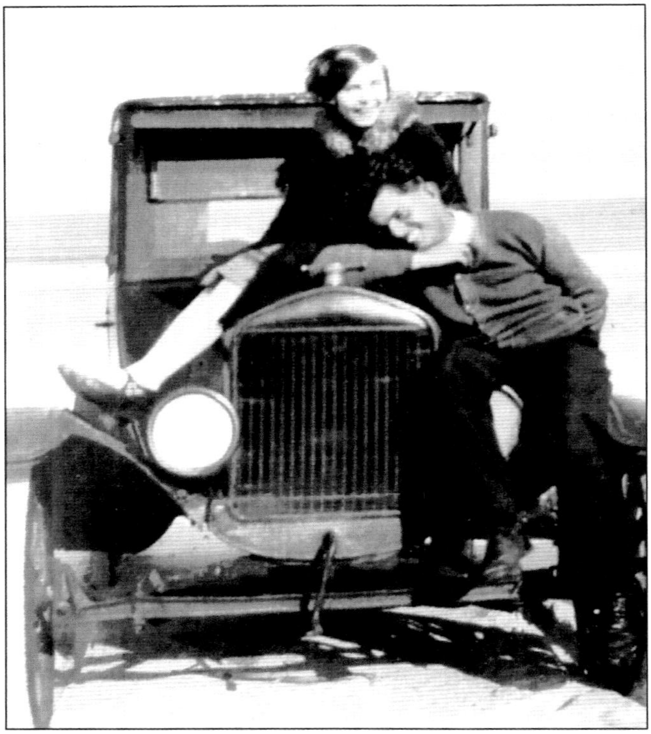

A young, loving couple, Francis E. and Mary Borum Usina enjoy the beach in the 1920s. This is one of the couple's first cars. They liked cruising the beach regularly. Hard-packed sands along the coast allowed for easy driving, racing, and other activities. (Courtesy of Mary Louise Usina Brown.)

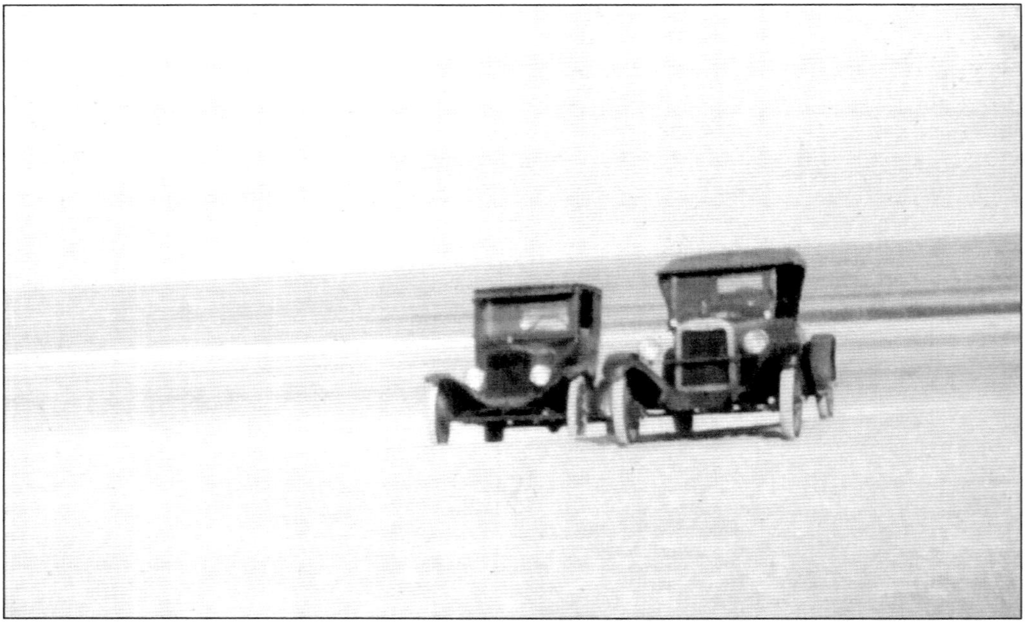

These are the 1920s cars of Francis E. and Mary Borum Usina. Before the Atlantic Alternate Route 1 (SRA1A) was constructed in 1946, travel between Pablo Beach (Ponte Vedra) and Vilano Beach was along the original coastal highway, built in 1926. The more common method of travel prior to the establishment of good roads was by car along the beach at low tide. (Courtesy of Mary Louise Usina Brown.)

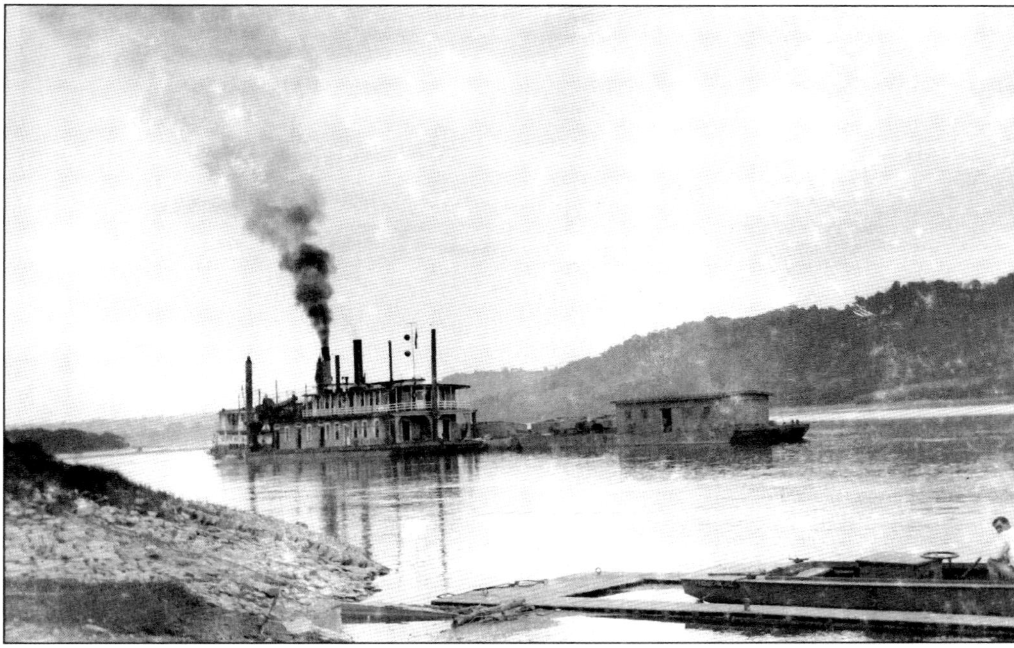

The St. Augustine Inlet, the North River, otherwise known as the Tolomato River, and other area waterways have needed periodic dredging to allow safe navigation for commercial travel over the years. Here is an early photograph of such operations, which continue along the coastline to manage changing shorelines. (Courtesy of Karen Harvey.)

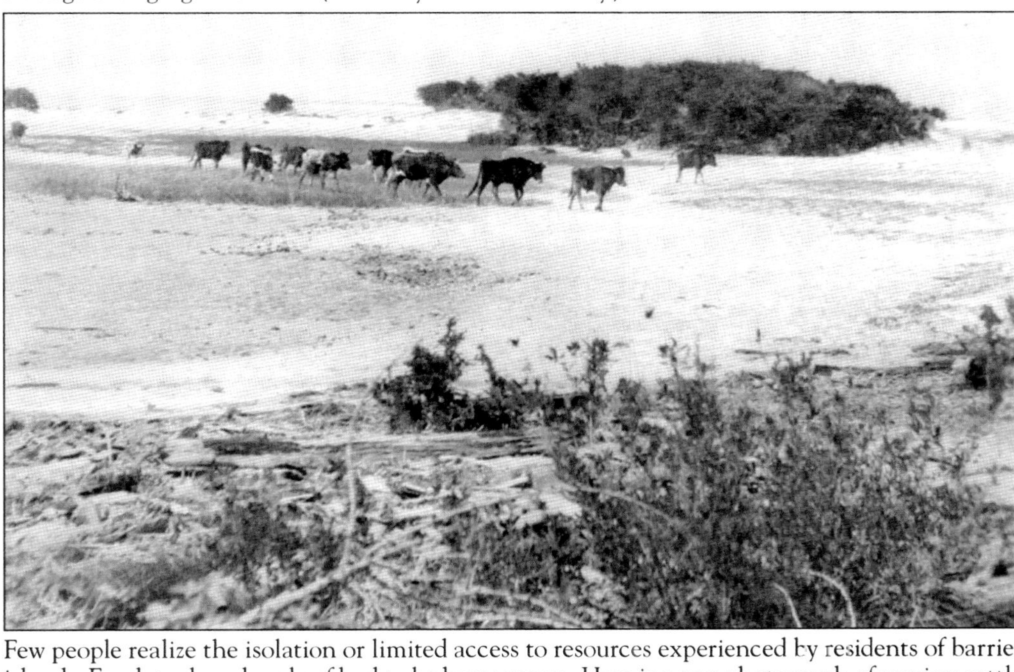

Few people realize the isolation or limited access to resources experienced by residents of barrier islands. Food stock such as beef had to be homegrown. Here is a rare photograph of grazing cattle in the coastal hammock along the beach. Herds were guided overland to shallow routes across the rivers. (Courtesy of Jackie and Nadine Connahay.)

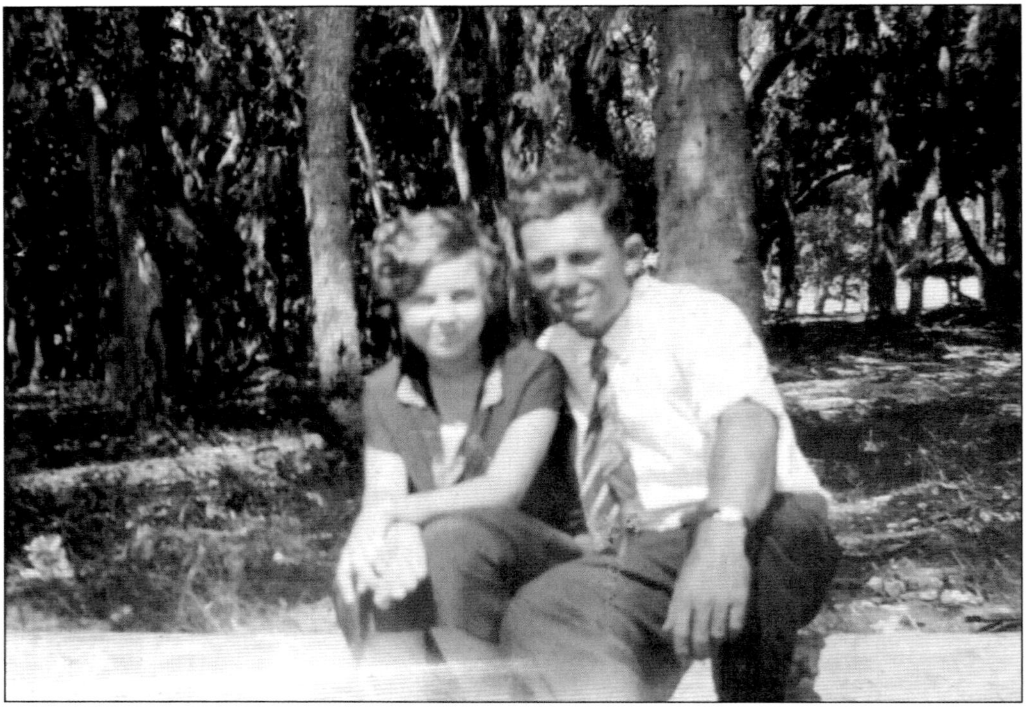

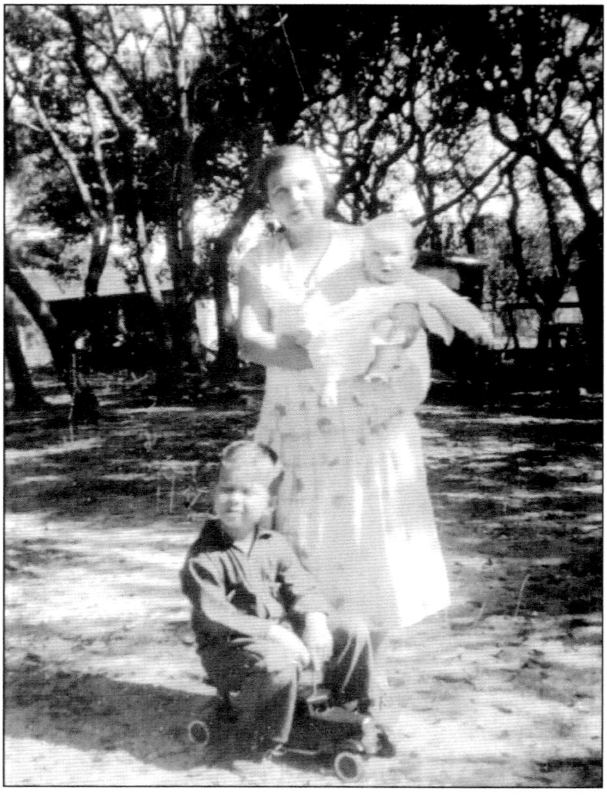

Francis E. and Mary Borum Usina pose in front of coastal scrub at North Beach. The unspoiled paradise was and still is "pleasant." These photographs reflect the idyllic times of the young couple, who lived in North Beach, raising Frank D., John F. "Jack," and Mary Louise Usina. (Courtesy of Mary Louise Usina Brown.)

"Mamie," John F. "Jack" (kneeling), and Frank D. Usina (right) enjoy outings with relatives at North Beach. Jack and Frank grew up to become boat captains of *Victory II*. Their grandparents were Frank Andreu and Catherine "Kate" Usina, who originally settled North Beach. All of the children were raised in North Beach and learned early how to fish, swim, and explore. (Courtesy of Mary Louise Usina Brown.)

Jack, the eldest of Francis E. and Mary Borum Usina's sons, is shown here at six months old. As an adult, he was known for his famous smiles and stories, being a seaworthy captain full of nautical tales. His descendants still work in the family businesses in North Beach. (Courtesy of Mary Louise Usina Brown.)

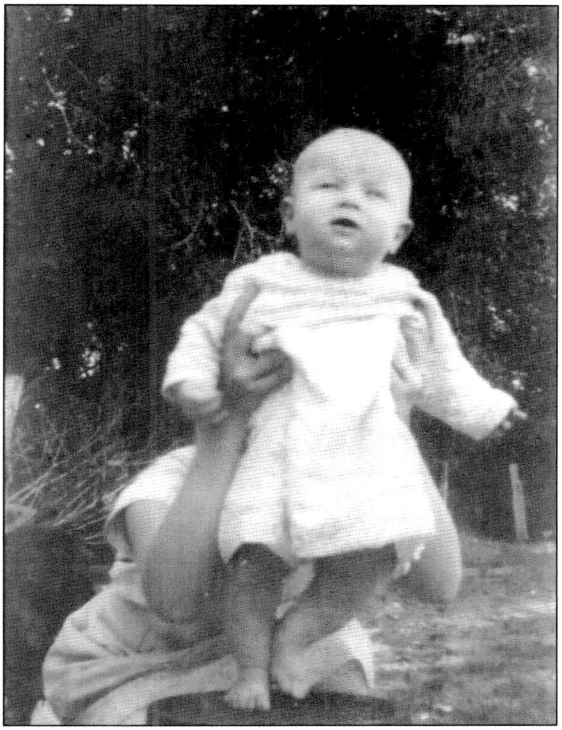

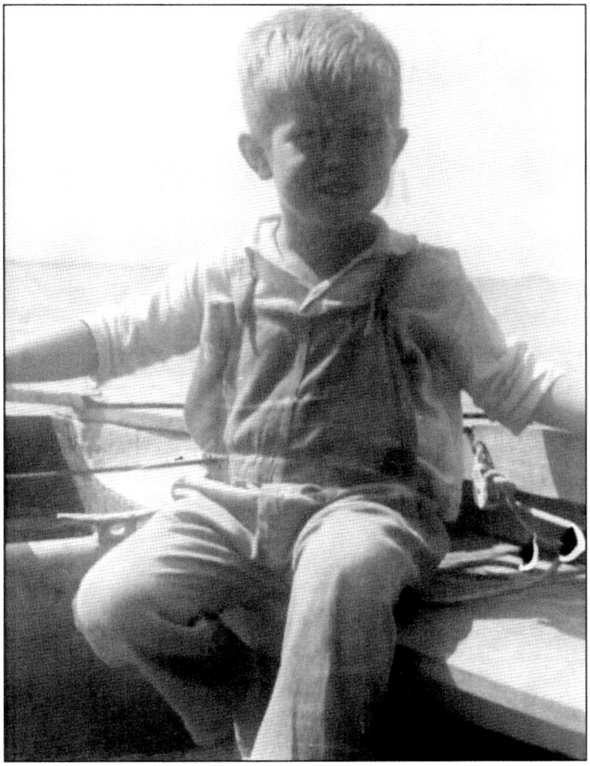

Young Jack Usina, son of Francis E. and Mary Borum Usina, loved the sea and showed it at the age of six. He later became captain of *Victory II* and aided in the family enterprises. Children were free to explore and fish on the river and marshes. (Courtesy of Mary Louise Usina Brown.)

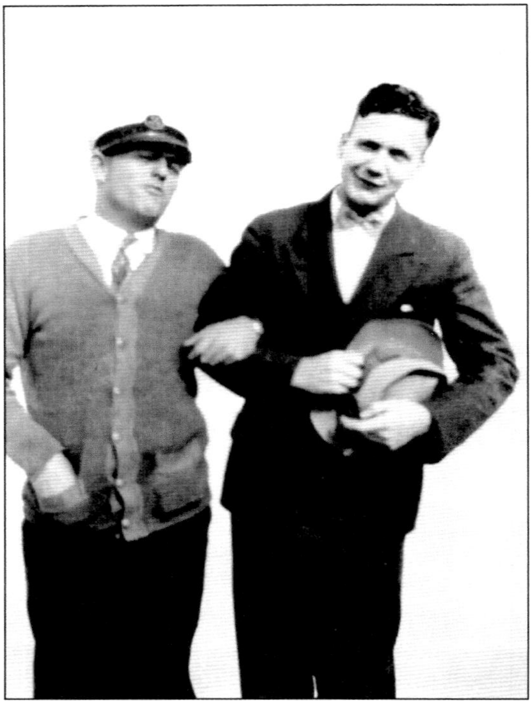

Francis E. Usina (left) hams it up on the beach with an unidentified friend. The caption reads: "The captain of the business and man sing 'Sweet Adeline.'" All was not work—play abounded! Car races, horseback riding, cycling, swimming, fishing, and more were common playtime activities. (Courtesy of Mary Louise Usina Brown.)

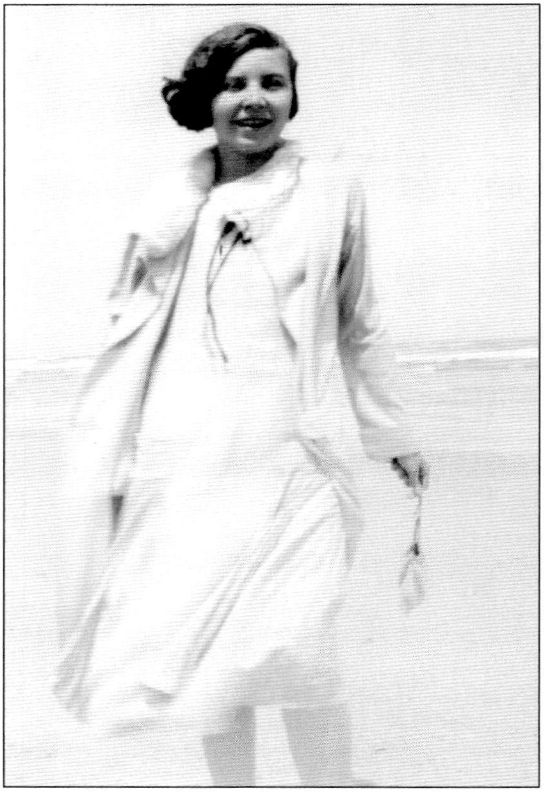

Mary Borum Usina is dressed up for a special occasion, posing in North Beach in the 1930s. (Courtesy of Mary Louise Usina Brown.)

Usina neighbors Victor and Clara Rahner are seen horsing around on the beach in the 1920s. Beaches were wide and flat and great for carefree, sun-filled antics. During the Roaring Twenties, dances were plentiful at nearby Surfside Casino. (Courtesy of Tom Rahner.)

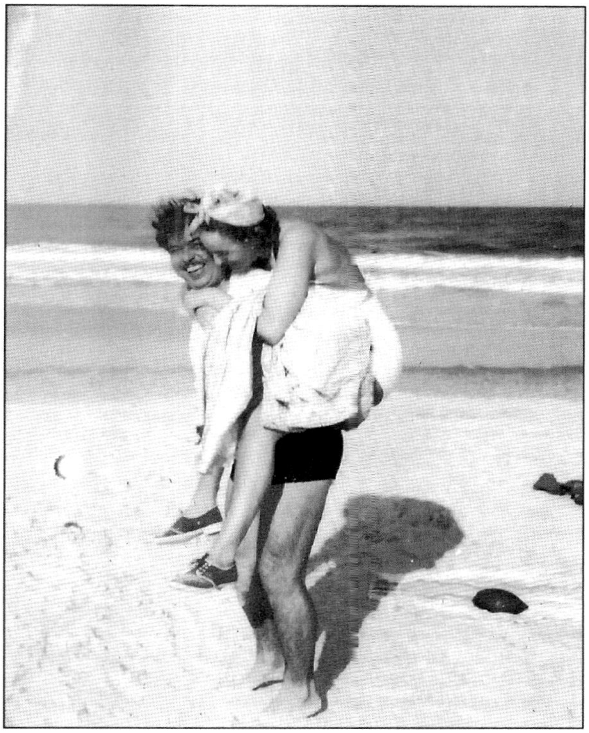

North Beach boyhood friends play on the docks, awaiting the return of sightseers circling the St. Augustine waterways around Salt Run and the North River. Youth at North Beach in the 1930s learned the ways of the sea early, as evidenced by fishing nets on this working dock. Jack (left), Victor Rahner Jr. and his dog (center), and Frank D. Usina (right) later went on to captain *Victory II* for years. (Courtesy of Tom Rahner.)

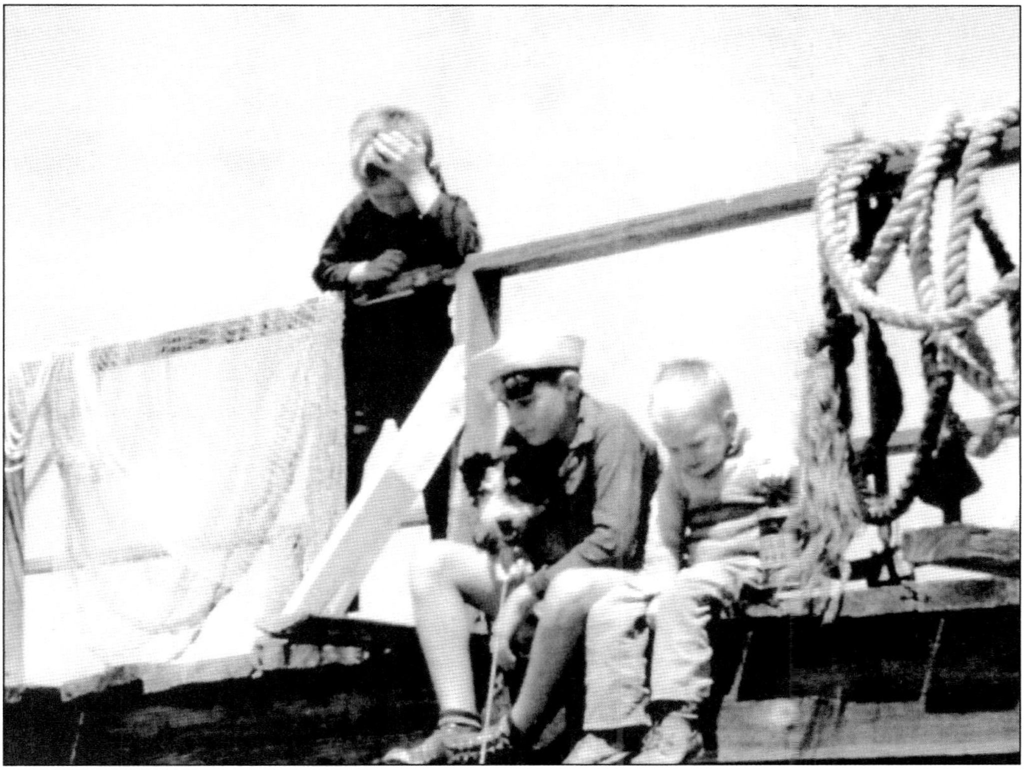

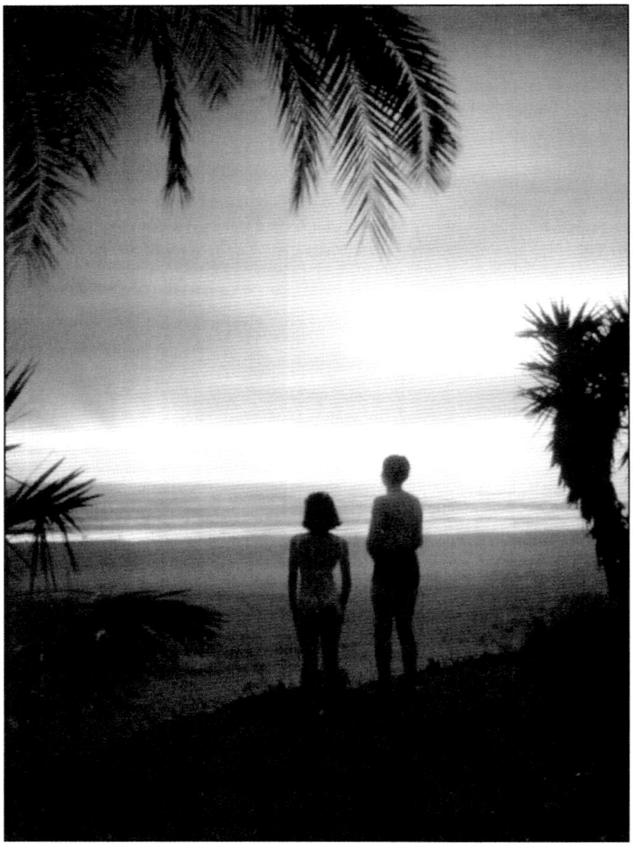

Victor Rahner Sr. was a renowned St. Augustine photographer. Here, he captures his children Victor Jr. and Martha Jane at sunrise in North Beach. The vistas highlight the beauty of the coastal setting, replete with palmettos and vivid views of the Atlantic Ocean. Many St. Augustine residents and out-of-town visitors had portraits taken by Rahner. (Courtesy of Tom Rahner.)

In the 1930s, the Rahner family was among the first settlers in North Beach. Times were hard during the Depression, and many resources for survival came from the coastal surroundings. Food sources were plentiful from the waterways and from homegrown crops suitable to the coastal terrain. Clara and her children, Victor Jr. (left), Tom (center), and Martha Jane pose for a family photograph taken by Victor Sr. (Courtesy of Tom Rahner.)

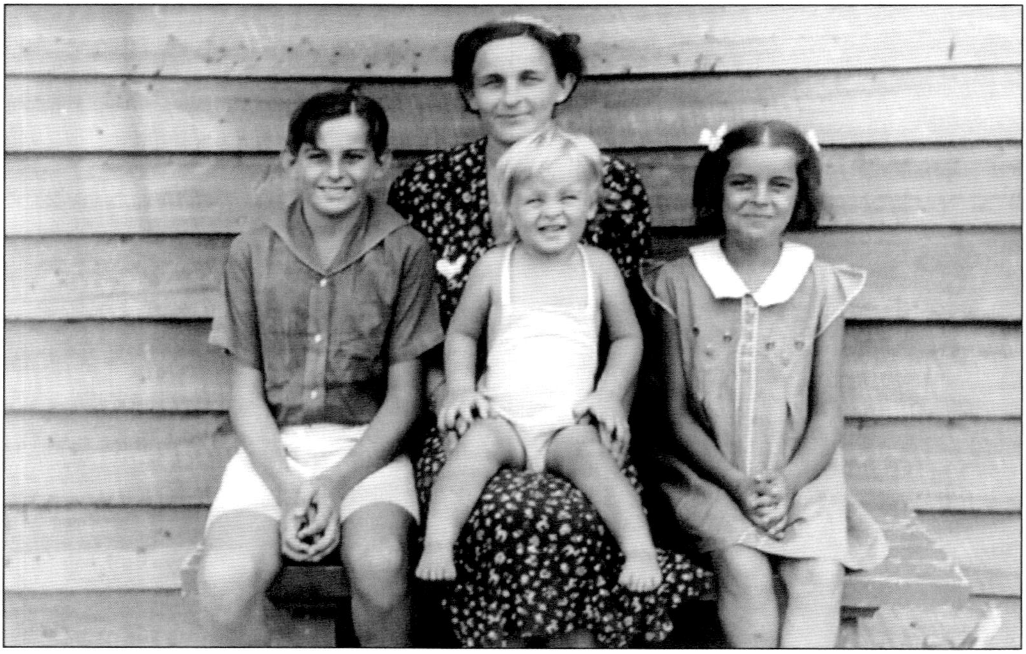

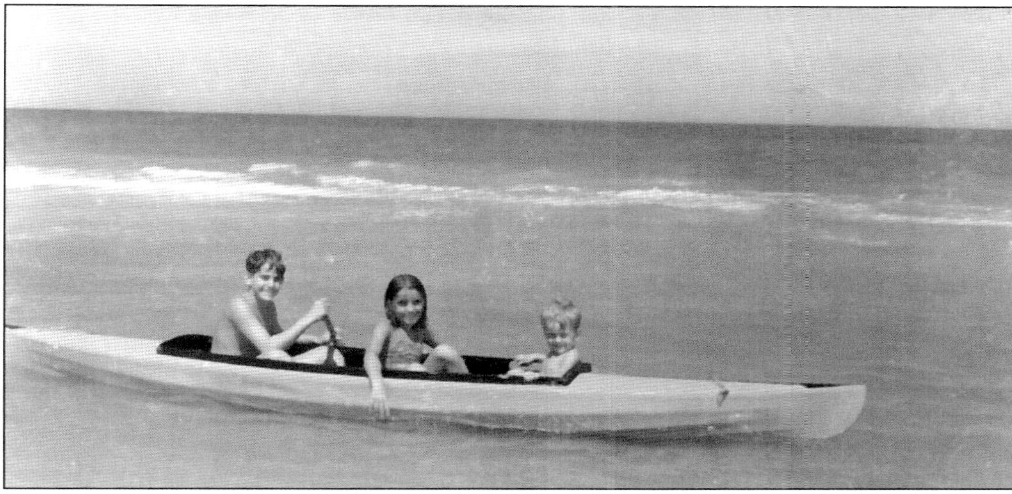

The Rahner children enjoy a day at sea in their kayak in front of their North Beach cottage. The coastal sloughs and sandbars make great natural play areas for children. There was little worry about children exploring the wooded areas and waterways; they grew up learning much about nature and what to watch out for to avoid danger. (Courtesy of Tom Rahner.)

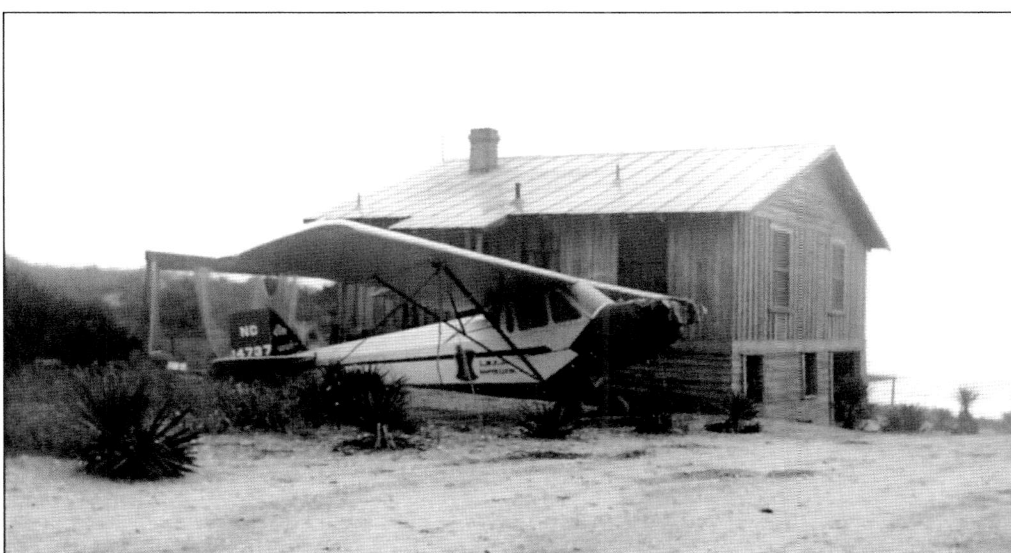

In 1937, an airplane running out of fuel over North Beach made an emergency landing. The Rahner home was in sight for this desperate pilot, L.W. Franklin Jr., a pharmacist from Danville, Virginia. A safe landing brought an overnight stay and much hospitality. The Rahner children, except for Tom, who was only two, experienced riding in the airplane in front of their oceanfront cottage. (Courtesy of Tom Rahner.)

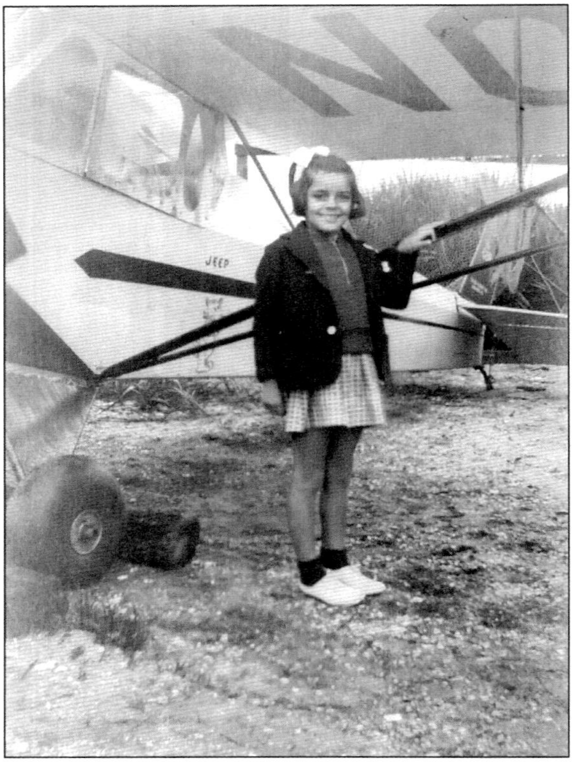

Martha Jane Rahner poses in front of an unlikely visitor's plane. She experienced her first flight on this plane, a Taylor E-2 Cub, nicknamed "Jeep." Her father, Victor Rahner Sr., captured this image. Tom Rahner researched long-forgotten information about the plane, tracked down the registration, and located the owner in North Carolina. At the age of 68, Tom had his turn to fly. (Courtesy of Tom Rahner.)

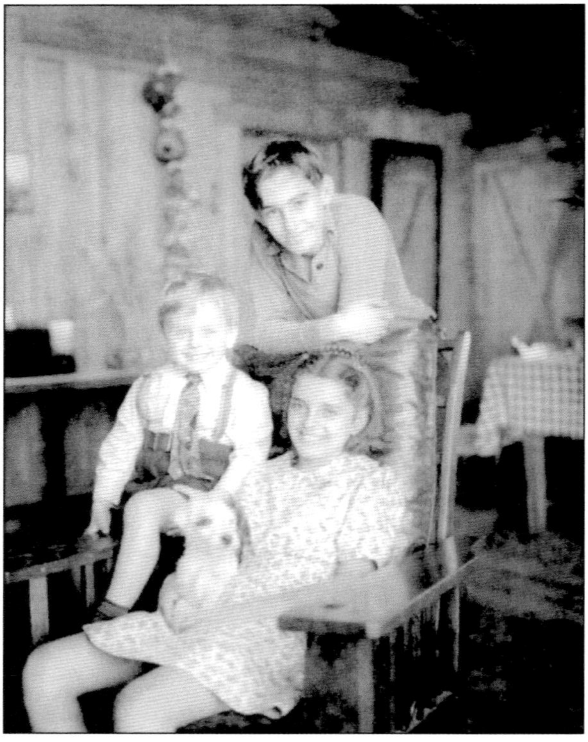

The Rahner children pose inside their North Beach cottage around 1939. Through economic necessity caused by the Depression, the family relocated to North Beach, where Victor built the home. They lived in relative isolation, with no telephone lines and a battery-operated radio. The kids became good friends with the neighboring Usina families. (Courtesy of Tom Rahner.)

Capt. Francis E. Usina enjoyed the river and the ocean, and the bountiful harvest of fresh seafood. It was not uncommon for a day on the river to yield gigantic catches. Note that the materials used for fencing included oyster shells. They were also used in road construction. (Courtesy of Elizabeth and Frank D. Usina.)

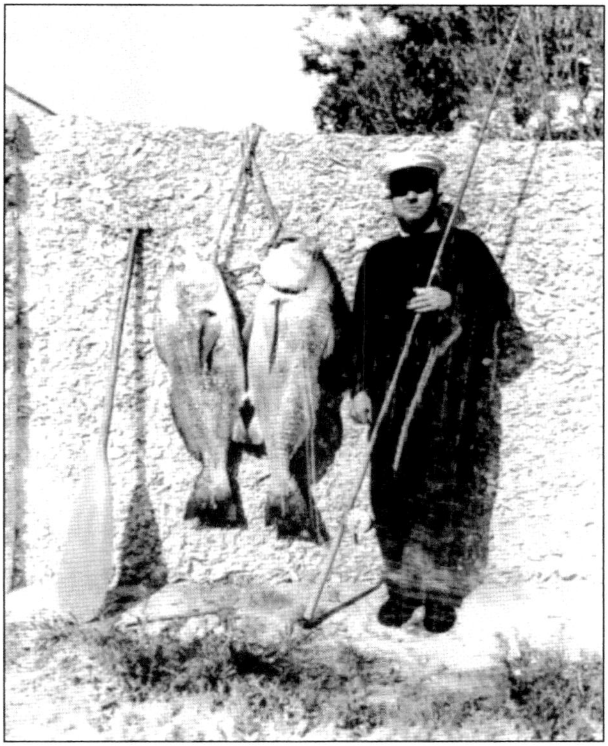

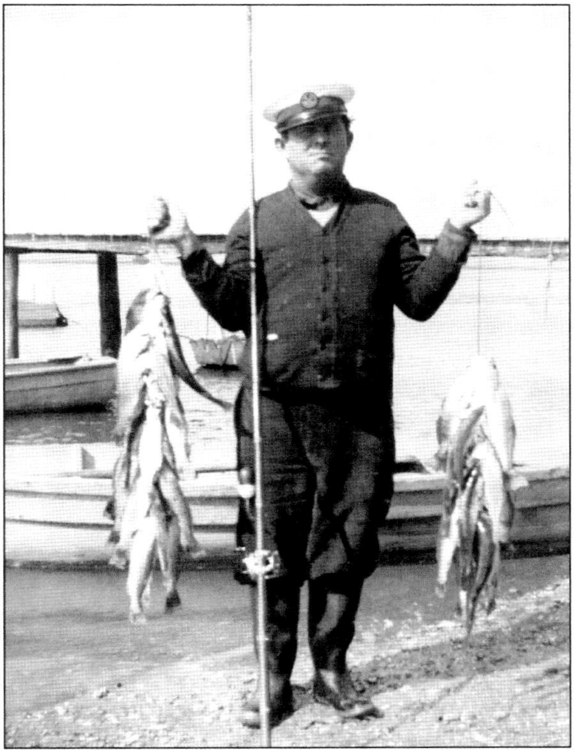

Capt. Francis E. Usina shows off his black drum fish in the 1930s. He enjoyed sharing his family knowledge of how to fish with everyone. After World War II, the family business expanded its camp-resort enterprises, embracing boating, fishing, and sightseeing endeavors. North Beach was the place to get out and away from the crowds. (Courtesy of Elizabeth and Frank D. Usina.)

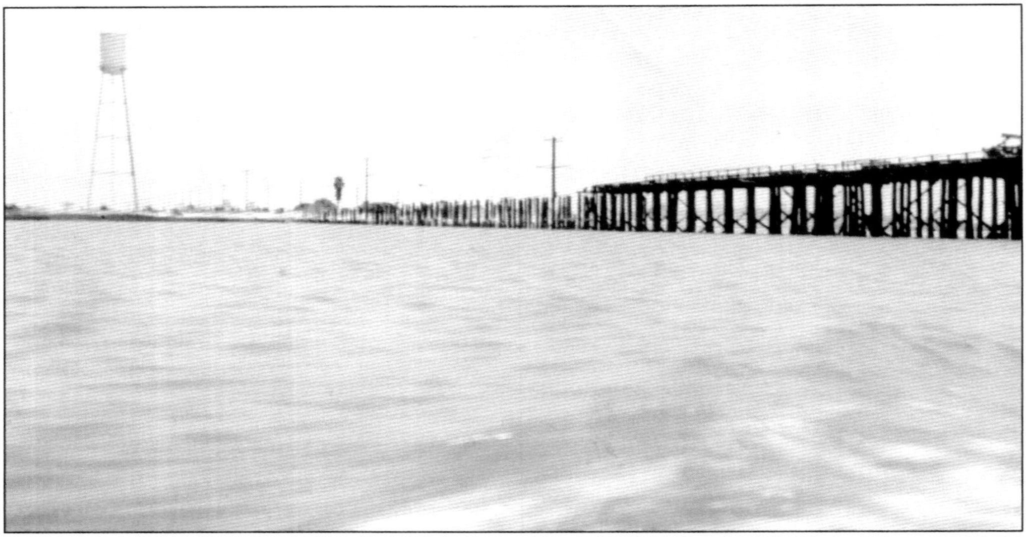

On June 13, 1938, fire destroyed the east end of the wooden Vilano Bridge. *Victory II* came to the rescue of coastal residents, providing ferry service while the bridge was undergoing temporary repairs. Even after a year, repairs were slow, with one-lane access, as shown here in 1939. Creosote and tar are obvious. The bridge was replaced in 1948. (Courtesy of Mary Louise Usina Brown.)

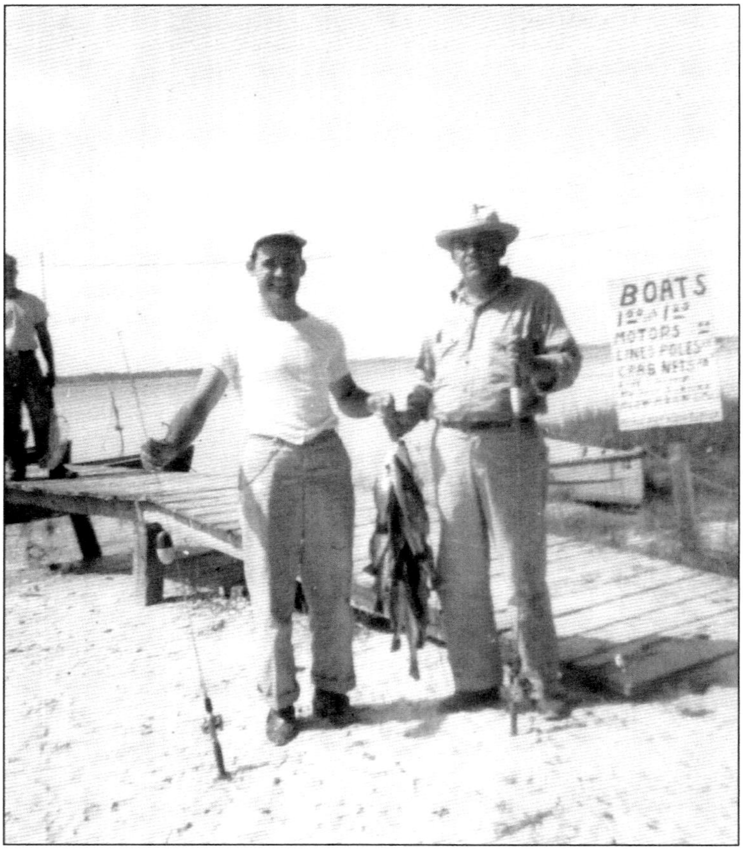

Unidentified fishermen at the dock at the end of Euclid Avenue show off their catches in the late 1940s. The dock and surrounding facilities were all part of the Usina fishing complex. Boat rentals, bait, and other necessities were available. (Courtesy of Elizabeth and Frank D. Usina.)

Three

Surfside Beach

Paul and Helen Capo came to what is now known as Surfside in 1904. They began bringing tourists from the St. Augustine bayfront on their boat, *Pauline II*, to a landing at the east end of Surfside Avenue. Tourists would then board a horse-drawn trolley for a half-mile ride to the beachfront. There was a bathhouse for changing into swimwear and a room for dancing upstairs. By 1914, Paul had registered a plat for this area and named it North Beach City. In 1926, this plat was renamed Surfside Beach. Lots were sold for homes to be built near the beach. Every street end and the public beach allowed these property owners plenty of public access to the beach. These free beach access areas remain in effect today.

The Surfside subdivision permitted right-of-way for the new coastal highway, which allowed automobile traffic to arrive from Ponte Vedra and continue through the new toll bridge, southward over the river and into St Augustine.

In the 1930s, a group of beachside cottages was built by Lucius Gibson "Shorty" Rees on the coastal highway. He rented them to passing tourists. These cottages remain today as small beach homes and rentals for individual owners. During World War II, the locals served as lookouts for German spies coming ashore, as had happened in nearby Ponte Vedra Beach. Residents were required to keep blackout curtains on their oceanfront windows.

The North Shores Improvement Association began meeting in 1939 at the Surfside Bathhouse. By the 1950s, this civic group acquired a donated block of land fronting on Meadow Avenue to build its own meetinghouse.

In the years after World War II, many permanent homes were built in this community. The new 1995 bridge entrance to St. Augustine is located in Surfside—and not in adjoining Vilano Beach, as it had been from 1927 until 1995. The Vilano Beach Town Center includes a portion of the southern side of the Surfside plat, which now includes a part of the site of the long-awaited Publix grocery store and pharmacy, which opened in 2012.

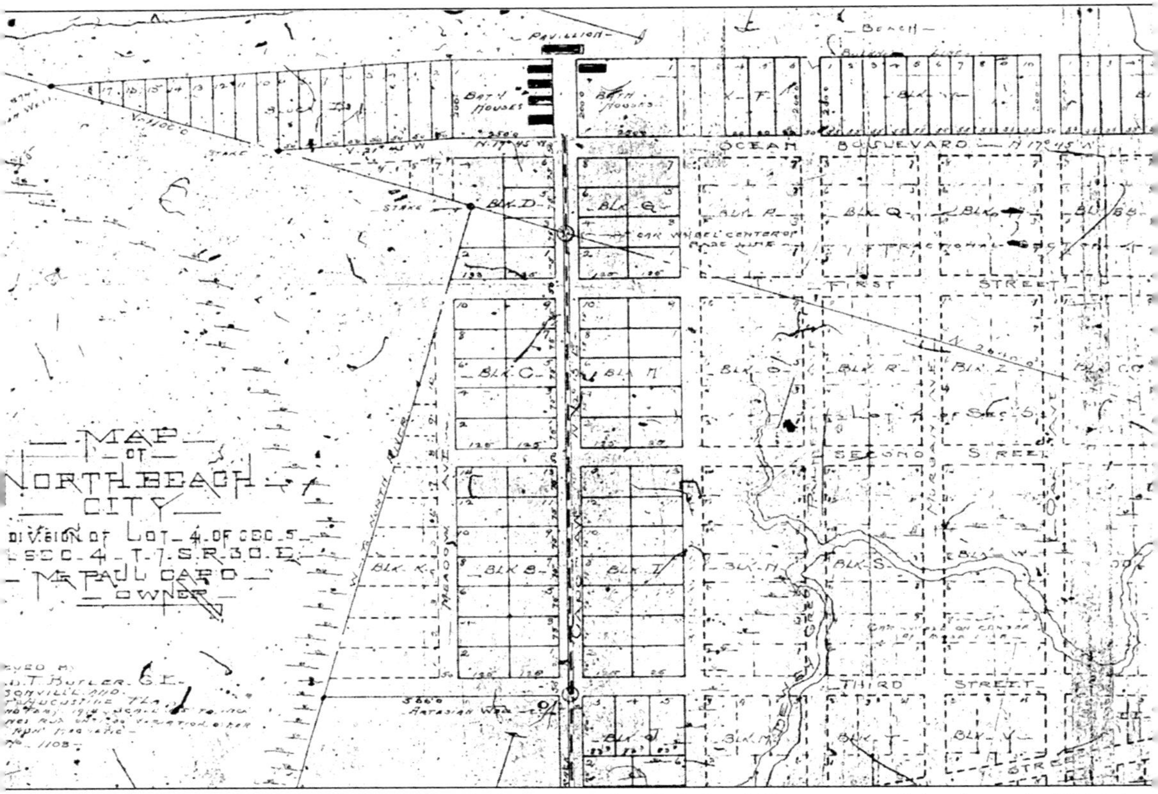

This 1914 plat map of North Beach City identifies "Mr. Paul Capo, owner." At the end of Third Street is a pavilion and artesian well. The old railway line is shown on "Capo Ave," leading to the beachside pavilions and bathhouses. Ocean Boulevard is the current A1A Scenic & Historic Coastal Byway. The Capos erected a boat landing, pavilion, and, later, a small hotel, and also built a horse-drawn trolley line to carry passengers across the dunes to the beach. Their operation was very similar to the Usinas. Paul Capo ferried passengers from downtown St. Augustine in his excursion boat, *Pauline II*. The Capo family had long been residents of the St. Augustine area. Paul, born in 1856, married Helen Capo, and they had sons Lon, Edmond, and Cecil and one daughter, Eunice. Eunice's granddaughter, Eunice Capo Banta Bowen, confirms that her grandmother built cottages at North Beach. (Courtesy of St. Johns County.)

Adolphus Pacetti was manager and later owner of the Capos' bathhouse on the bayfront of Hypolita Street. This was a popular place in the 1890s to enjoy hot, cold, seawater, and sulphur baths. Beachgoers departed from downtown and headed across the bay to Capo's Landing in North Beach City. (Courtesy of the St. Augustine Historical Society.)

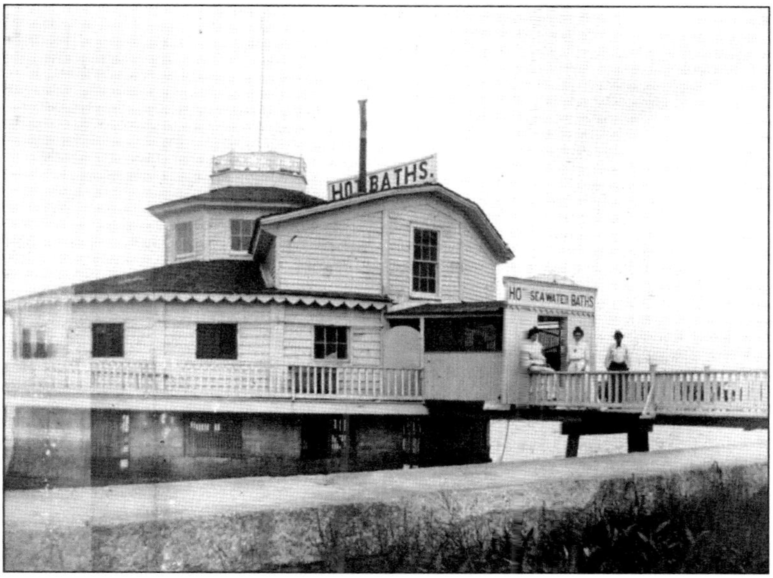

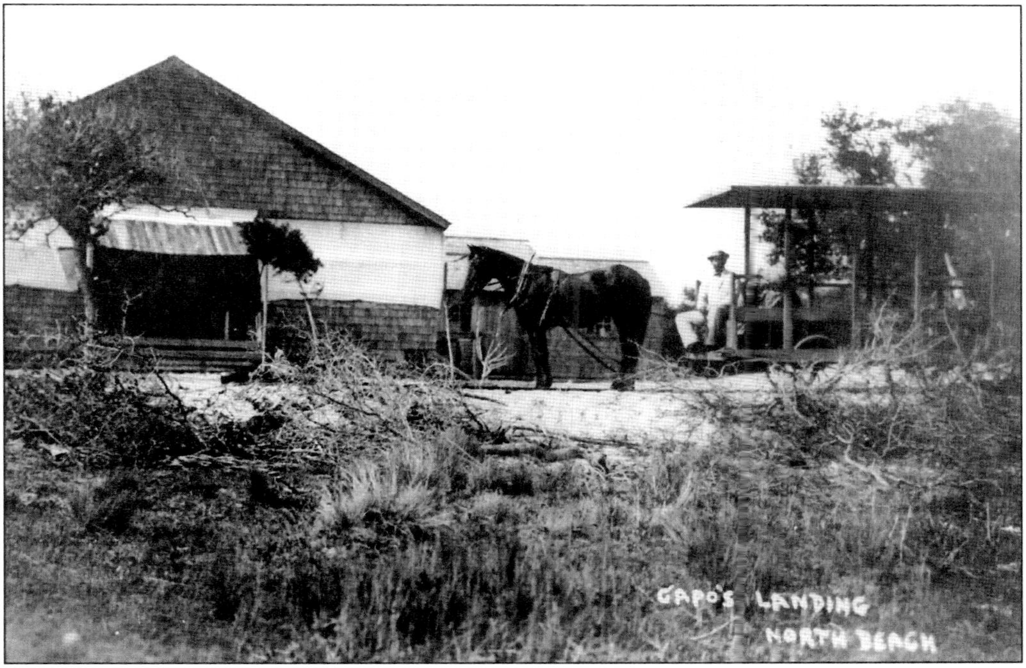

Some of the Capo family settled in the North Beach City area around 1904. Public records show Capo relatives throughout downtown. Paul Capo later developed a thriving business for tourists by building a pavilion and horse-drawn trolleys. Meals offered included Minorcan dishes, such as roasted oysters, pilau, chowder, and fish. Later additions to the establishment included a small hotel. (Courtesy of Elizabeth and Frank D. Usina.)

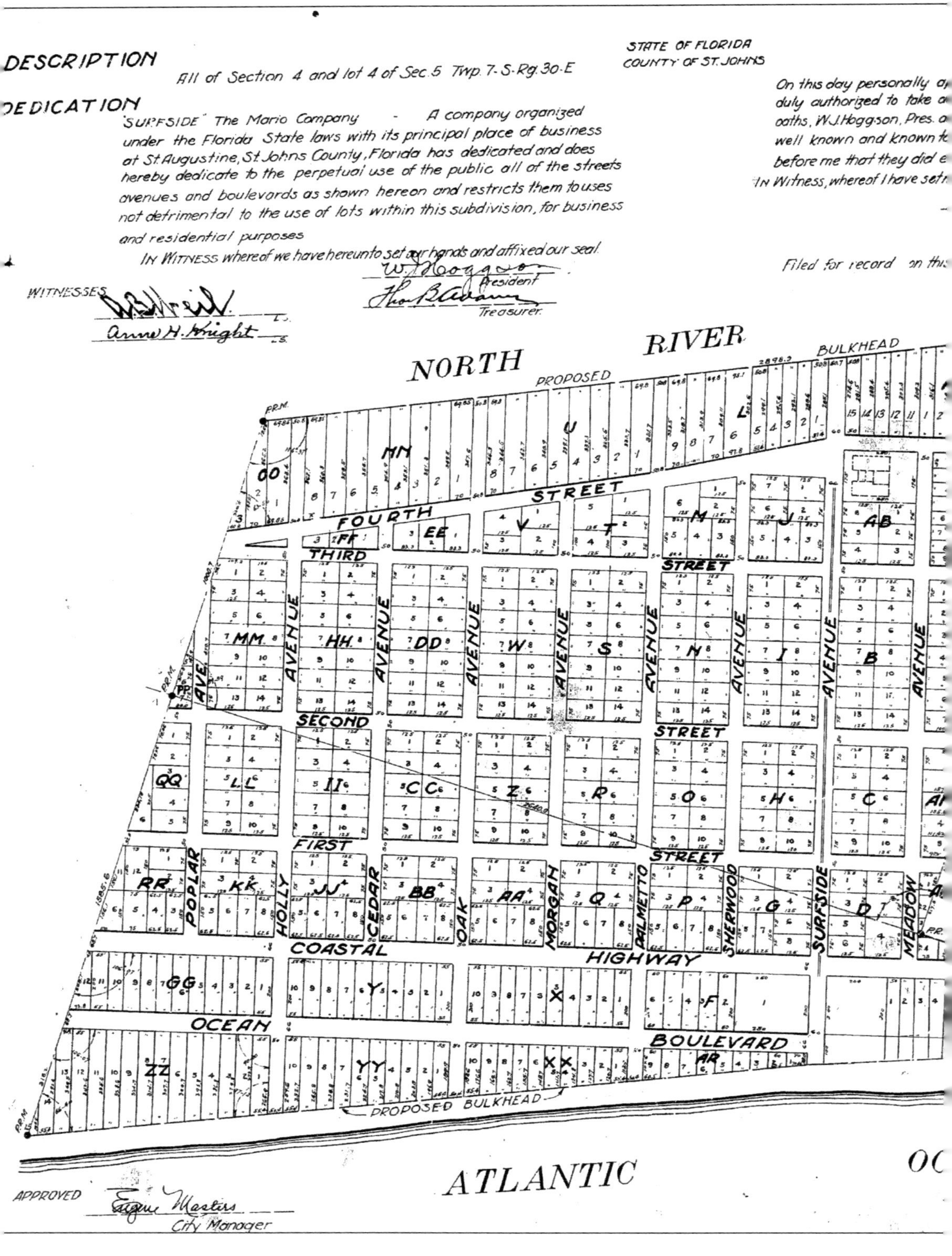
DESCRIPTION
All of Section 4 and lot 4 of Sec. 5 Twp. 7-S-Rg. 30-E
DEDICATION
"SURFSIDE" The Mario Company - A company organized under the Florida State laws with its principal place of business at St. Augustine, St. Johns County, Florida has dedicated and does hereby dedicate to the perpetual use of the public all of the streets avenues and boulevards as shown hereon and restricts them to uses not detrimental to the use of lots within this subdivision, for business and residential purposes
IN WITNESS whereof we have hereunto set our hands and affixed our seal.
President
Treasurer.
WITNESSES
Anne H. Knight
STATE OF FLORIDA
COUNTY OF ST. JOHNS
On this day personally a
duly authorized to take a
oaths, W.J. Hoggson, Pres. a
well known and known t
before me that they did e
IN Witness, whereof I have set
Filed for record on thi
NORTH
RIVER
PROPOSED
BULKHEAD
FOURTH
STREET
THIRD
STREET
SECOND
STREET
FIRST
STREET
COASTAL
HIGHWAY
OCEAN
BOULEVARD
POPLAR
HOLLY
CEDAR
OAK
MORGAH
PALMETTO
SHERWOOD
SURFSIDE
MEADOW
AVENUE
PROPOSED BULKHEAD
ATLANTIC
OC
APPROVED
Eugene Masters
City Manager

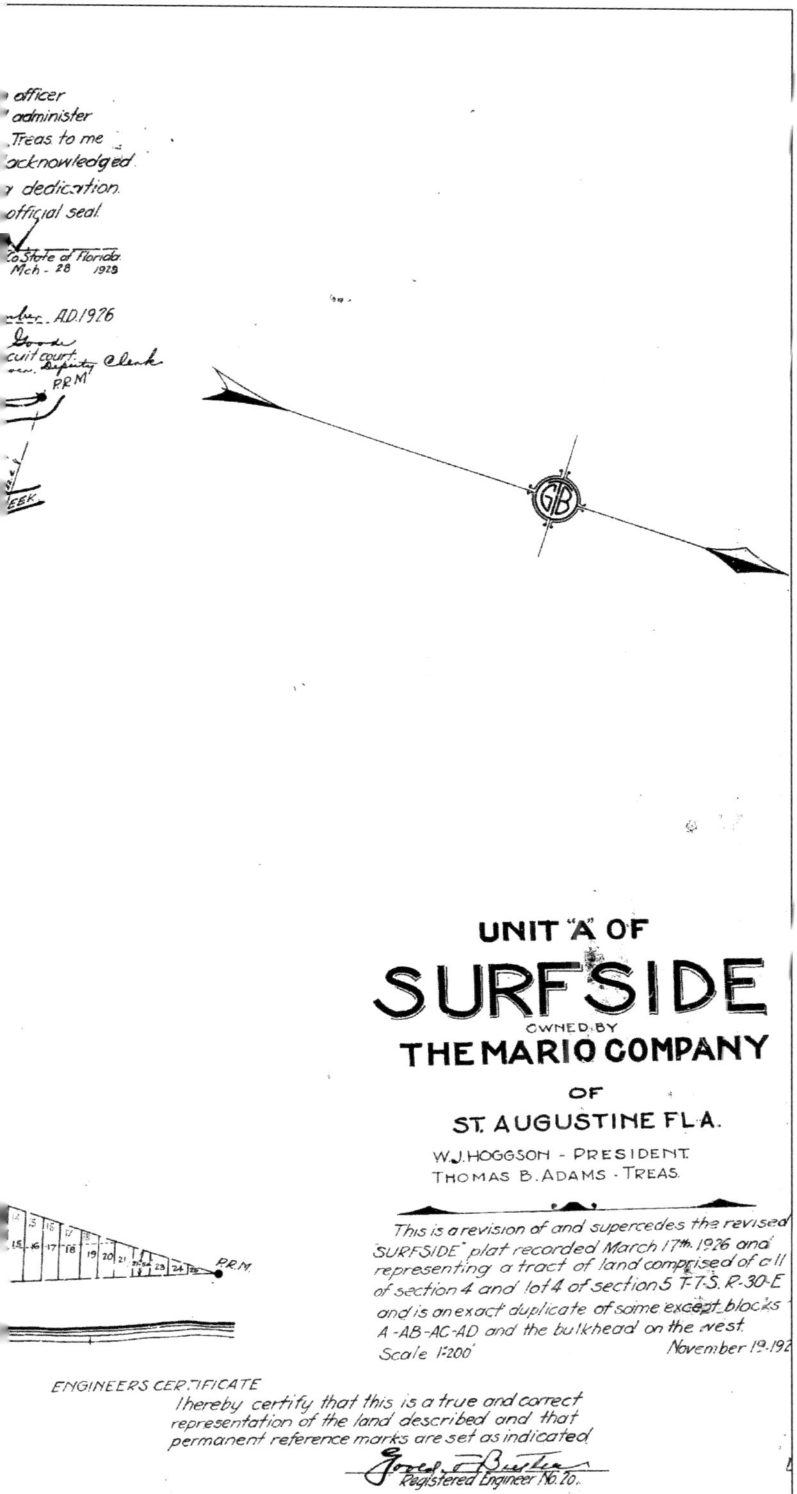

The Surfside subdivision was platted and filed in 1926. The previous plat on the same site (North Beach City) included some of the same road names and lot sizes. This subdivision was platted after the coastal highway, which ran from Ponte Vedra through this area, was built. The public beach was located at the corner of Coastal Highway and Surfside Avenue. This beach included an entertainment building with a dance floor as well as a bathhouse for beachgoers. The North Shores Improvement Association met there after it was established as a local civic group in 1939. In the 1950s, this group built its own community center, located at 120 Meadow Avenue, where it currently meets. This plat adjoins the Vilano Beach plat (1927) and shares a portion of the Vilano Town Center with Vilano Beach. (Courtesy of St. Johns County.)

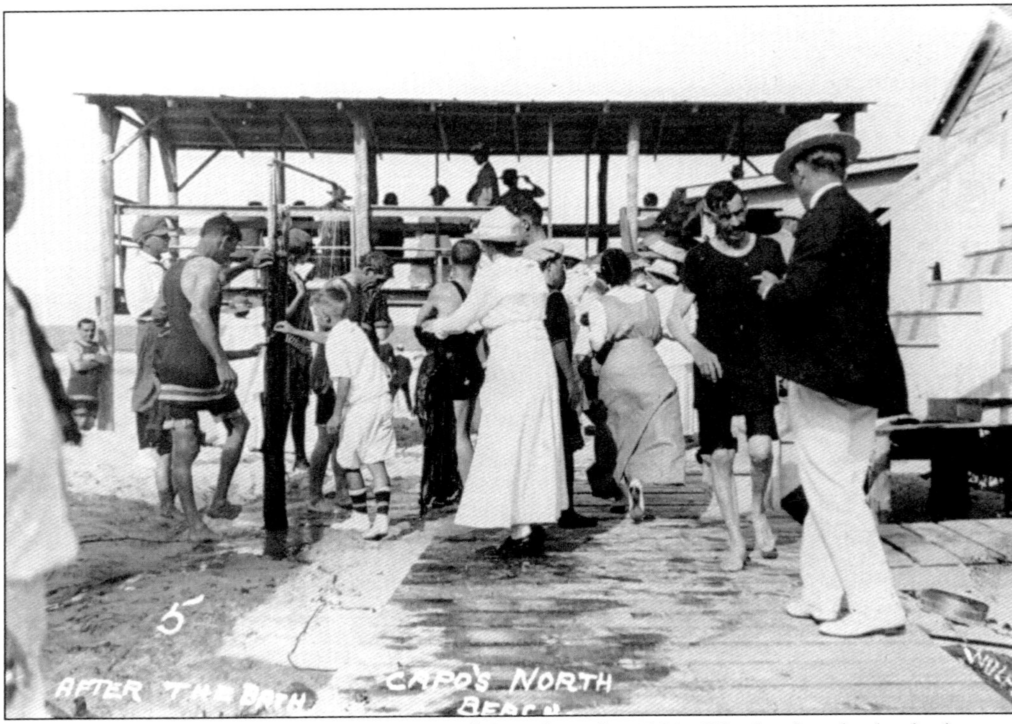

Beachgoers travel to Capo's Landing at North Beach in the 1920s. The landing had refreshments and changing facilities for guests to use after their swims in the ocean. It was south of the Usina docks and pavilion. The wide beaches accommodated motorcars, horses, and airplanes. (Courtesy of the St. Augustine Historical Society.)

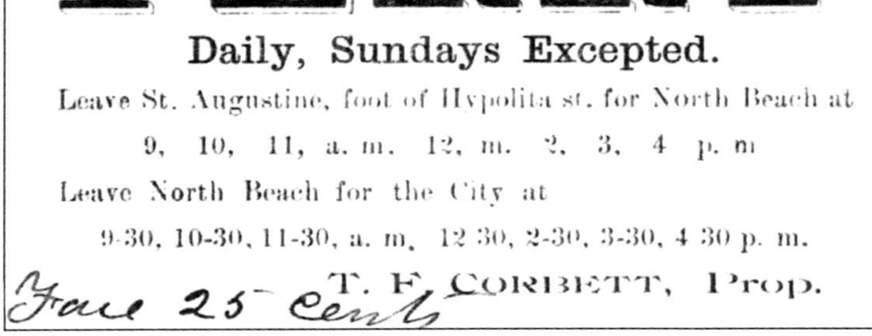

HOURLY TRIPS to NORTH BEACH.

NORTH BEACH

FERRY

Daily, Sundays Excepted.

Leave St. Augustine, foot of Hypolita st. for North Beach at

9, 10, 11, a. m. 12, m. 2, 3, 4 p. m

Leave North Beach for the City at

9-30, 10-30, 11-30, a. m. 12-30, 2-30, 3-30, 4-30 p. m.

T. F. CORBETT, Prop.

Fare 25 Cents

This 1890s ferry schedule identifies hourly trips, excepting Sundays, to North Beach offered by T.F. Corbett. Captain Corbett operated the *Ida*, a private steam launch providing regular runs to the barrier islands. Fare was 25¢. A rivalry was beginning to develop with competing private boat companies. (Courtesy of the St. Augustine Historical Society.)

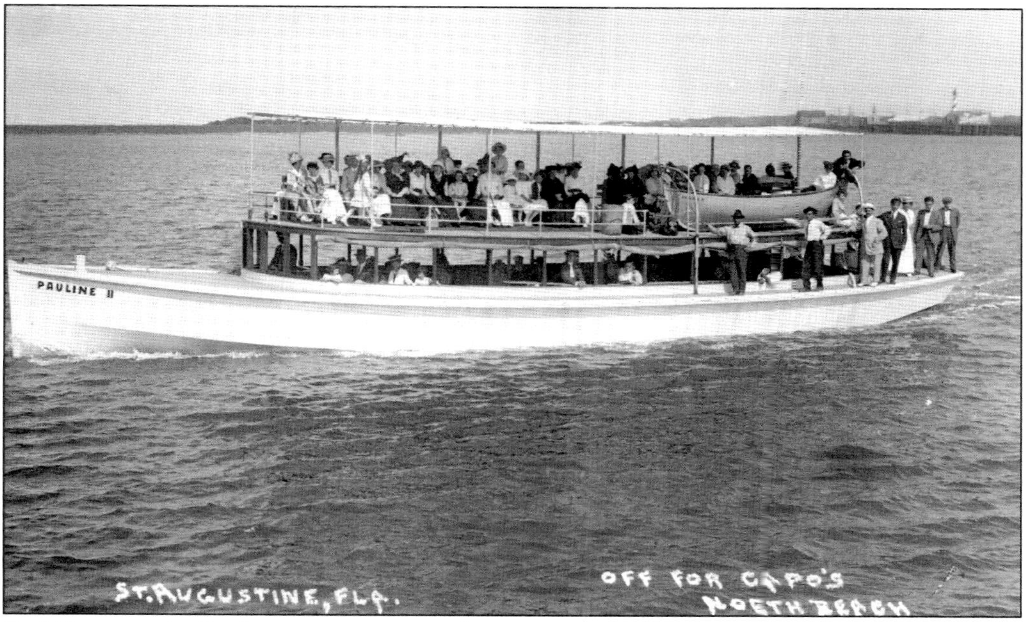

Paul Capo sought St. Augustine tourists to be passengers on his excursion boat, *Pauline II*. From the city docks, the boat traveled north to Capo's North Beach landing, where passengers were met by horse-drawn trolley, which took them to the beach. This service also was available by the Usina excursion boat *Victory II*. As can be imagined, there was rivalry between the two operations. (Courtesy of Jackie and Nadine Connahay.)

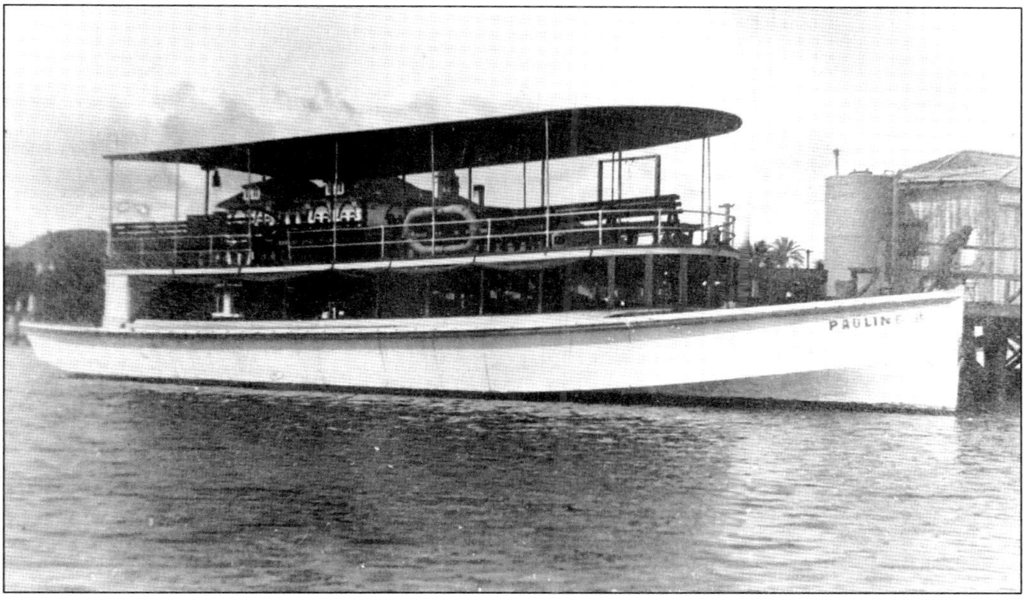

Like the Usinas' *Victory*, *Pauline II* carried guests to North Beach regularly. The extended family of Capos were of Minorcan decent and well established in St. Augustine. There was a parallel development of business enterprises of the two families. The Usinas were first to settle in North Beach, in 1890, while the Capos moved in later, in 1904. The expansion of the two businesses followed different timelines. (Courtesy of Karen Harvey.)

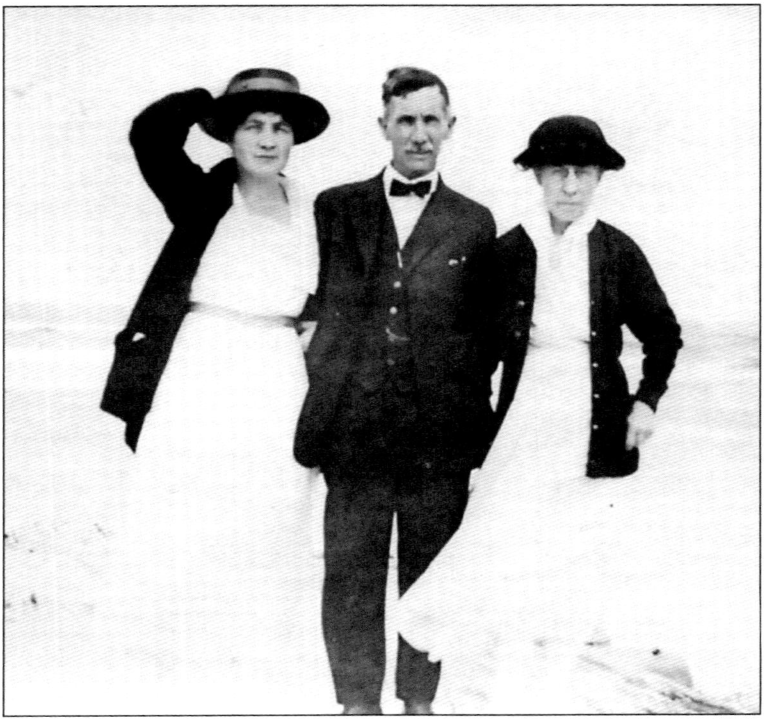

In March 1922, Mr. and Mrs. Walter H. Moore of Tennessee (pictured) visited their daughter, Telitha Moore McCartney (left). They are shown here, enjoying a day at the beach. Telitha, an auditor for the Florida East Coast Railway, resided in St. Augustine. Telitha's fiancé was a volunteer lifeguard on weekends and holidays, from Memorial Day to Labor Day. It was during that time that the two courted and later married. (Courtesy of Walter Daniels.)

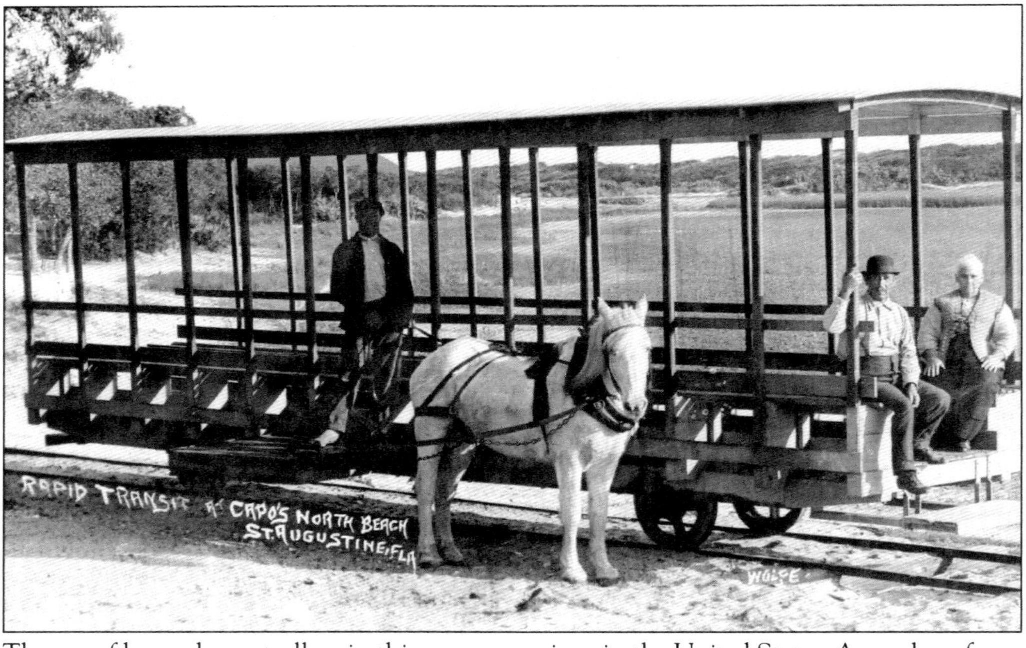

The use of horse-drawn trolleys in this area was unique in the United States. A number of cars operated almost year-round. Covered cars offered protection from the sun. It was not only North Beaches that used these horse-drawn cars; downtown St. Augustine had similar trolleys crossing the Matanzas, heading to Anastasia Island. (Courtesy of Karen Harvey.)

Beginning in 1904, a horse-drawn trolley operated by the Capo family would meet *Pauline II*, a boat also owned by the family. The trolley then took tourists coming from the St. Augustine bayfront to Capo's Landing, which had a bathhouse building complete with a dance and party area upstairs. As seen here, wild hogs roamed the area. (Courtesy of Jackie and Nadine Connahay.)

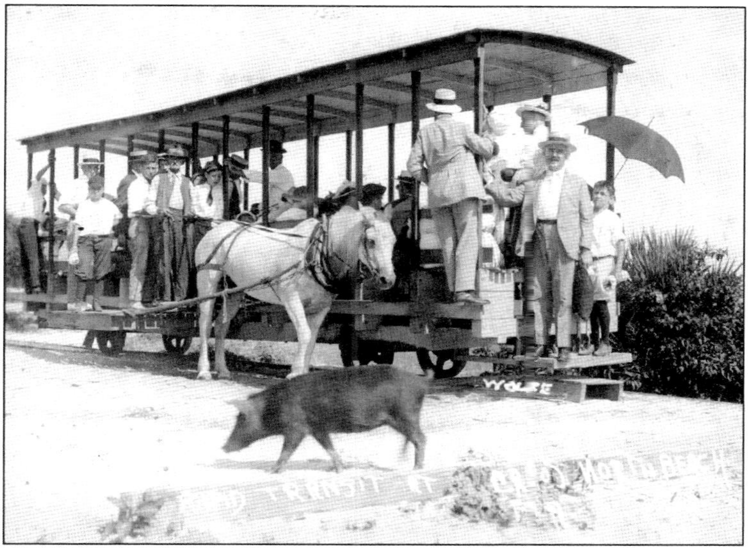

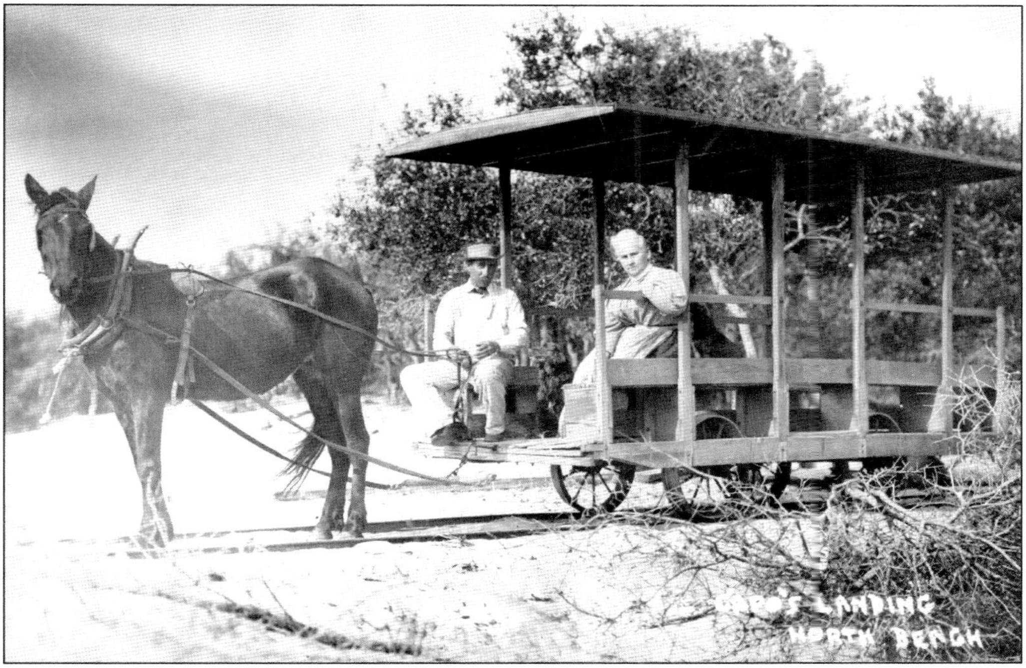

Henry Flagler's northern visitors could choose between the South Beach on Anastasia Island and the North Beach located across the Matanzas Inlet. At North Beach, beachgoers could also select from services provided by the Usina or Capo families. This photograph of Capo's "rapid transit" clearly shows how horses were hitched onto railcars. (Courtesy of Elizabeth and Frank D. Usina.)

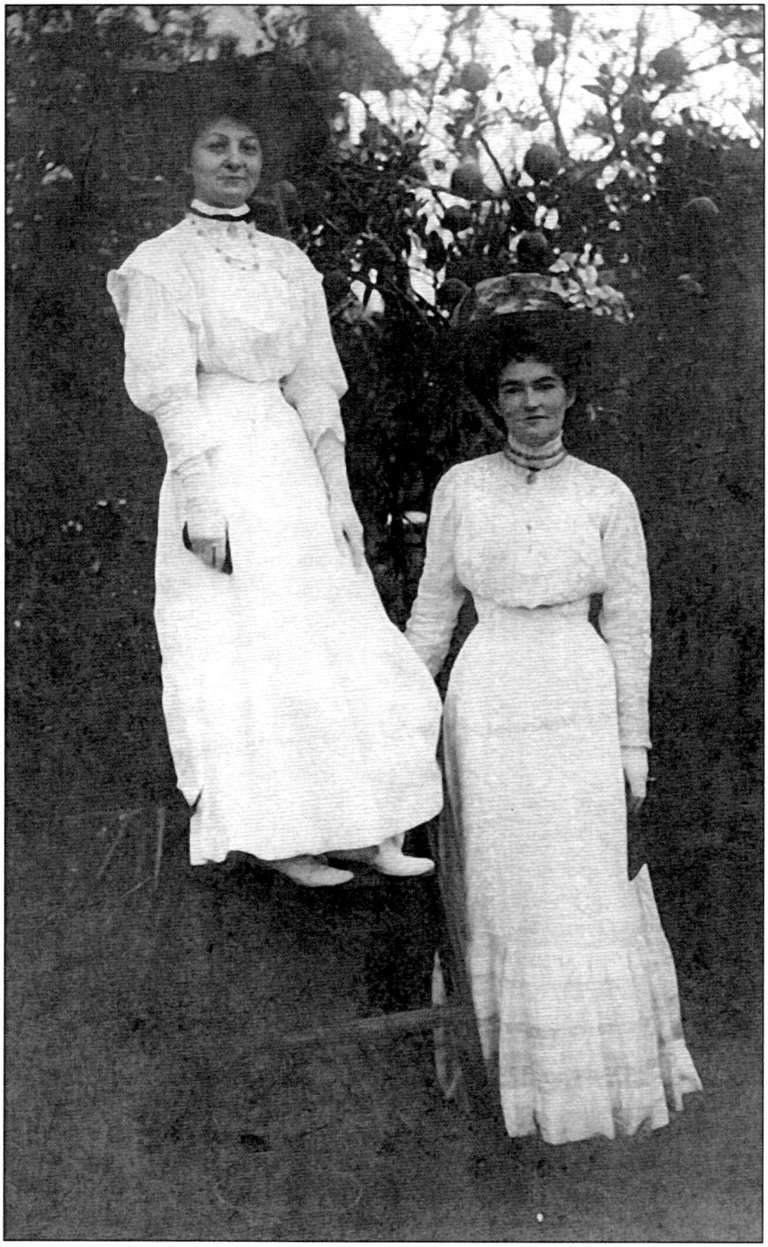

Here, two ladies show off styles of the early 1900s while perhaps on a day excursion to the beaches. The long dresses of the day made climbing the dunes difficult. Attire for beach activity was similarly nonrevealing. Before the turn of the century, showing one's ankles was considered daring and exciting. After a few decades, beach attire changed to reflect more revealing elements of design for ladies and men. Towels were something of a luxury over 100 years ago, as well. Visitors often rented towels on their day excursions to avoid the necessity of labor-intensive laundering. These ladies are in an orange grove, of which there were many in the area. Florida-themed messages in later years included orange-juice stands. Fresh fruit and warm days were great draws for visitors. (Courtesy of Karen Harvey.)

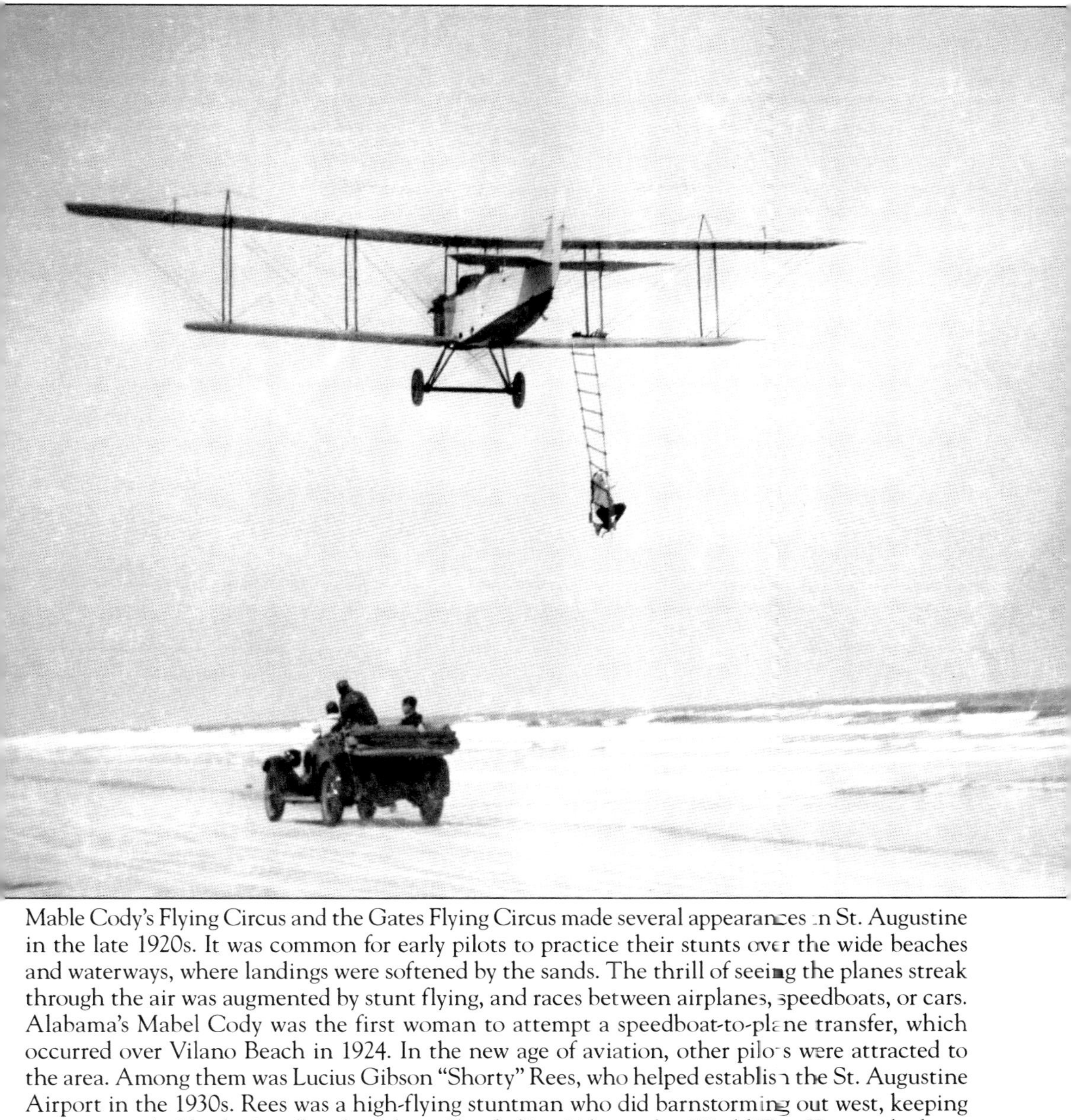

Mable Cody's Flying Circus and the Gates Flying Circus made several appearances in St. Augustine in the late 1920s. It was common for early pilots to practice their stunts over the wide beaches and waterways, where landings were softened by the sands. The thrill of seeing the planes streak through the air was augmented by stunt flying, and races between airplanes, speedboats, or cars. Alabama's Mabel Cody was the first woman to attempt a speedboat-to-plane transfer, which occurred over Vilano Beach in 1924. In the new age of aviation, other pilots were attracted to the area. Among them was Lucius Gibson "Shorty" Rees, who helped establish the St. Augustine Airport in the 1930s. Rees was a high-flying stuntman who did barnstorming out west, keeping company with Charles Lindbergh. Gibson "landed" in Vilano after World War II to settle down in Surfside Beach. (Courtesy of Florida Memory.)

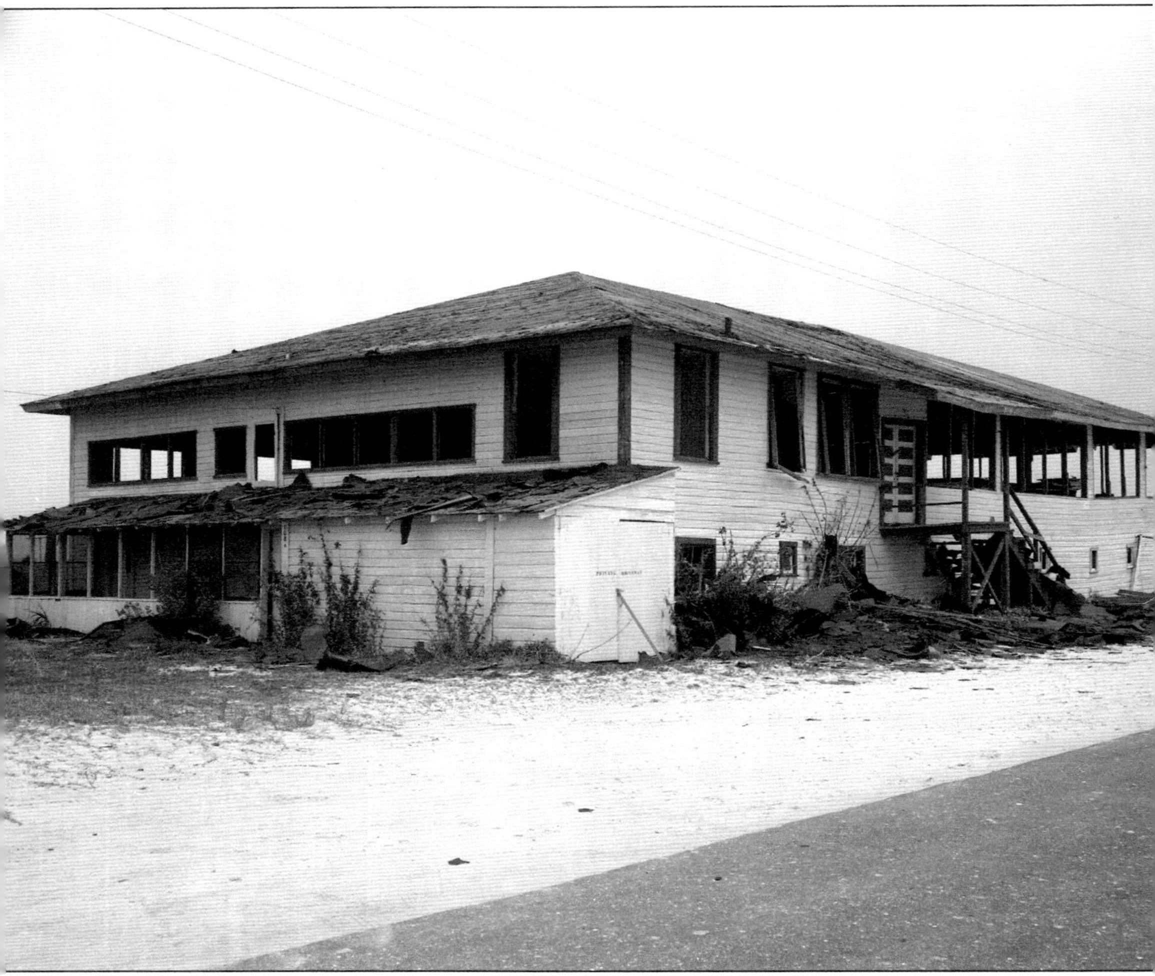

The Surfside Dance Hall and Bathhouse stood along Ocean Highway from the 1900s to the 1970s, when the aging building was torn down and replaced by a county park, now known as Surfside Park. Surfside was built as part of the Capo family resort, which covered 165 acres at North Beach. Paul Capo's yacht, *Pauline II,* carried visitors from the bayfront to North River at the west end of Surfside Avenue, where they could stay at Capo's Hotel, complete with a 120-seat restaurant. Horse trolleys transported guests to the seashore, where the casino offered an upstairs dance hall and a downstairs bathhouse. A variety of organized sports, such as horse racing, airplane stunts, car racing, and marathons were viewed from this high ocean overlook. In 1939, the North Shores Improvement Association began meeting here to improve the community. During and after World War II, Surfside was popular with servicemen, as it had jukebox music and inexpensive entertainment. (Courtesy of the St. Augustine Historical Society.)

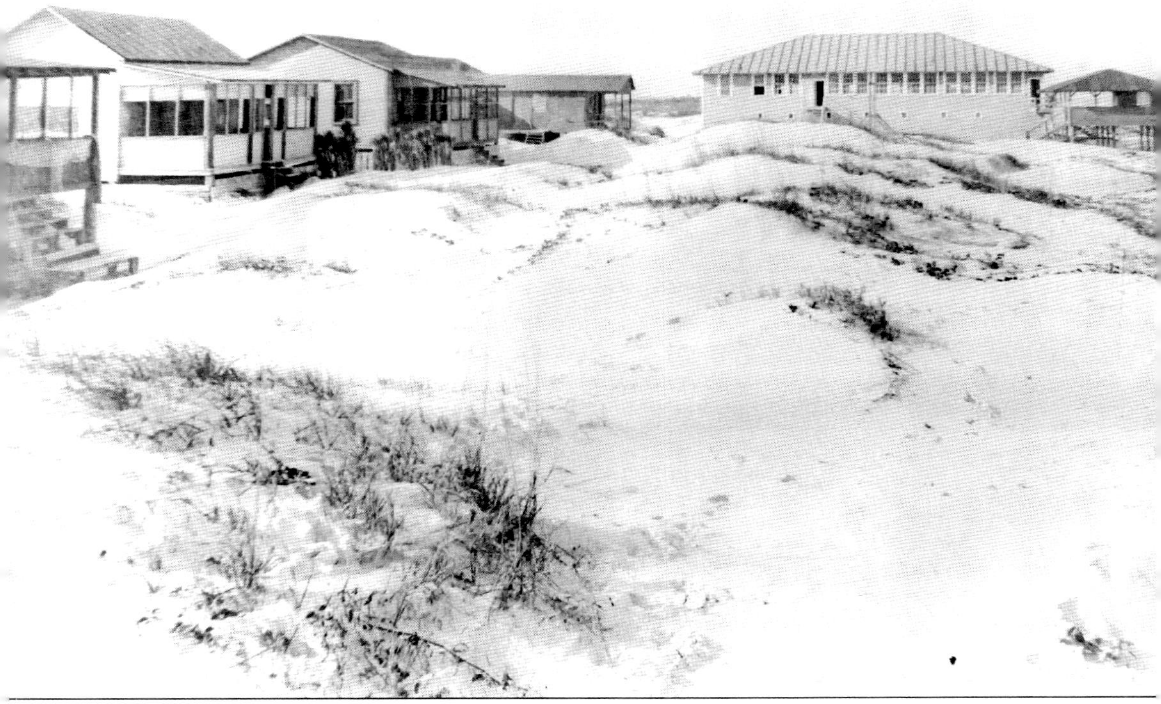

After a decade, the original North Beach City subdivision was replatted and became known as Surfside Beach. With the improved roads for automobiles in the late 1920s, visitors stayed longer. Many beach cottages sprang up and remain today in the subdivision. Surfside Casino was built in 1922, when only a few houses existed along "Capo Avenue," now Surfside Avenue. In 1935, and again in the late 1940s and 1950s, additional cottages were built. Eunice Capo Banta Bowen lived in one of the four oldest houses in Surfside until 2000, when she relocated to Albany, Georgia, to be near family. In 2010, at the age of 97, she left a legacy of 1 son, 12 grandchildren, 28 great-grandchildren, and 5 great-great-grandchildren. Among her relatives was Capt. Ronnie Capo, who also resided in Surfside Beach. (Courtesy of Karen Harvey.)

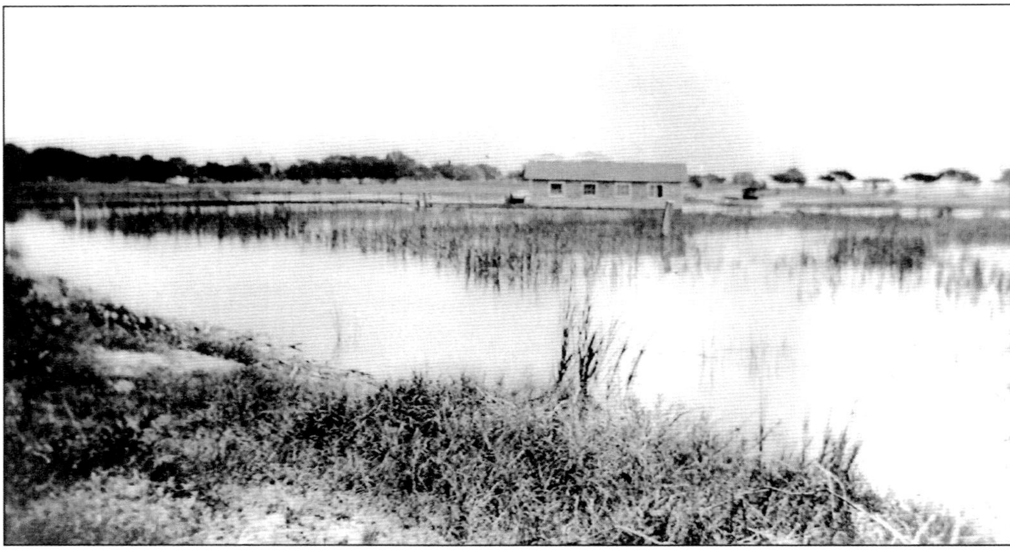

The land in and around Surfside and North Beach was bordered by waterways. Marshlands along the Tolomato, or North River, were plentiful. This, however, did not dissuade builders from constructing homes on them in the early days. This house is located on a tidal creek with access to the North River. (Courtesy of Karen Harvey.)

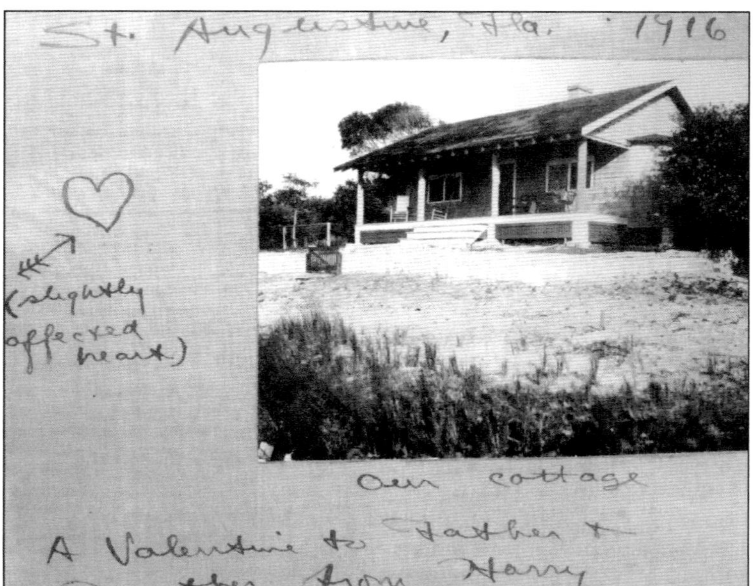

This house in Surfside was rented for a while by Sinclair Lewis and his wife, Grace. He sent this photograph of "Our Cottage" to his parents for Valentine's Day in 1916. A close look reveals Lewis writing on the back porch, possibly working on his novel *Main Street*. Lewis graduated from Yale University, which maintains a collection of his memorabilia. (Courtesy of Dawn Jones.)

As businesses boomed in the 1920s, jobs became available. At Surfside Beach, regular and part-time lifeguards were always in demand. Here, Victor Rahner (center) relaxes at the foot of a beach walkover at Surfside Casino. Lifeguarding was a popular part-time job for many young men. (Courtesy of Tom Rahner.)

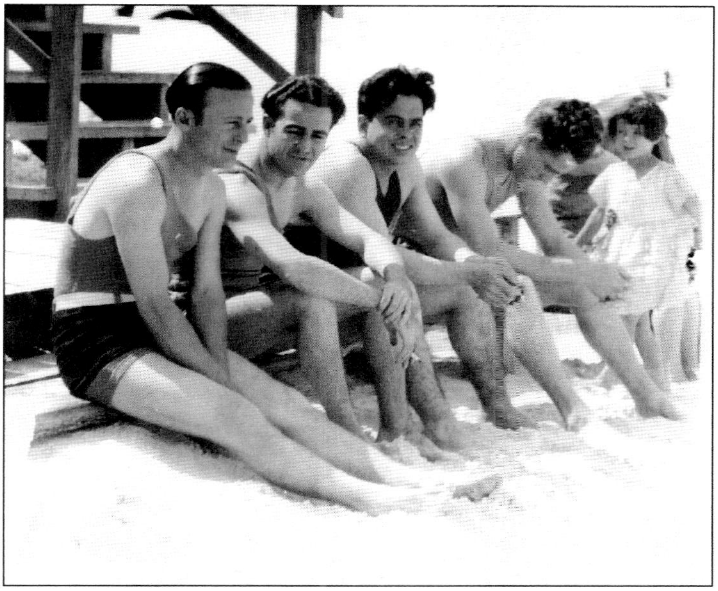

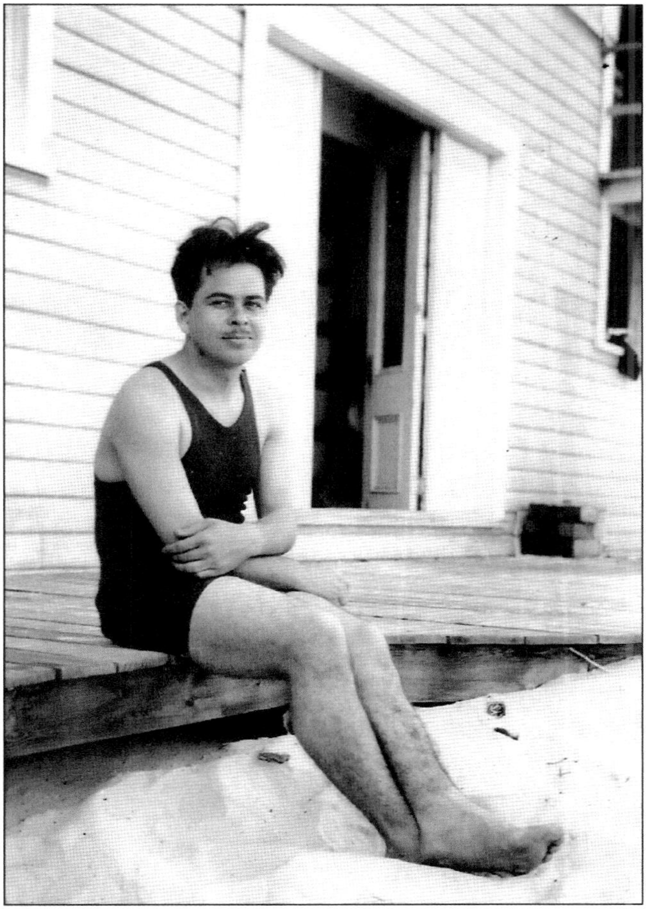

Victor Rahner Sr. was involved with the Life Saving Corporation, a group operating through the American Red Cross since 1912. When it began, the Florida East Coast Railroad supported lifeguards with monthly payments. The service lifeguards provided was important for ongoing beach safety and future visitors. (Courtesy of Tom Rahner.)

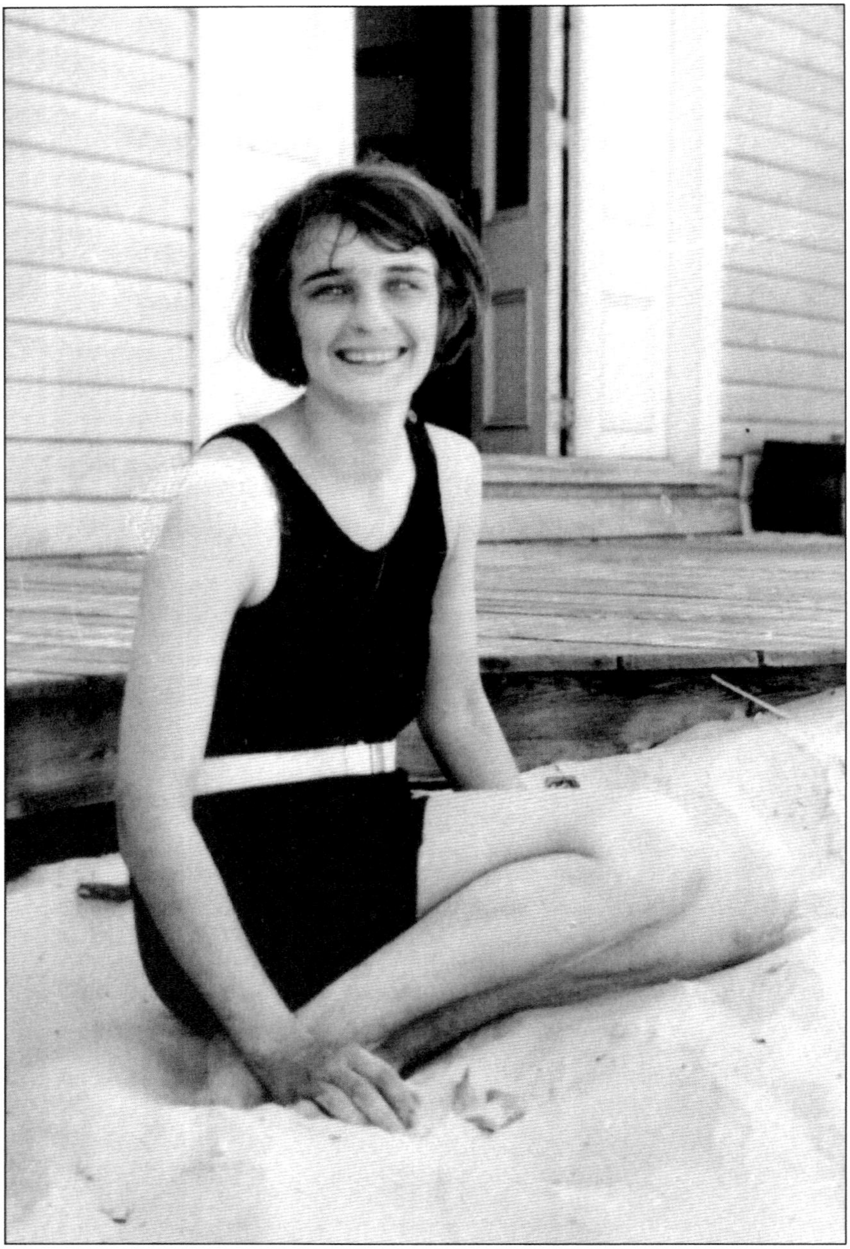

Clara and Victor Rahner shared a lifelong love of the beach. Out of economic necessity, after the stock market crash in 1929, the Rahners moved to North Beach in 1936, where Victor built the family's cottage by hand. His children—Victor Jr., Martha Jane, and Tom—also loved the ocean. Young Victor Rahner would become one of the area's prominent photographers. Here, Clara sits in front of the Surfside Dance Hall and Bathhouse, located four miles south of the family cottage, which was the last home on the road heading north to Pablo Beach. They did not get many visitors, being in such a remote location, and they relied on the radio. The Rahners moved away from the beach in 1941, having purchased property from pilot Lucius Gibson "Shorty" Rees, making the story of the aeroplane visitor most ironic. (Courtesy of Tom Rahner.)

Ronnie Capo, captain of the *Porpoise*, worked for Marine Studios as first person in charge of rounding up species of fish and sea mammals for Marineland. Barbara Capo Ezelle recalled her uncle as the first man to fry shrimp at Capo's Jungle Inn. Favorite Capo pastimes included playing poker, building rowboats, and knitting mullet/shrimp nets with hand-carved needles. (Courtesy of the St. Augustine Historical Society.)

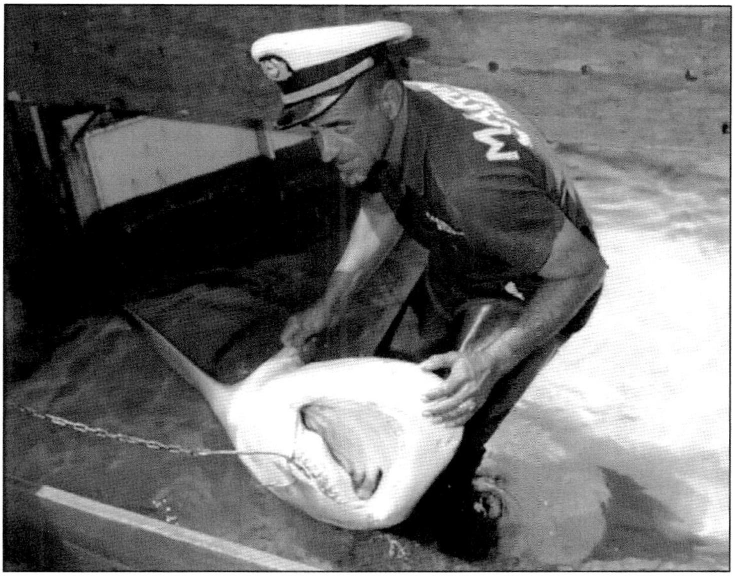

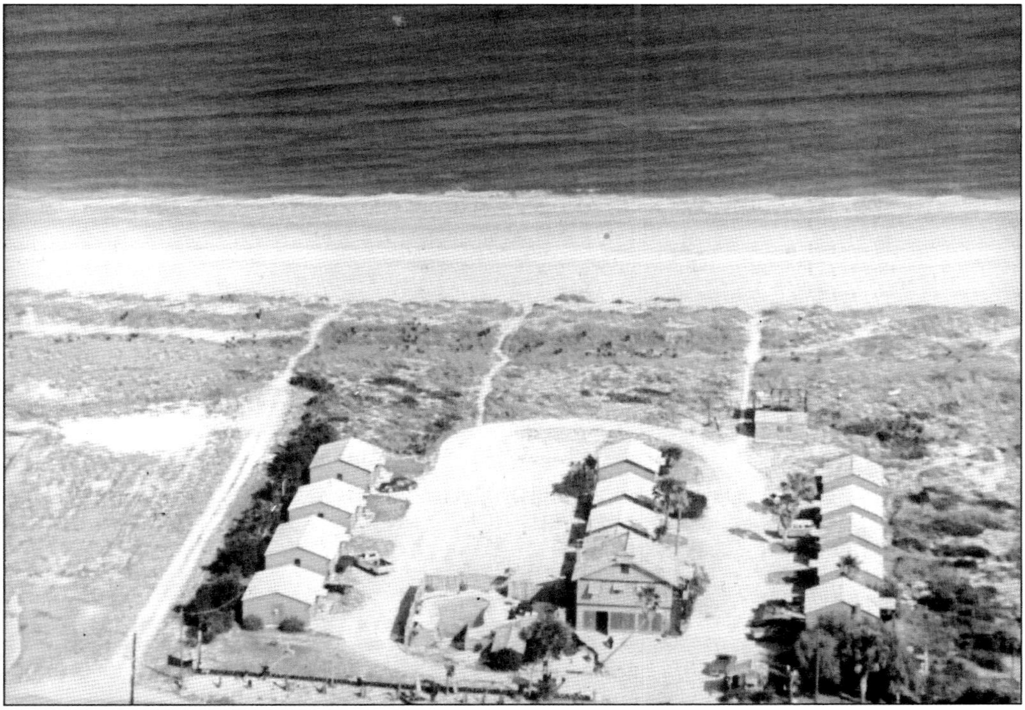

This aerial photograph of the Lucius Gibson "Shorty" Rees property shows 12 cottages and a large house, where the family lived. The compound is situated in the Surfside Subdivision, directly in front of the intersection of Coastal Highway and A1A as one comes off the Usina Bridge. (Courtesy of Sue "Rainbow" Williams.)

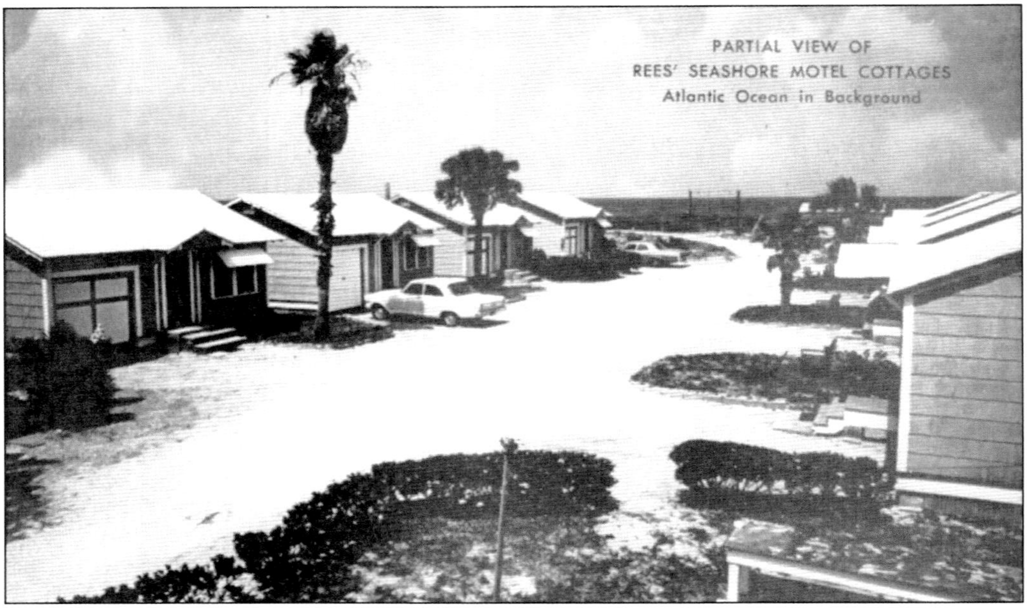

The Rees' Seashore Motel Cottages were built by Shorty Rees. The motor-court-style cottages allowed beachgoers close access to the ocean. Shorty settled in St. Augustine after World War II, starting this business with his family. Each member pitched in for cleaning and needed jobs. This property later changed hands and became known as the Pagoda Cottages. (Courtesy of Nadine and Jackie Connahay.)

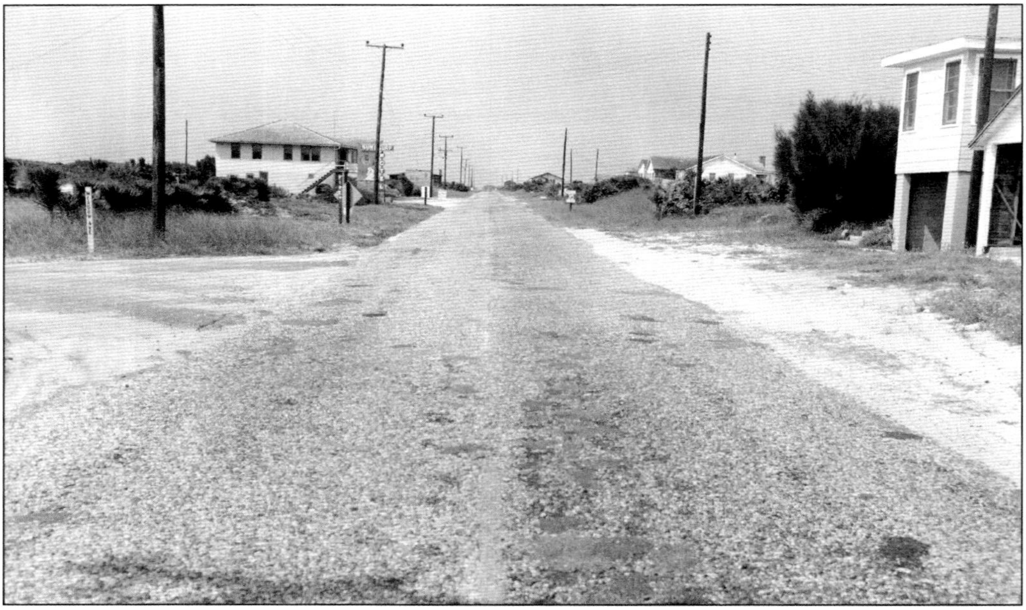

The original coastal road was renamed State Road A1A in 1946. At the same time, the wooden bridge was replaced with a unique drawbridge. There were only a few lift bridges in Florida. This was a welcomed improvement, after the wooden bridge partially burned in 1938. Meadow Avenue and First Avenue is the home of the North Shores Improvement Association Community Center and old firehouse. (Courtesy of Florida Memory.)

Four

Vilano Beach Beginnings

Vilano Beach was established by August Heckscher, a New York industrialist. He filed the official plat in 1927. That same year, a toll bridge and causeway to St. Augustine opened. They had been under construction by the previous owners, Mr. and Mrs. W.J. Hoggson, and were made part of the Vilano Beach subdivision. A grand recreation and entertainment mecca was built to attract buyers for the surrounding home lots. In Vilano, the casino (no gambling) opened in 1927 with a restaurant, dance floor, saltwater pool, and bathhouse overlooking the ocean. It was destroyed by a storm in 1938.

Very few homes or businesses were built in Vilano Beach in the Depression years. In 1939, the Usina family of North Beach built a small grocery store and gas station at the corner of Vilano Road and Coastal Highway. Mary Borum Usina ran the store during World War II, providing gas and groceries for locals. The store became a series of restaurants through the years. P.J. Manucy and family built a fish camp with a fishing dock, called Riverside Cottages, at the base of the recently built Vilano Bridge in 1948. Lloyd Small started St. Augustine Marina in the 1950s on the river adjacent to the Vilano Bridge to provide bait and tackle, boat sales, and repair. This remains a family-run institution.

Newt Haley passed through Vilano Beach as a military man stationed nearby, then came back after the war to settle in Vilano. He built most of the area's mom-and-pop motels in the 1940s and 1950s. These motels, still operating today, were enjoyed by tourists who vacationed here to swim in the ocean, fish, and visit St. Augustine, just across the bay via the drawbridge. By 1958, two of the community's current buildings were erected: the Art Deco Vilano Beach Motel, decorated with pink flamingos (now the Magic Beach Motel); and the Art Deco building that began as Gla-May Restaurant and then operated for decades as Barrancotto's Roma Restaurant. With these buildings, the 1950s came to a close.

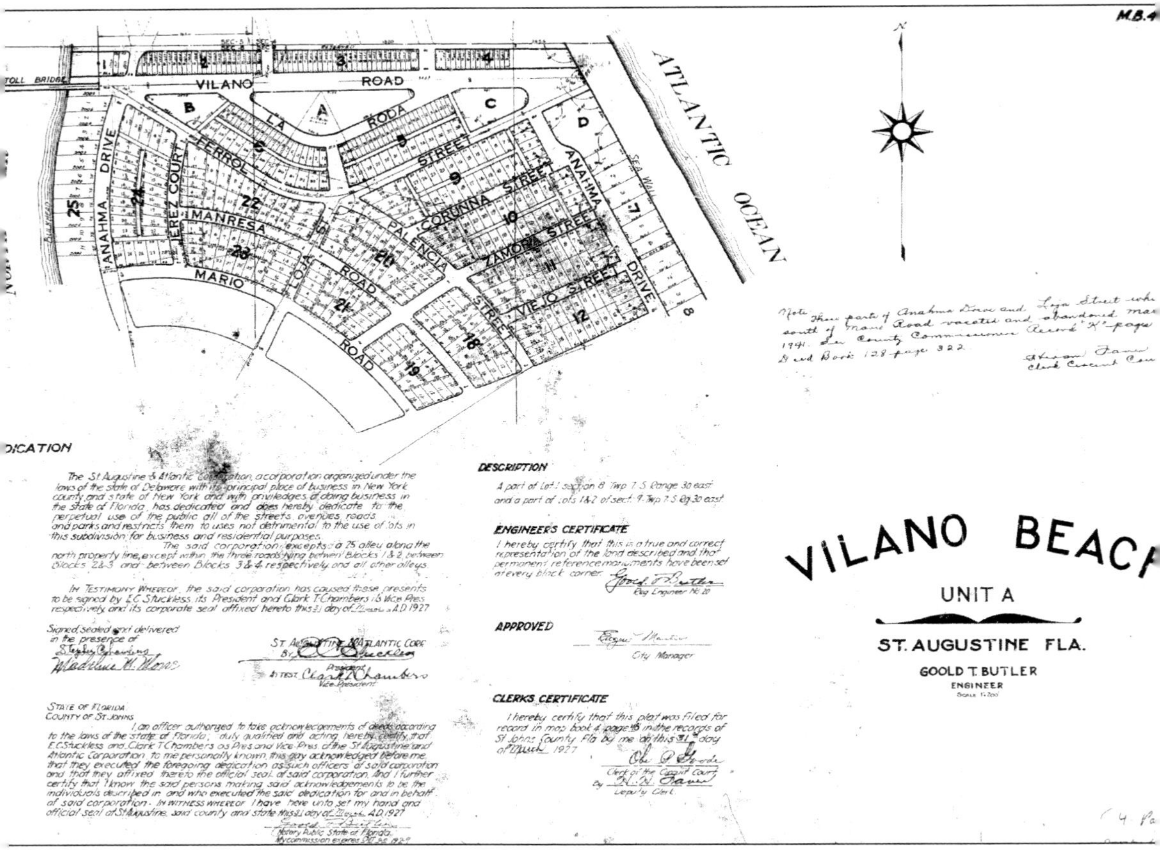

The Vilano Beach plat was filed with St. Johns County on March 31, 1927. The toll bridge on the left of the map had been started years earlier as a private enterprise to connect the new A1A coming south along the coast to the city of St Augustine. Note that Vilano Road is a 100-foot-wide boulevard. The thin, 25-foot lots were designed to allow the first buyers to adjust the amount of front footage they wanted to purchase along Vilano Road. The Vilano Beach Casino (1927–1938) was built on Parcel D, fronting Anahama Drive and the oceanfront. Parcels A, B, and C, along with La Roda, were replatted in 1950. The alleys located behind the frontage lots on both sides of Vilano Road were designed like small towns in the Northeast. (Courtesy of St. Johns County.)

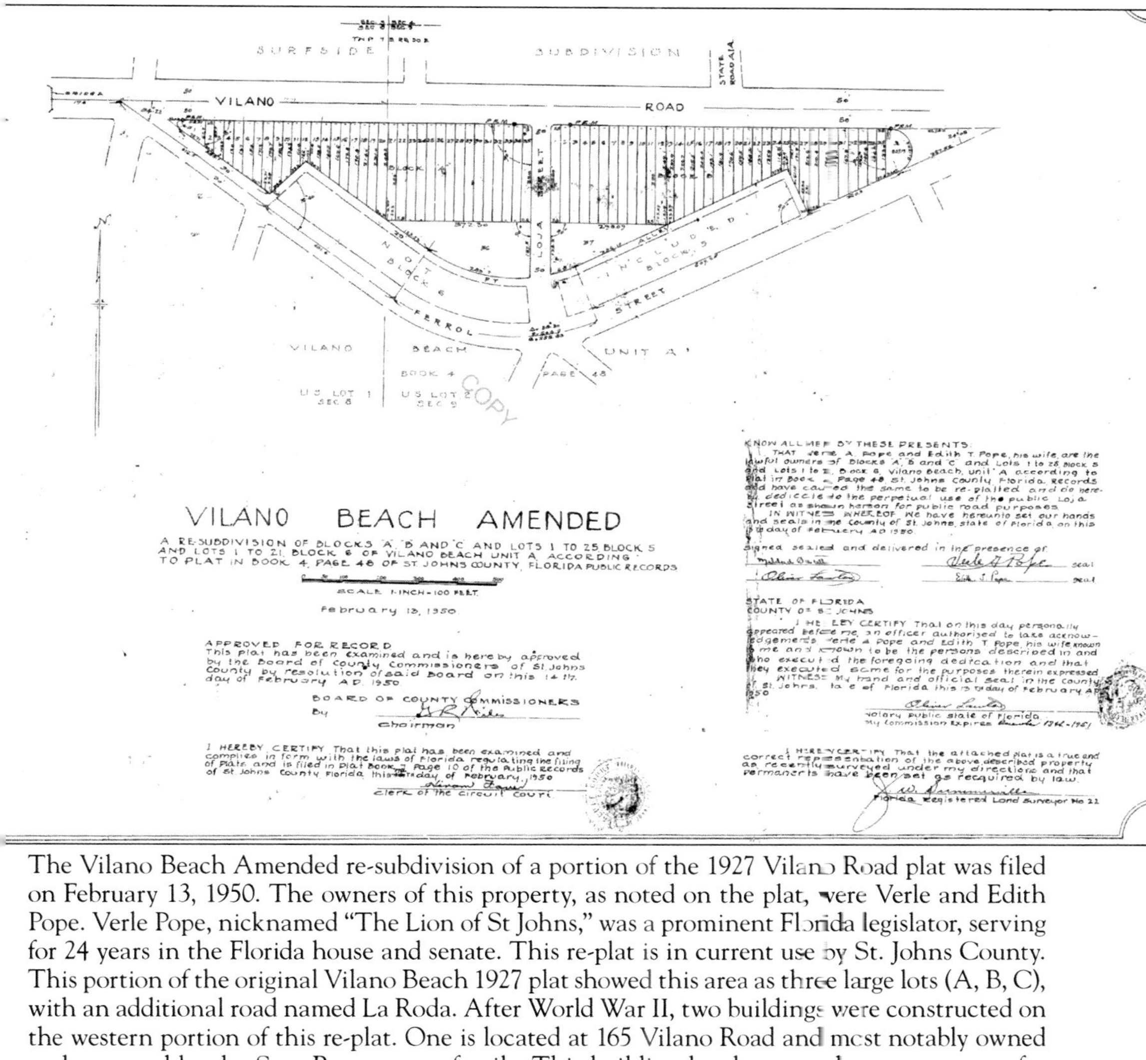

The Vilano Beach Amended re-subdivision of a portion of the 1927 Vilano Road plat was filed on February 13, 1950. The owners of this property, as noted on the plat, were Verle and Edith Pope. Verle Pope, nicknamed "The Lion of St Johns," was a prominent Florida legislator, serving for 24 years in the Florida house and senate. This re-plat is in current use by St. Johns County. This portion of the original Vilano Beach 1927 plat showed this area as three large lots (A, B, C), with an additional road named La Roda. After World War II, two buildings were constructed on the western portion of this re-plat. One is located at 165 Vilano Road and most notably owned and operated by the Sam Barrancotto family. This building has been used as a restaurant for decades. It is a good example of Art Deco architecture. Next to it is a small motel at 155 Vilano Road. It has been renovated in Art Deco style by Vilano Springs Development, LLC. (Courtesy of St. Johns County.)

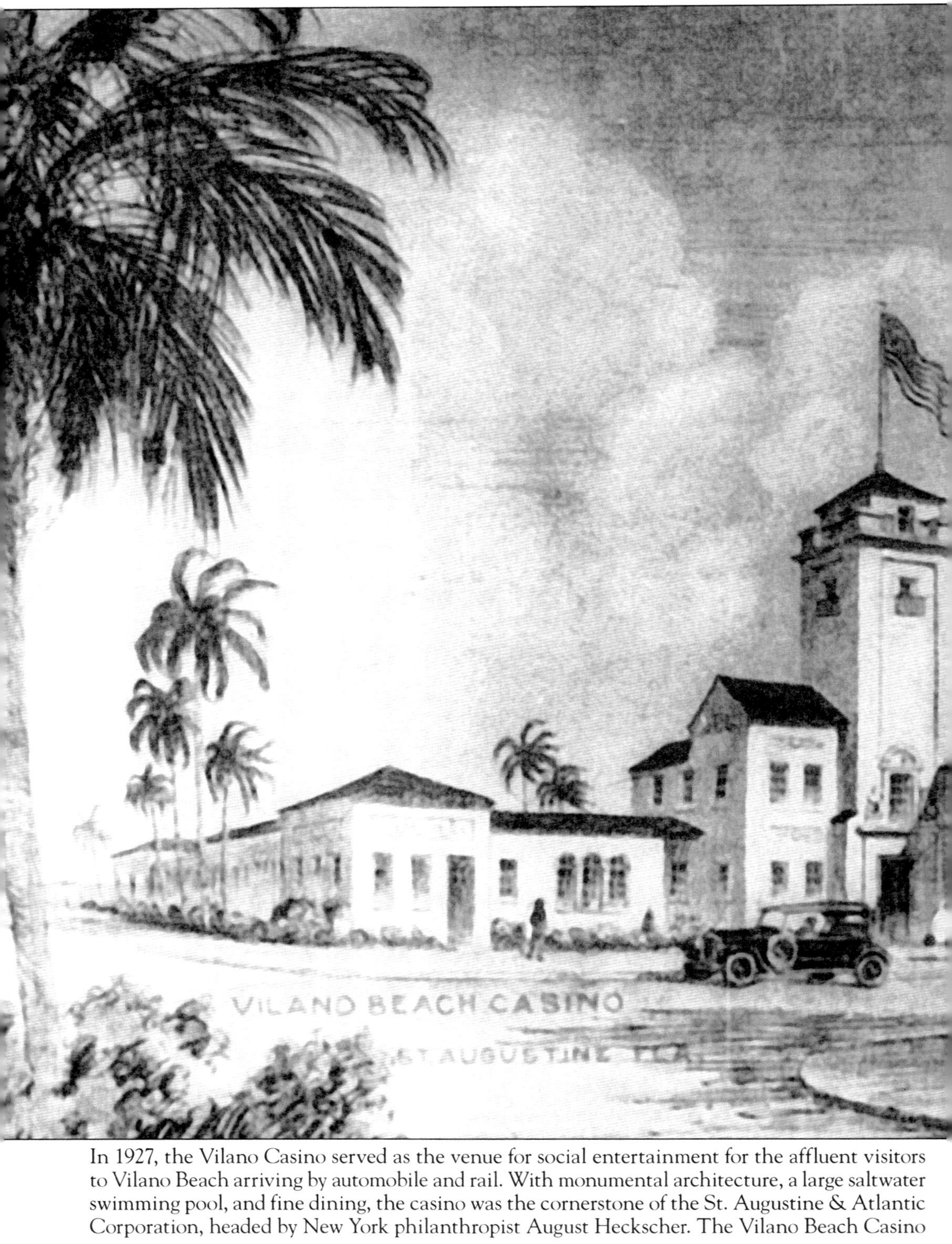

In 1927, the Vilano Casino served as the venue for social entertainment for the affluent visitors to Vilano Beach arriving by automobile and rail. With monumental architecture, a large saltwater swimming pool, and fine dining, the casino was the cornerstone of the St. Augustine & Atlantic Corporation, headed by New York philanthropist August Heckscher. The Vilano Beach Casino

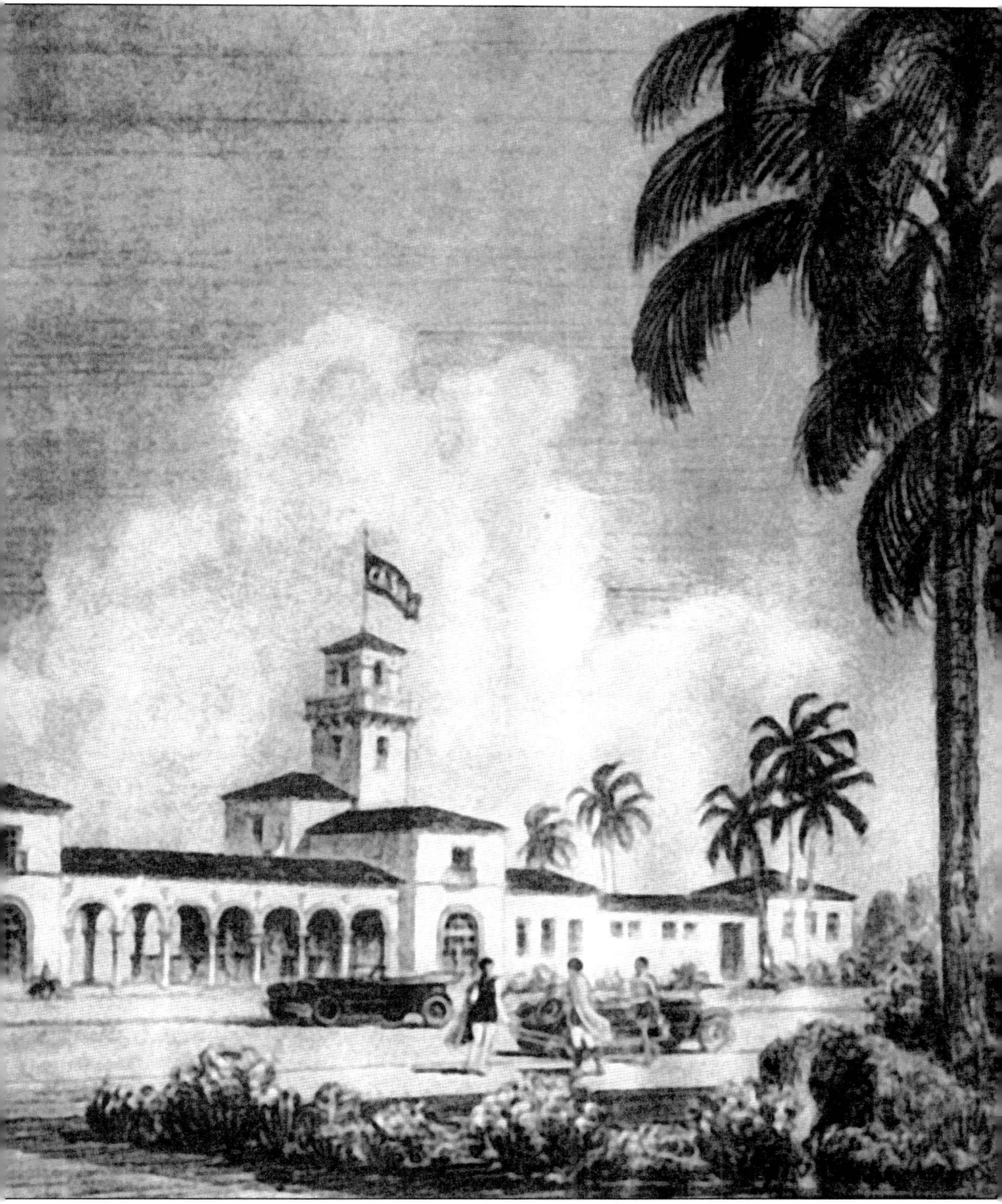

was not a gambling site, but, rather, a gathering place for big-name bands, vaudeville acts, theme parties, and dances. Crowds enjoyed the ocean view and luxurious setting across the bay from St. Augustine. Gala events drew visitors from far and wide. Storms in 1938–1939 washed away the casino. (Courtesy of the St. Augustine Historical Society.)

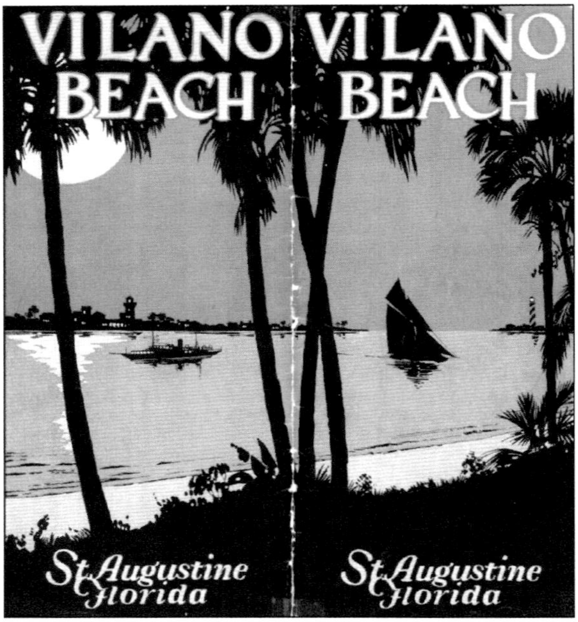

August Heckscher's 1927 sales brochure touts beautiful Vilano Beach as the place to live, "where the St. Augustine & Atlantic Corporation is building a modern city." Heckscher promoted the area as "the ideal location for the ideal home for the person who enjoys comfort and progressiveness midst ideal surroundings." He claimed, "What we promise, we do." (Courtesy of the St. Augustine Historical Society.)

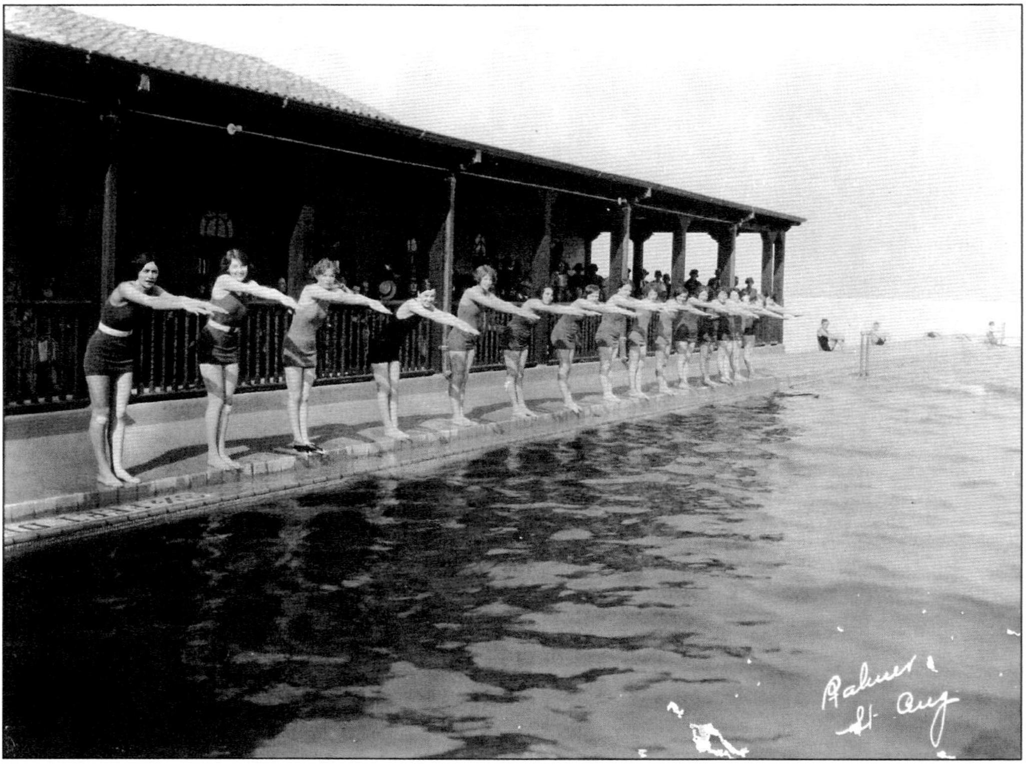

The view of the ocean was unrivaled from the Vilano Casino Pool. Swimmers enjoyed patio bathing and competitive recreational dives. After a dip in the saltwater pool, guests enjoyed fine dining. Unfortunately, the development's land sales also took a dive after the stock market crash of 1929. (Courtesy of the St. Augustine Historical Society.)

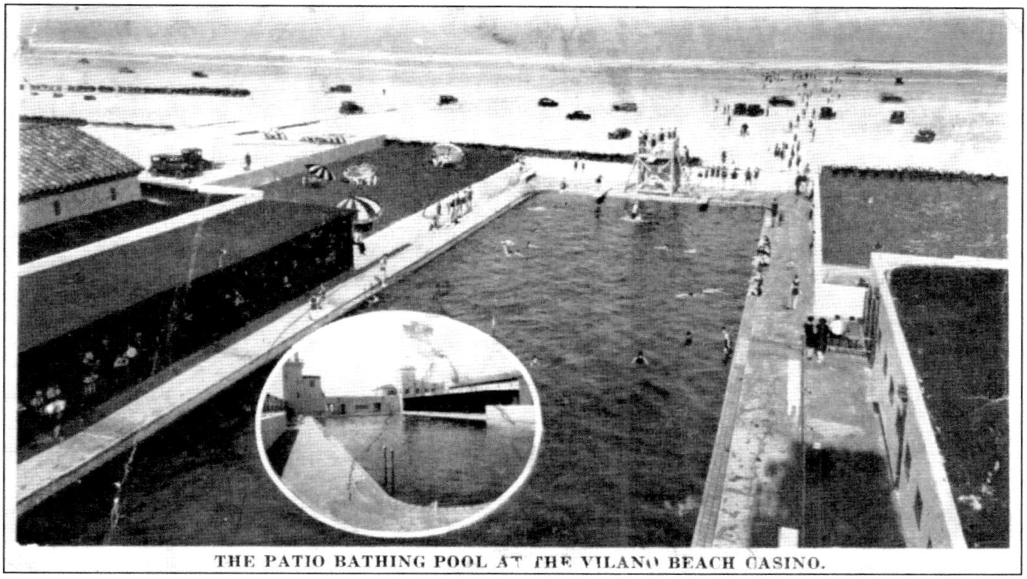

The Vilano Beach Casino, built in 1926, had a swimming pool that was 150 feet long and 50 feet wide, with a diving tower. The pool water came from the ocean. Attractive all-wool bathing garments were available at the main entrance. As seen here, for the convenience of beachgoers, automobiles could be parked on the hard-packed sand, right on the oceanfront. (Courtesy of Jackie and Nadine Connahay.)

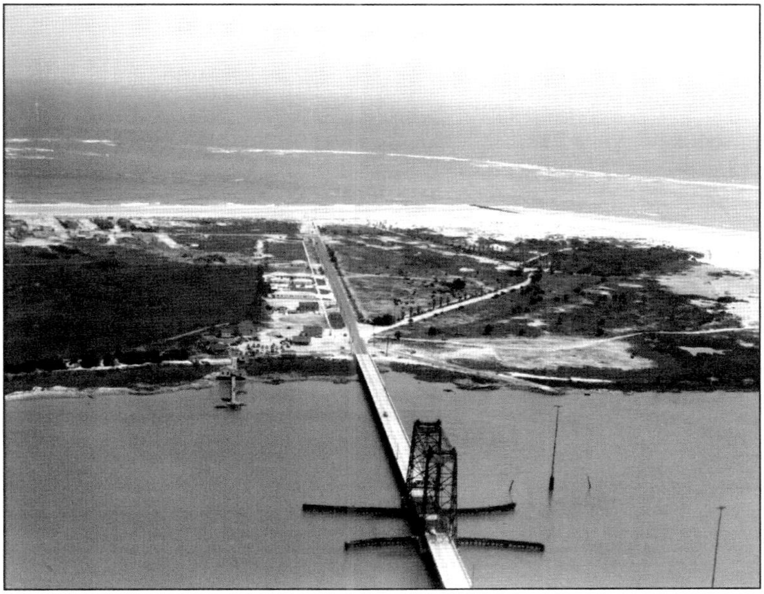

The first bridge connecting Vilano Beach to the mainland was placed in service on March 31, 1927. It was a privately built bridge made of wood. The second bridge (pictured), opened in 1948, had a bridge tender's house located in the middle. Daniel Webster Borum, father of Mary Usina, was the first bridge tender. (Courtesy of the St. Augustine Historical Society.)

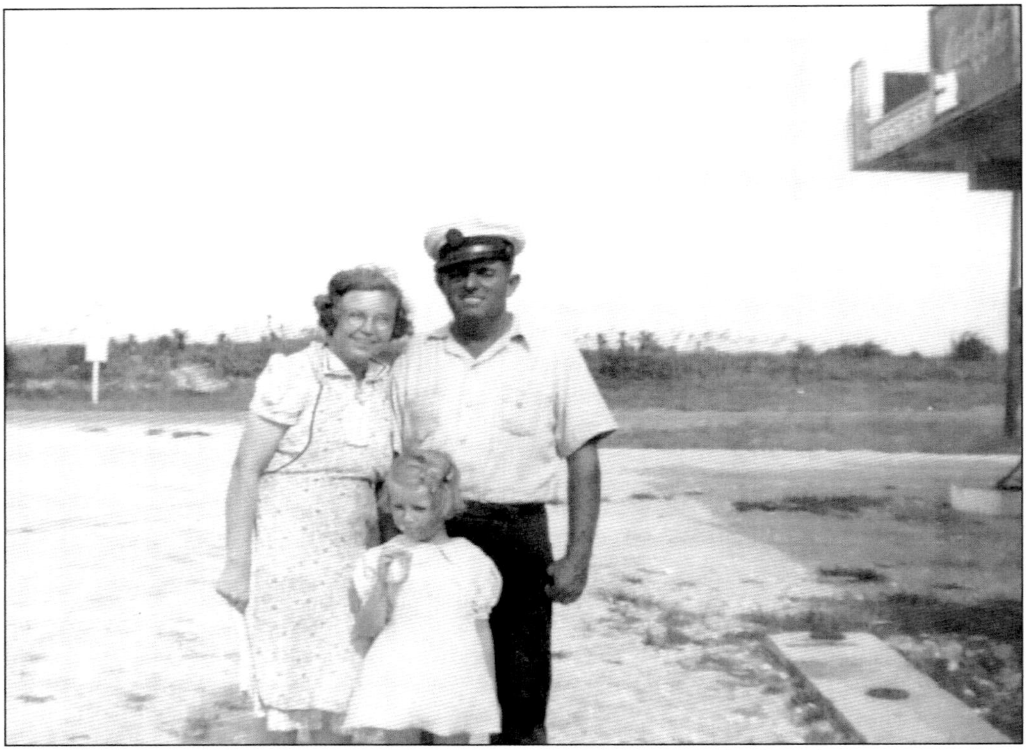

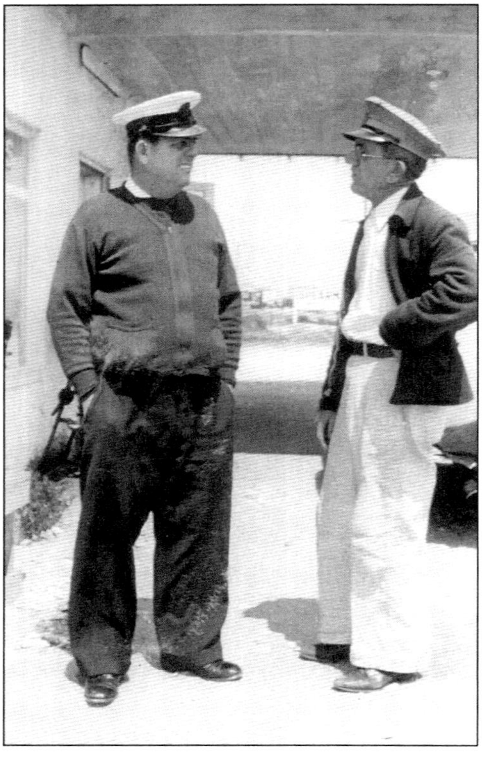

In 1939, the Usinas built Seabreeze Service Center at the corner of Vilano Road and Coastal Highway. This was the gas store east of the bridge. Building blocks, handmade from beach sand, coquina, and cement, were formed in a small machine that made two blocks at a time. The structure was used as restaurants from the 1960s and was removed in 2011 to clear the building site for Publix. Pictured are Mary Borum Usina (left), Mary Lou Usina (center) and Francis E. Usina. (Courtesy of Mary Louise Usina Brown.)

During World War II, gas, steel, and other materials were in scarce supply. The Usinas filled a community need by developing a small store in Vilano. The new store soon became the gathering place for locals. Here, Francis E. (left) chats with Francis Hubert Carcaba, probably about the catch of the day. (Courtesy of Elizabeth and Frank D. Usina.)

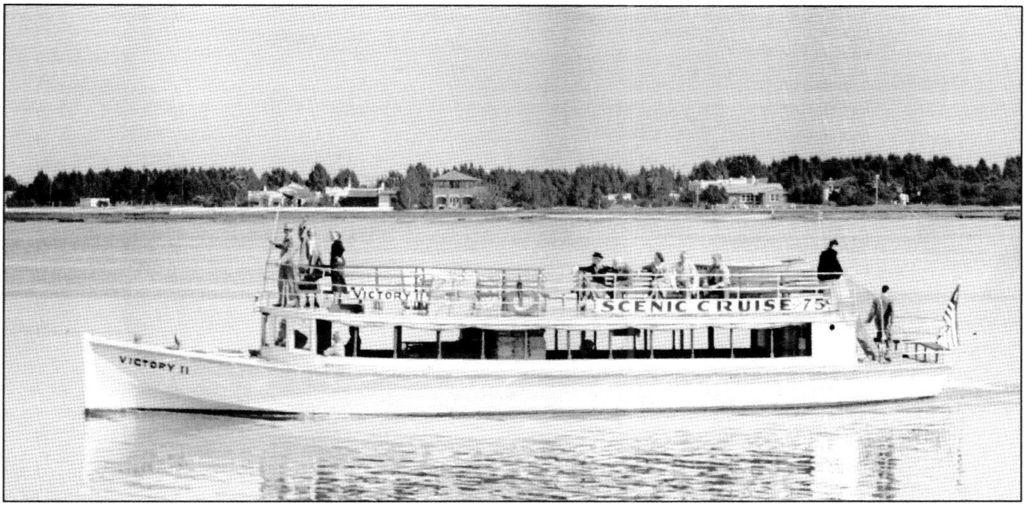

The Usinas operated docks at the bayfront, which also served as a boarding spot for passengers for the transport ferry *Victory II*. The vessel often came to the aid of the Florida Department of Transportation, assisting by ferrying residents to and from the mainland when troubles beset the lift bridge. By 1949, operation of the full-time sightseeing boat resumed. (Courtesy of Elizabeth and Frank D. Usina.)

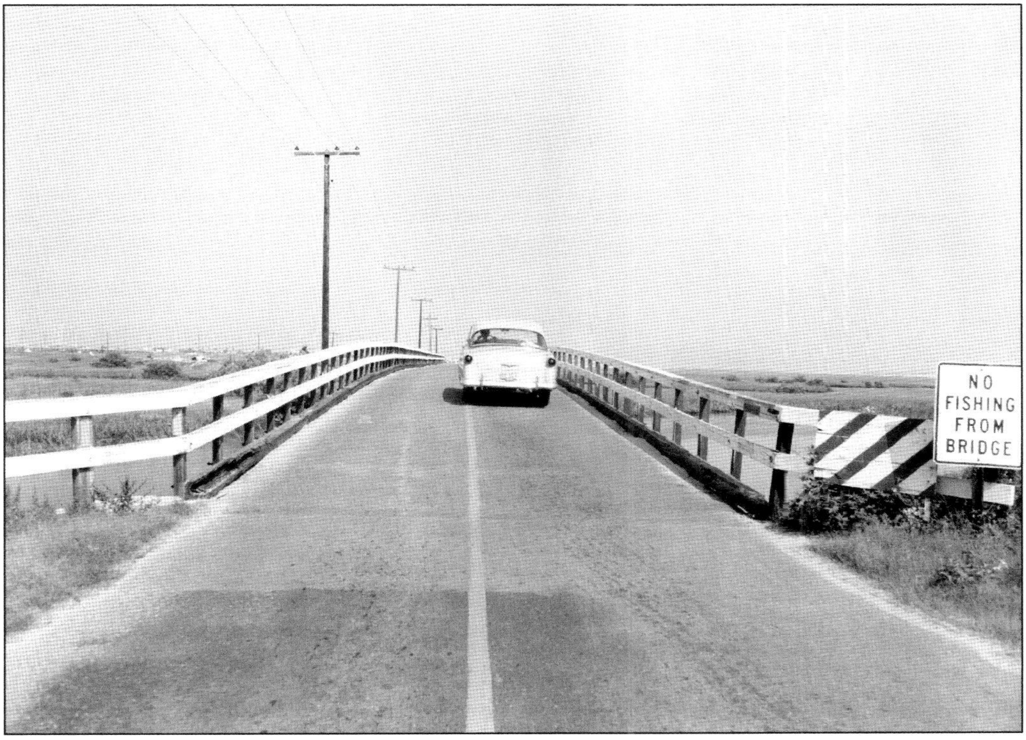

In order for August Heckscher to complete the Vilano Bridge, the causeway approach needed roadwork, and smaller sections needed work. Hospital Creek lies across from the south entrance of the Florida School for the Deaf and Blind and between May Street and the Vilano Causeway. (Courtesy of Florida Memory.)

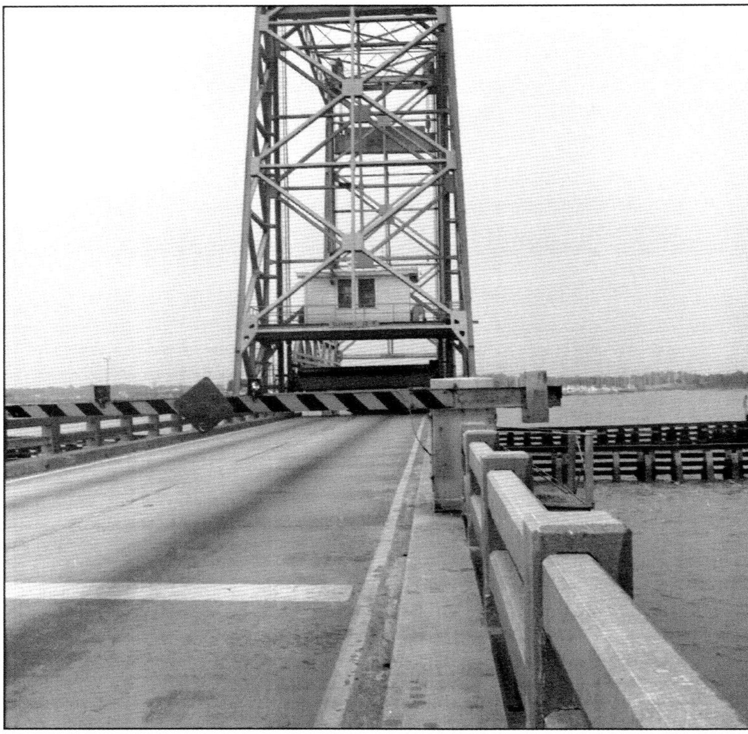

The view in this 1955 photograph looks east toward Vilano Beach. This second bridge was constructed in 1948 as a lift drawbridge. As such, tenders were needed in case of mechanical problems. A new bridge, which bypassed the commercial district of old Vilano Beach, was built in 1995. (Courtesy of the St. Augustine Historical Society.)

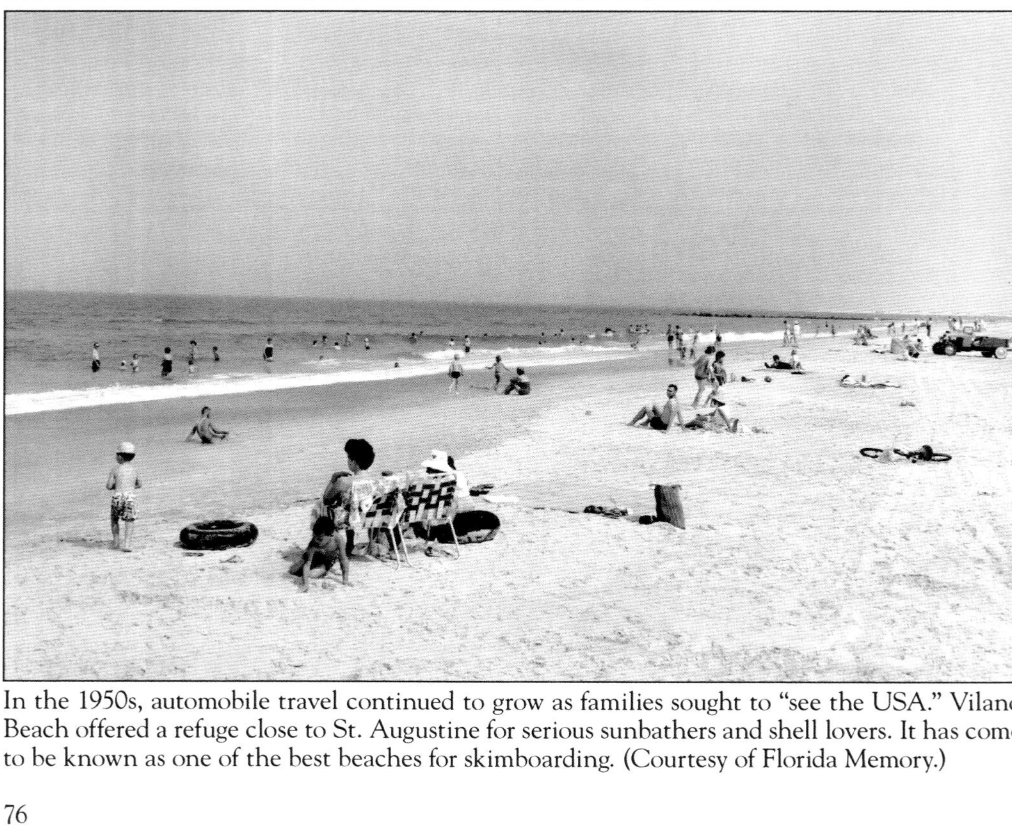

In the 1950s, automobile travel continued to grow as families sought to "see the USA." Vilano Beach offered a refuge close to St. Augustine for serious sunbathers and shell lovers. It has come to be known as one of the best beaches for skimboarding. (Courtesy of Florida Memory.)

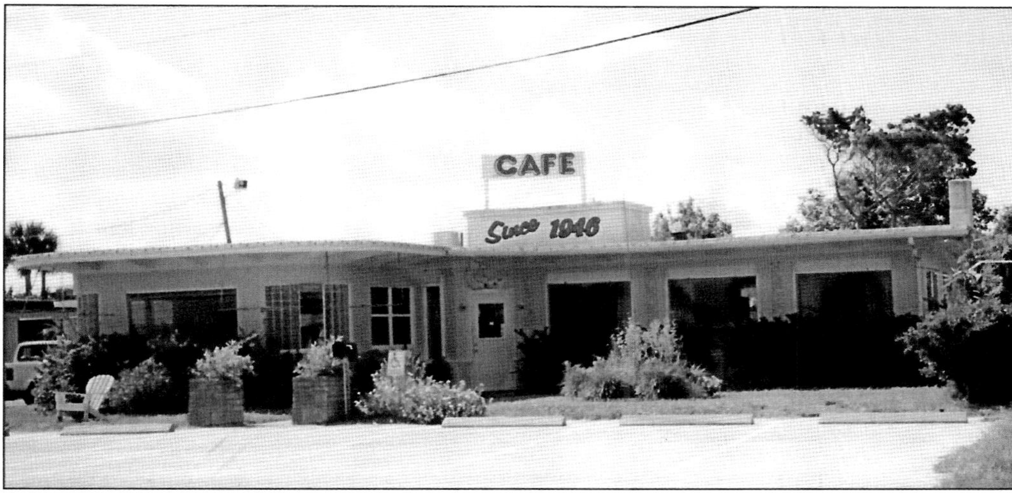

This building at 165 Vilano Road opened as the Gla-May Restaurant in 1958. It was operated by Fred and Miriam Spires for about six years. They sold it to Sam Barrancotto Sr., who relocated his popular restaurant business here in 1964 from the Crawford Hotel on San Marco Avenue. The Barrancotto's Roma Restaurant was a beloved institution until it closed in the 1990s. Several businesses followed. The Art Deco building is currently Casa Benedetto's, renowned regionally. (Courtesy of Florida Memory.)

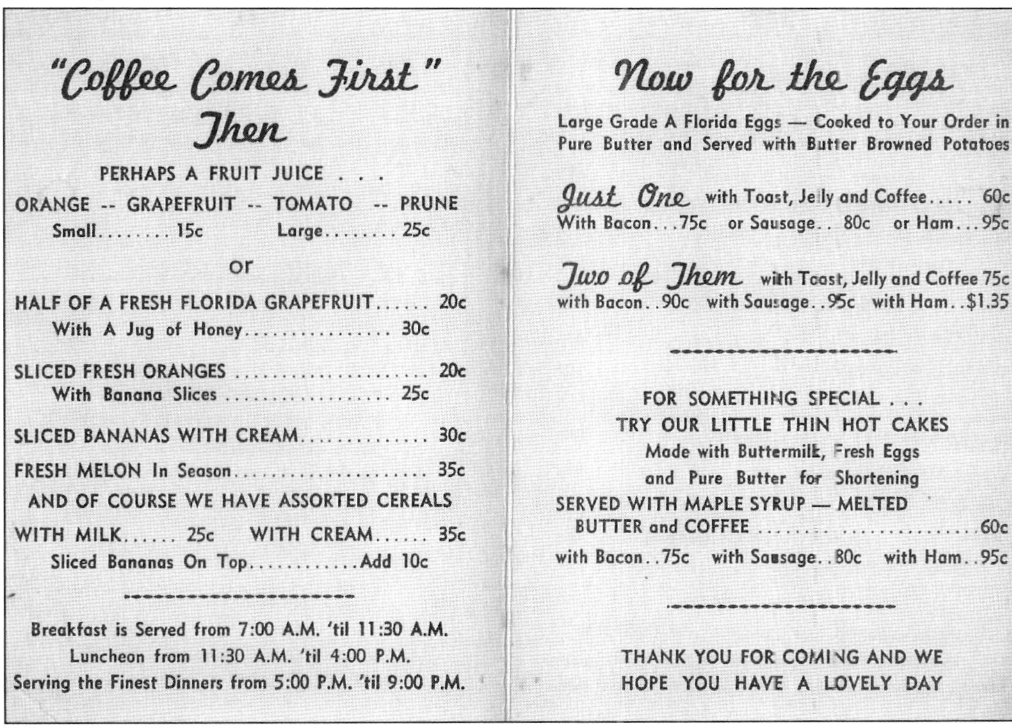

"Coffee Comes First" Then

PERHAPS A FRUIT JUICE . . .

ORANGE -- GRAPEFRUIT -- TOMATO -- PRUNE
Small........ 15c Large........ 25c

or

HALF OF A FRESH FLORIDA GRAPEFRUIT...... 20c
With A Jug of Honey.............. 30c

SLICED FRESH ORANGES 20c
With Banana Slices 25c

SLICED BANANAS WITH CREAM............. 30c

FRESH MELON In Season.................... 35c

AND OF COURSE WE HAVE ASSORTED CEREALS

WITH MILK...... 25c WITH CREAM...... 35c
Sliced Bananas On Top...........Add 10c

Breakfast is Served from 7:00 A.M. 'til 11:30 A.M.
Luncheon from 11:30 A.M. 'til 4:00 P.M.
Serving the Finest Dinners from 5:00 P.M. 'til 9:00 P.M.

Now for the Eggs

Large Grade A Florida Eggs — Cooked to Your Order in Pure Butter and Served with Butter Browned Potatoes

Just One with Toast, Jelly and Coffee..... 60c
With Bacon...75c or Sausage.. 80c or Ham...95c

Two of Them with Toast, Jelly and Coffee 75c
with Bacon..90c with Sausage..95c with Ham..$1.35

FOR SOMETHING SPECIAL . . .
TRY OUR LITTLE THIN HOT CAKES
Made with Buttermilk, Fresh Eggs
and Pure Butter for Shortening
SERVED WITH MAPLE SYRUP — MELTED
BUTTER and COFFEE 60c
with Bacon..75c with Sausage..80c with Ham..95c

THANK YOU FOR COMING AND WE
HOPE YOU HAVE A LOVELY DAY

The Spires family operated the Gla-May Restaurant on Vilano Road from 1958 to 1964. It offered affordable breakfasts and fresh fruits, as well as steaks, finely cooked by its owner. On this menu, prices for breakfast are under $1. Steaks for dinner were the owner's specialty. (Courtesy of Bo Pitts.)

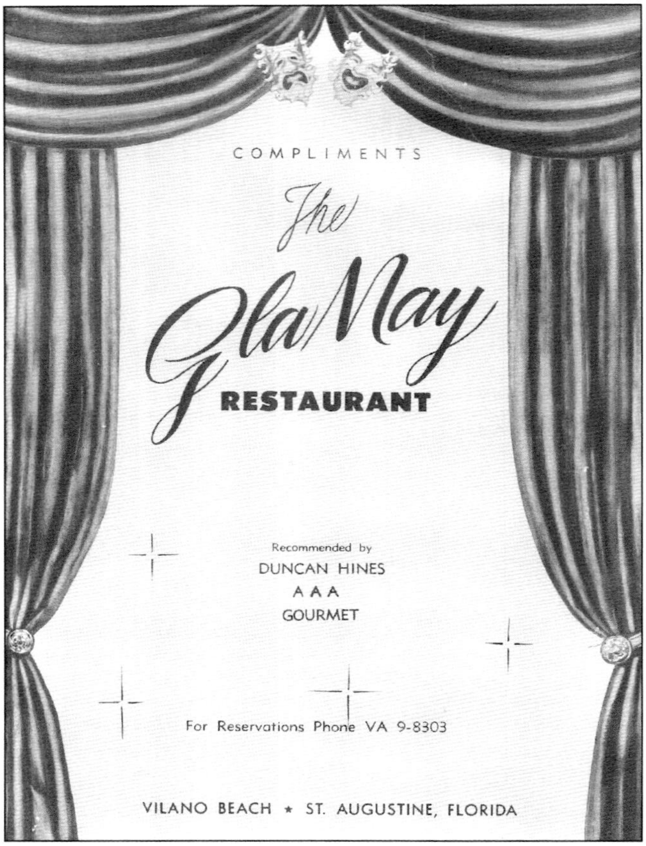

In the 1950s, restaurants of renown were awarded special recognition. The Gla-May received the Duncan Hines and AAA seals of approval. Hines was more commonly known for developing cake mixes, not his culinary skills. He traveled extensively through the country as a chef evaluator for restaurants. (Courtesy of Mark and Cindy Scott.)

The property at 180 Vilano Road was built in 1950 and has housed a series of restaurants over the years. For over a decade, Benito's Restaurant served mainly Italian food. The site operates today as 180 Vilano Grill, one of Vilano Beach Town Center's favorites because of its historical look. (Courtesy of Sacha Martin.)

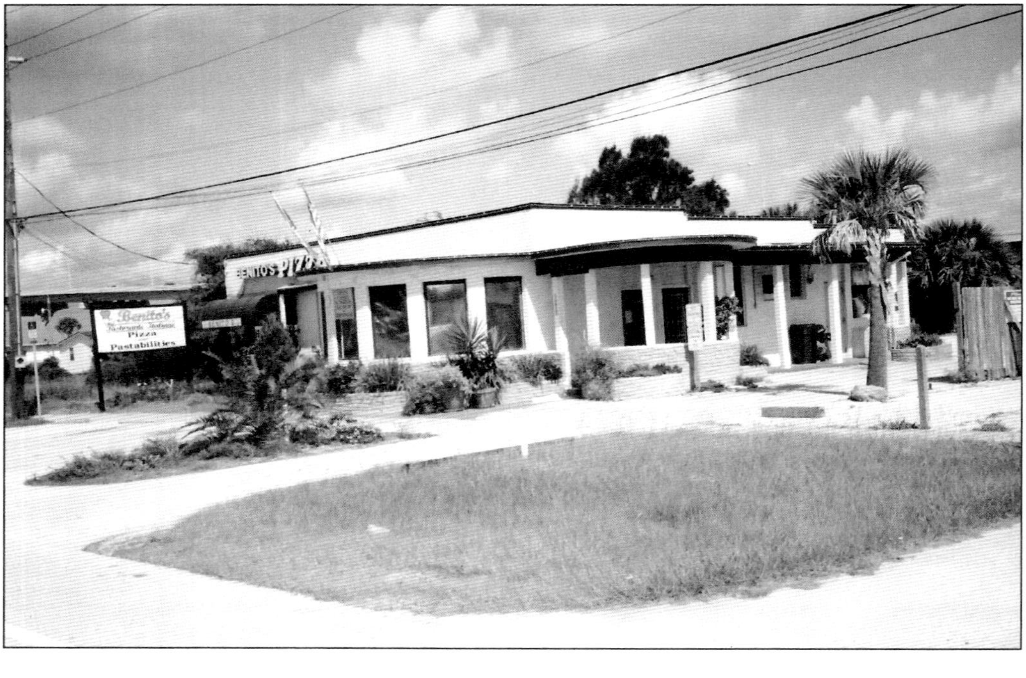

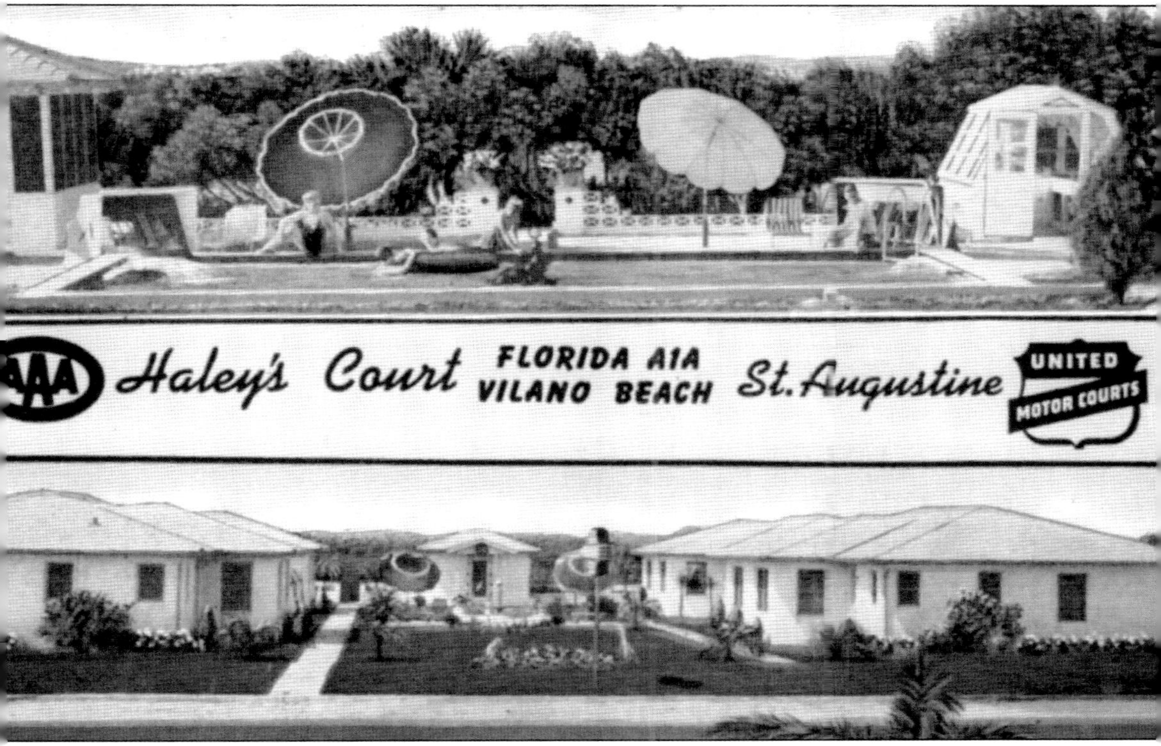

This Haley's Motor Court postcard advertises AAA approval and a "Swimming Pool for Guests Only." In the 1940s and 1950s, Americans took to the road to enjoy affordable vacations and "motor court" hotels. Offering "electric kitchens" and air-conditioning in some rooms, managing owner Newt Haley also owned Newt's Motel and Exclusive Trailer Park on A1A in Vilano Beach. Haley's holdings included Haley's Court, where semipermanent residents enjoyed the area year-round. The property located at 176 Vilano Road was operated as a motel with a pool, enjoyed by locals and tourists until the site was transformed for other uses. The 1950 masonry vernacular architecture of the structure, along Vilano Road, is reminiscent of the era. Haley acquired much of his holdings after returning from service in World War II and settling in the area. (Courtesy of Jackie and Nadine Connahay.)

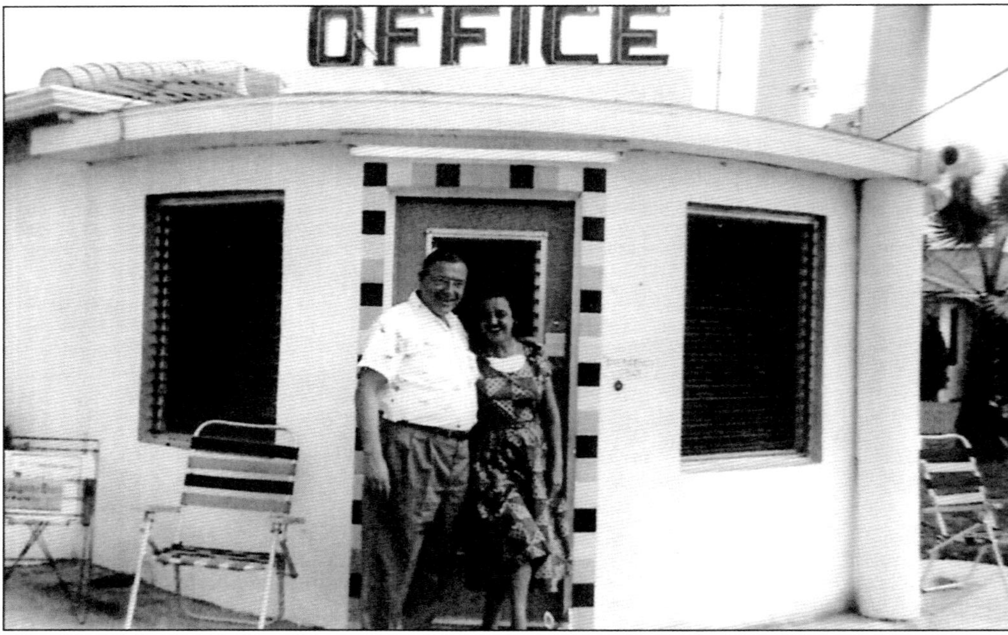

The Greens, property owners, stand in front of Haley's Court. The posts of the historic Haley's Court sign are seen adjacent to the building. This sign was most visible from atop the bridge. Another landmark was the Bluebird, across the street at 155 Vilano Road. A favorite advertising slogan used by notary Wilda Russell was "We're the first bird on the right after you get off the bridge." (Courtesy of Sacha Martin.)

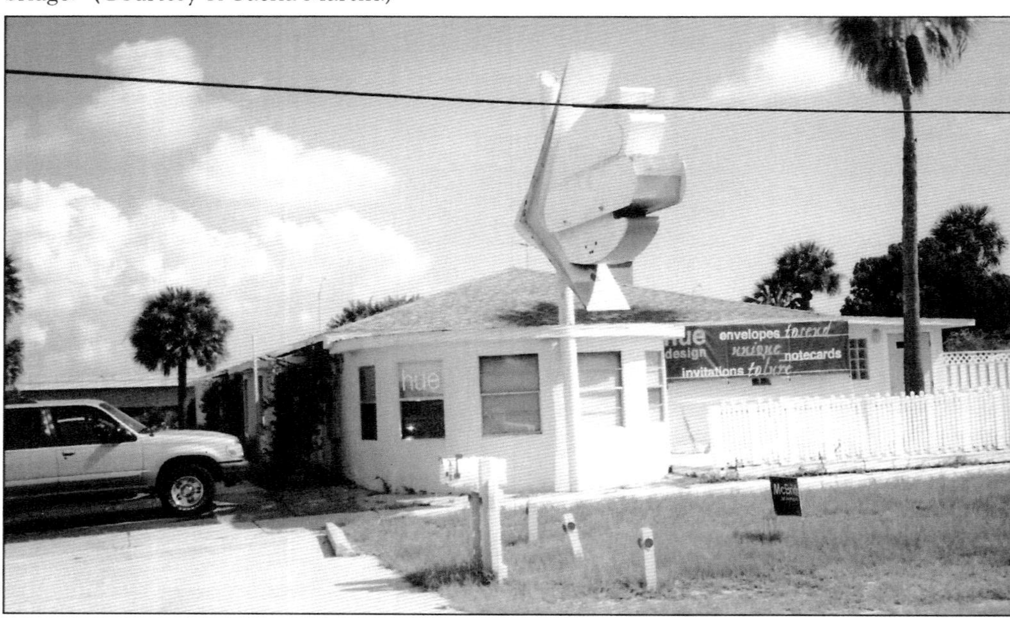

The hotel sign seen here on the original Haley's Court is today a historical marker located in the streetscape on Vilano Road. The masonry vernacular architecture is still intact. The pool was filled in and is only a distant memory for former vacationers. Newt Haley resided in the area for over 50 years. (Courtesy of Bo Pitts.)

The Lazy Sands and its menu changed hands several times. Mr. and Mrs. Heckendorf were the proprietors and knew everyone in the area. At that time, the main traffic flowed in front of the bar, as travelers came from the city heading north on A1A. The building was removed in 2013 because of its poor condition. (Courtesy of Bo Pitts.)

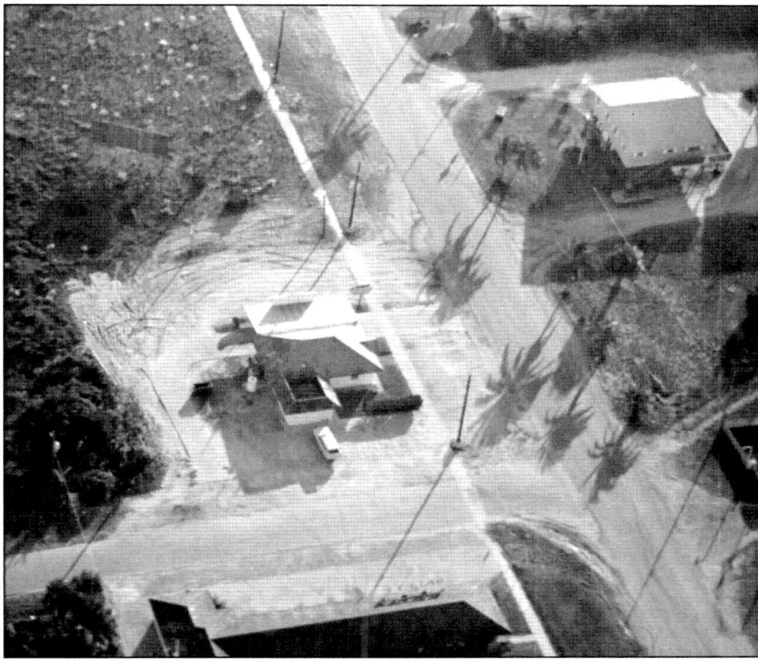

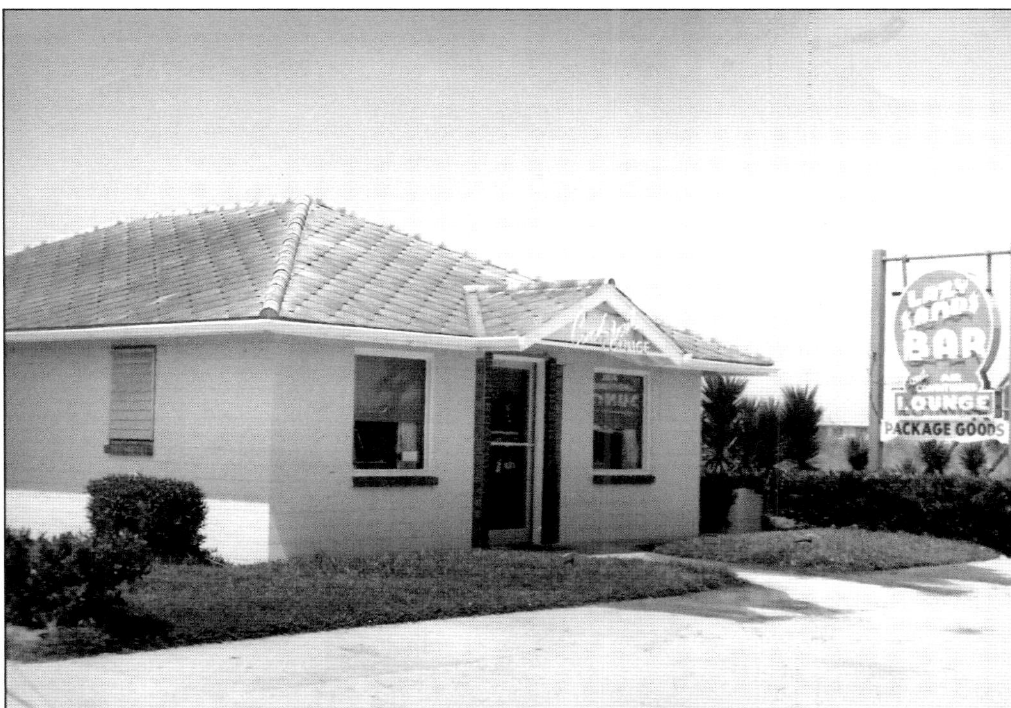

Built and owned by the Heckendorfs, the Lazy Sands, at 140 Vilano Road, was, like television's *Cheers* bar, a place where "everybody knows your name." The small building had a bar and grill, but its favorite and most important feature was a drive-thru for purchasing bottles. The owners lived around the corner on Ferrol Road and knew most of their customers. (Courtesy of Bo Pitts.)

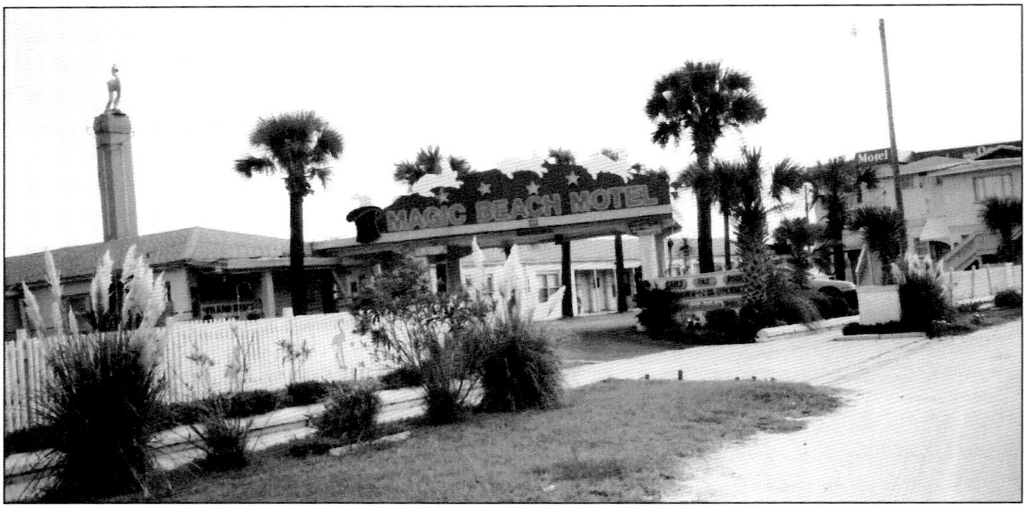

The motel located at 50 Vilano Road features 1950s Art Deco architecture. It has operated continuously as a motel, first known as the Vilano Beach Motel. After using the motel as a television set in the 1990s, Hollywood left its sign for the motel behind. The iconic flashing letters identify it as the Magic Beach Motel. (Courtesy of Florida Memory.)

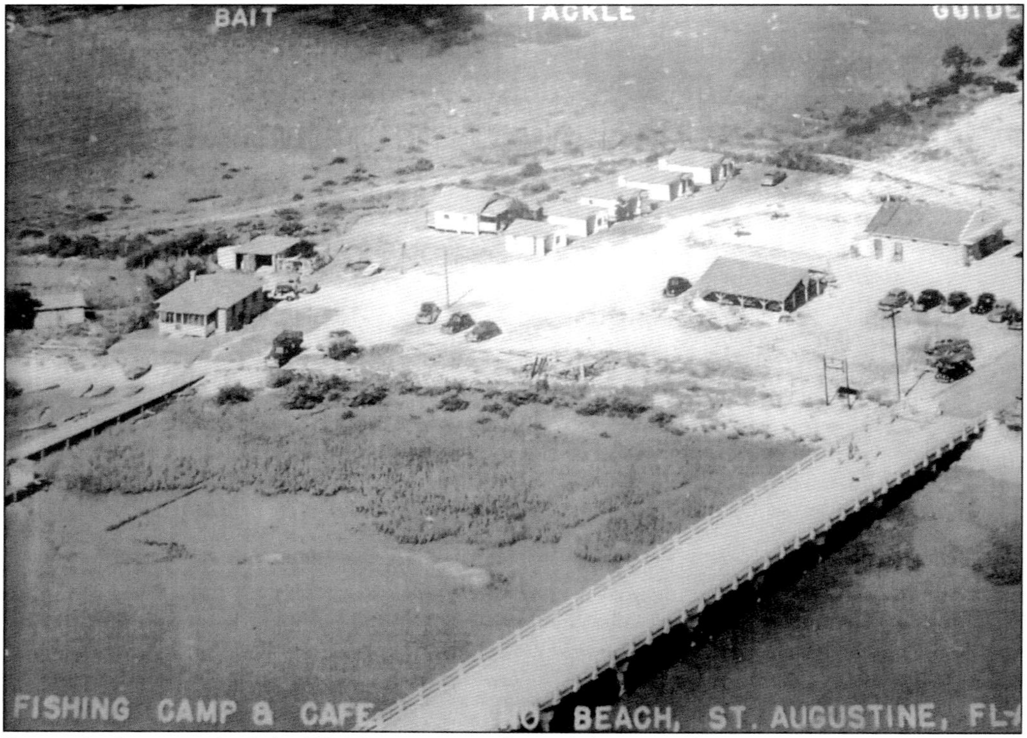

Riverside Cottages, built by P.J. Manucy, served as a fisherman's haven, where groceries, fishing tackle, boats, motors, and bait were available. These structures were built in the mid-1930s and survived for decades. There were six cottages situated on the property adjacent to docks along the North River, just under and south of the Vilano drawbridge. (Courtesy of Elizabeth and Frank D. Usina.)

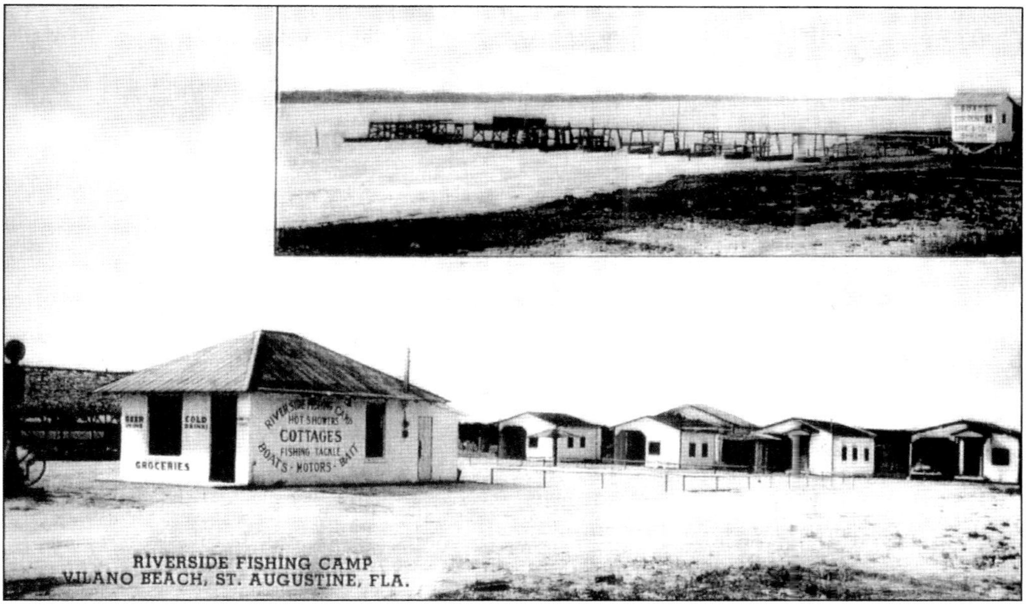

The postcard shows a few of the Riverside Fishing Camp cottages up close. Groceries and bait and ice were necessities for fishermen. The inset shows the North River and the boat dock. Not only were these small motels great for visiting fishermen and vacationers, they were also favorites of the emerging boating club enthusiasts who traveled far and wide to race. (Courtesy of Elizabeth and Frank D. Usina.)

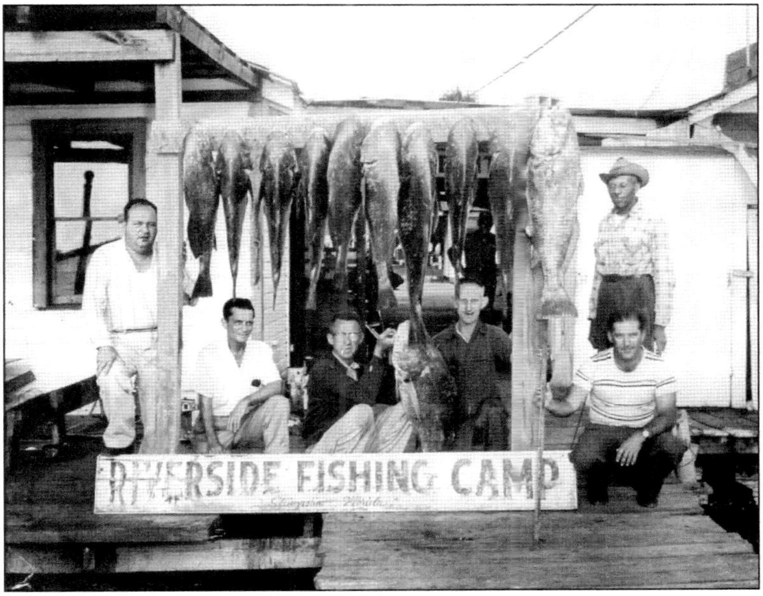

Taken in the late 1940s, this photograph depicts the bountiful catches common along the Tolomato River (often called the North River) and the nearby St. Augustine Inlet. P.J. Manucy (left) ran the Riverside Fishing Camp, located by the Vilano drawbridge. Son C.J. Manucy continued the recreational fishing retreat until the late 1980s. (Courtesy of Bunny Manucy.)

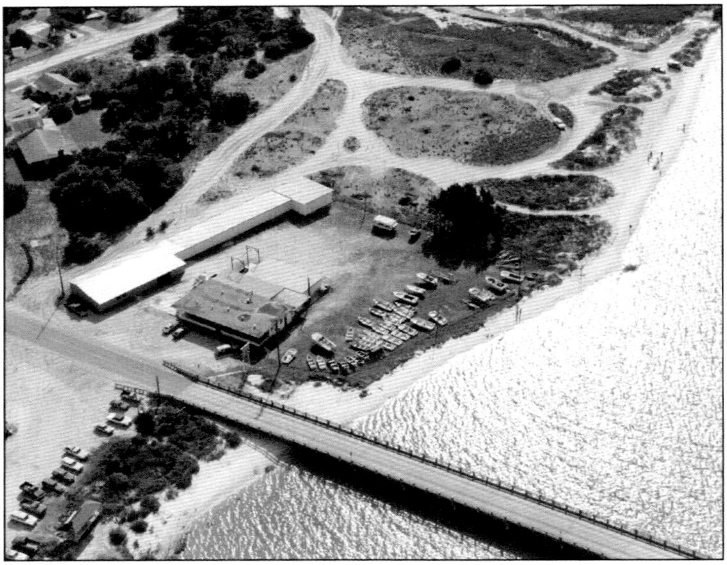

Lloyd Small and, later, Jimmy Beach, who married Lloyd's daughter, Marilyn, have operated a marina at the west end of Vilano Road. St. Augustine Marina is a popular place to get bait, tackle, boats, and most fishing gear needed to catch the "big ones." Now the oldest continuously operated business in Vilano, the St. Augustine Marina supports local fishing tournaments and kids' fishing camps. (Courtesy of Sacha Martin.)

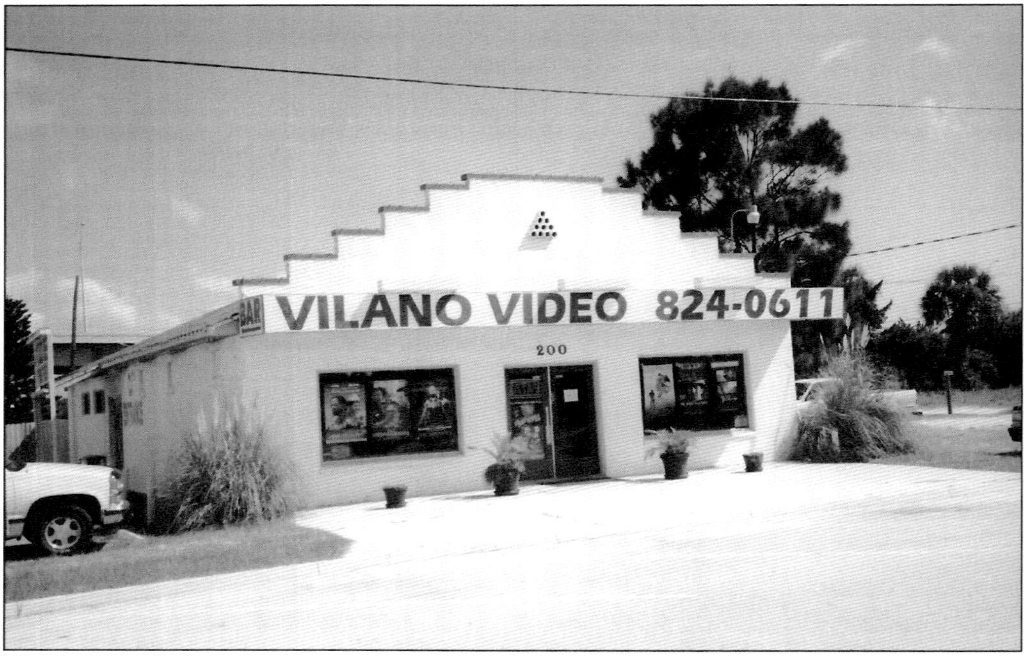

This building had many uses over the years, including as a bait store, bar, and video store. It has been vacant for several years. Vilano Beach Main Street has worked with several possible tenants to renovate/occupy and preserve the building. The community especially supported a theater group, but the restoration and permitting was beyond its budget. (Courtesy of Sacha Martin.)

Five

Life along the North Beaches

Through the 1940s and 1950s, North Beach residents coexisted with tourist motor courts, local businesses, and wild native flora and fauna. Neighborhoods included the Vilano Beach, Surfside, and North Beach subdivisions.

During World War II, gas rations were approved by the USO to allow *Victory II* to take servicemen on sightseeing excursions. North Beach residents listened to explosions of depth charges in the Atlantic Ocean and were educated in ship and plane identification. Many served as lookouts on the Vilano Beach Bridge. Blackout shades were mandatory. A few miles away, the Coast Guard station in South Ponte Vedra Beach was base for the Mounted Beach Patrol, with stables behind the building. Many Navy families lived in cottages in Surfside and socialized with locals.

Construction began on a new west end and draw for the Vilano Beach Bridge in 1946. The State of Florida contracted *Victory II* to operate as a passenger ferry between Riverside Fish Camp and the mainland. The bridge reopened in 1948.

In the late 1940s, artesian wells were driven at Myrtle Street near Perpall's Fish Camp, now Cap's Restaurant. The St. Augustine Boating Club's clubhouse was built at Eighteenth Street, which was renamed Boating Club Road. The St. Augustine Boating Club, still in operation, held cruises, races, and oyster roasts for its members.

In South Ponte Vedra Beach, timber harvesting continued from the 1930s through the 1970s. Land was leased for cattle and hog grazing. In 1957, the state leased the 12,000-acre Guana Peninsula to preserve wildlife habitat and provide outdoor recreation. The construction of the Guana River Dam created Guana Lake, enhancing habitat for waterfowl.

In the late 1950s, architect Robert C. Broward, who apprenticed with Frank Lloyd Wright, designed a two-story A-frame house that still stands today. On September 10, 1964, Hurricane Dora came ashore six miles north of St. Augustine with winds of 125 miles per hour. Many of the oceanfront homes were destroyed, but the A-frame survived. After the devastation, oceanfront property could be bought for a song.

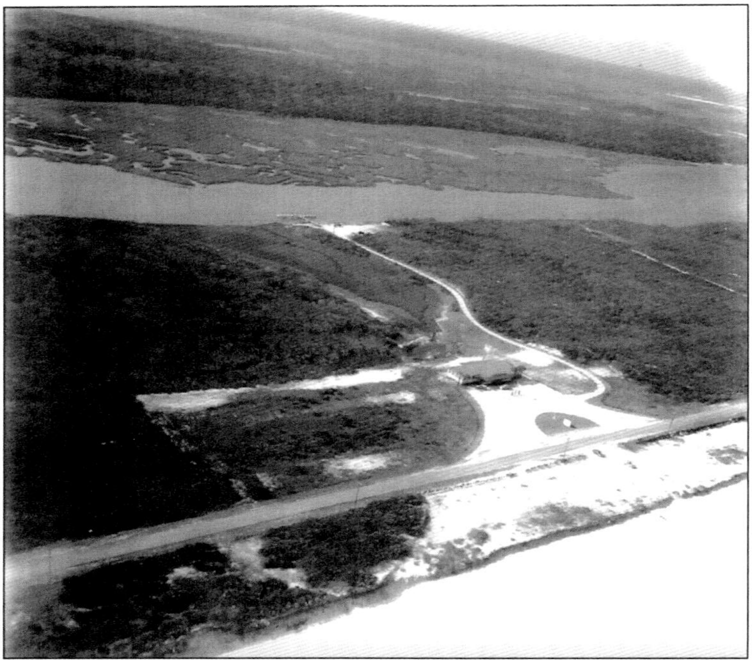

During World War II, a Coast Guard station was established at South Ponte Vedra to watch for German submarines. The 1930s facility near the present-day Guana Lake Dam was owned by Stockton, Whatley, Davin & Company. Without electricity or running water, and with limited amenities, the station provided quarters for the men and stables for the horses used in daily mounted patrols. (Courtesy of the St. Augustine Historical Society.)

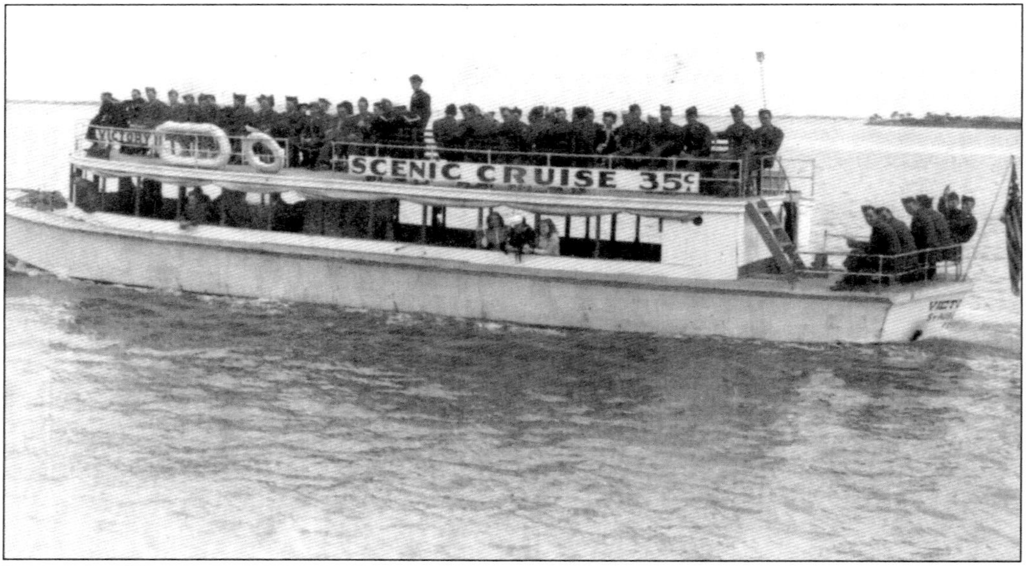

During World War II, St. Augustine became a military service town, and a halt was placed on fishing excursions. Gas rations approved by the USO allowed *Victory II* to take servicemen on sightseeing excursions. The state chartered *Victory II* to assist in ferrying residents during construction of a new bridge. By 1949, operation of the full-time sightseeing boat resumed. (Courtesy of Elizabeth and Frank D. Usina.)

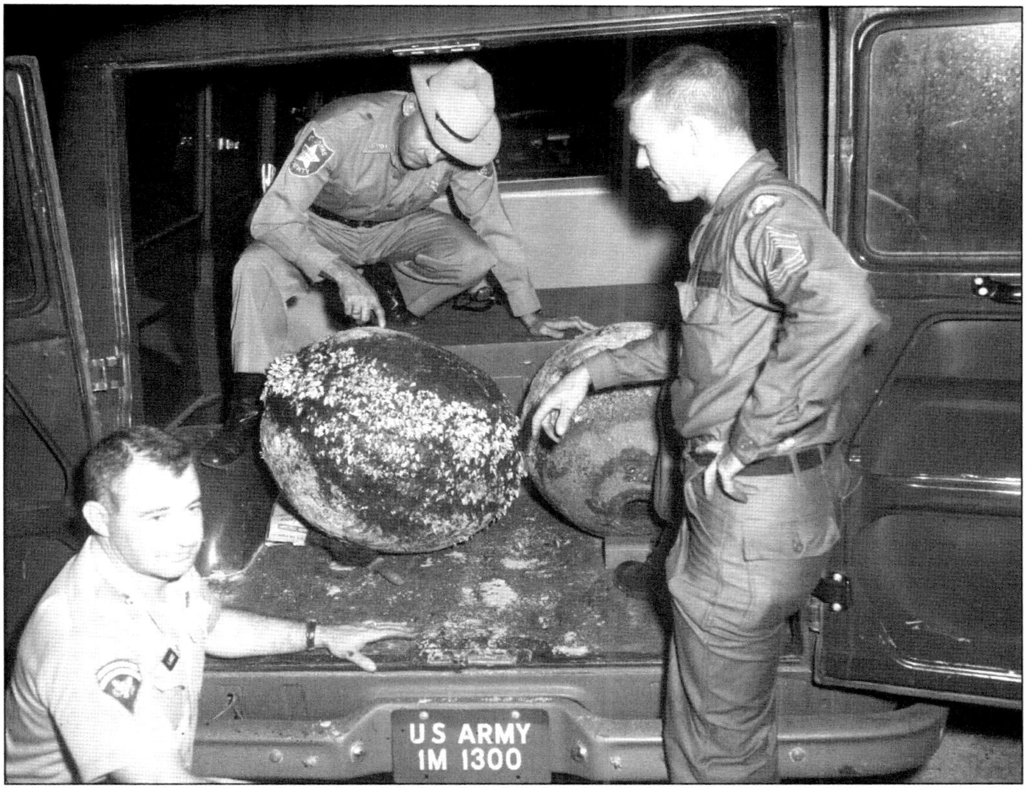

After World War II, it was not uncommon for beach patrols to discover land mines. Here, US Army officers safely remove these civilian threats. Even years after the war, these bombs were still sometimes located. It was risky business for the Army to disarm the mines. (Courtesy of St. Augustine Historical Society.)

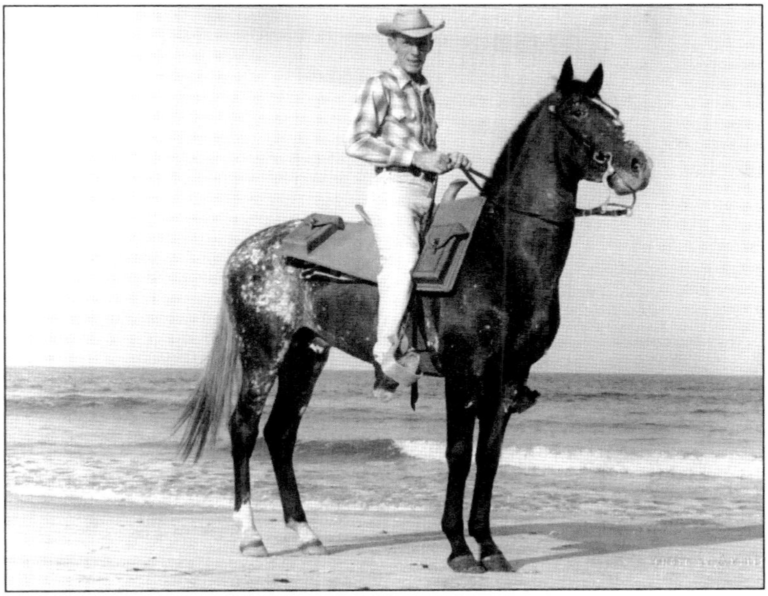

Transportation along the remote beaches of Northeast Florida was difficult at times. The easiest path to travel was along the unobstructed shoreline. Mail couriers, as seen here in Ponte Vedra, took advantage of the ocean ride, but only at low tides and in good weather. (Courtesy of Beaches Museum and History Park.)

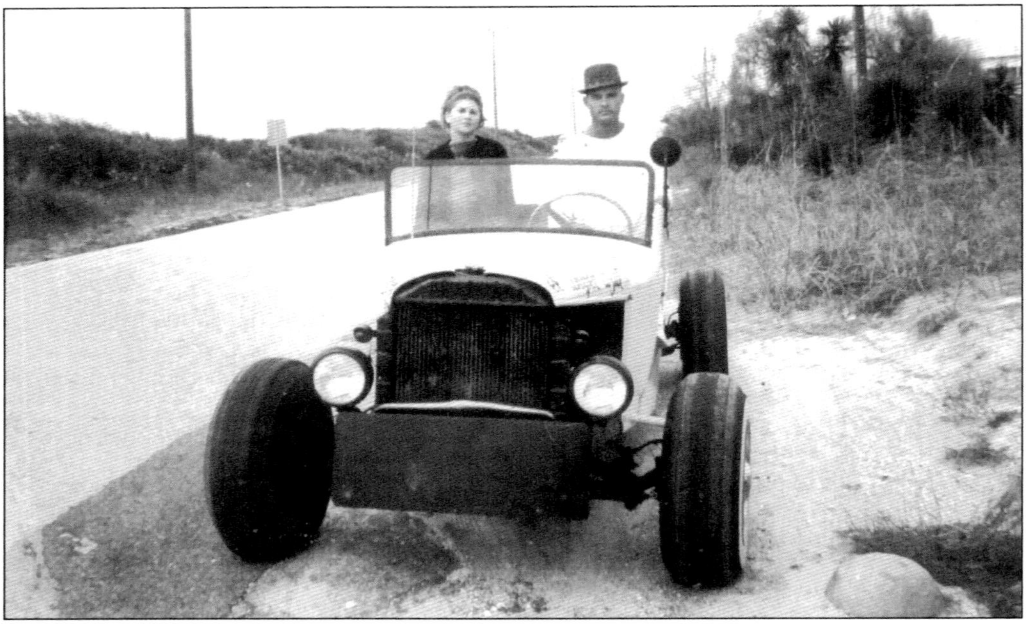

In the 1950s, along State Road A1A in the Surfside Subdivision, Freddie Lee drives a female passenger in an old "beach skeeter." State Road A1A connecting Ponte Vedra Beach to Vilano Beach was a favorite for motoring after World War II. People flocked to the beach and open roads to enjoy sun, surf, and shellfish along the coquina shores. (Courtesy of Elizabeth and Frank D. Usina.)

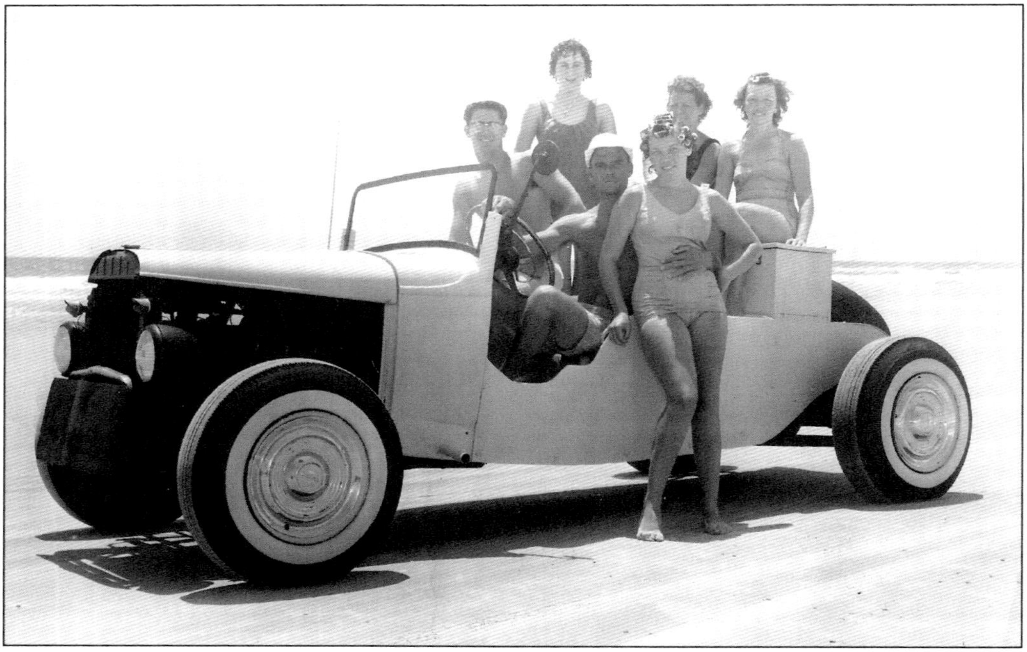

Ready to have fun on a hot Sunday afternoon in 1946? Just gather some good friends and a racy beach skeeter and go buzz the beach! After World War II, gas restrictions were lifted, and people went looking for entertainment. These cars were all the rage. (Courtesy of Bo Pitts.)

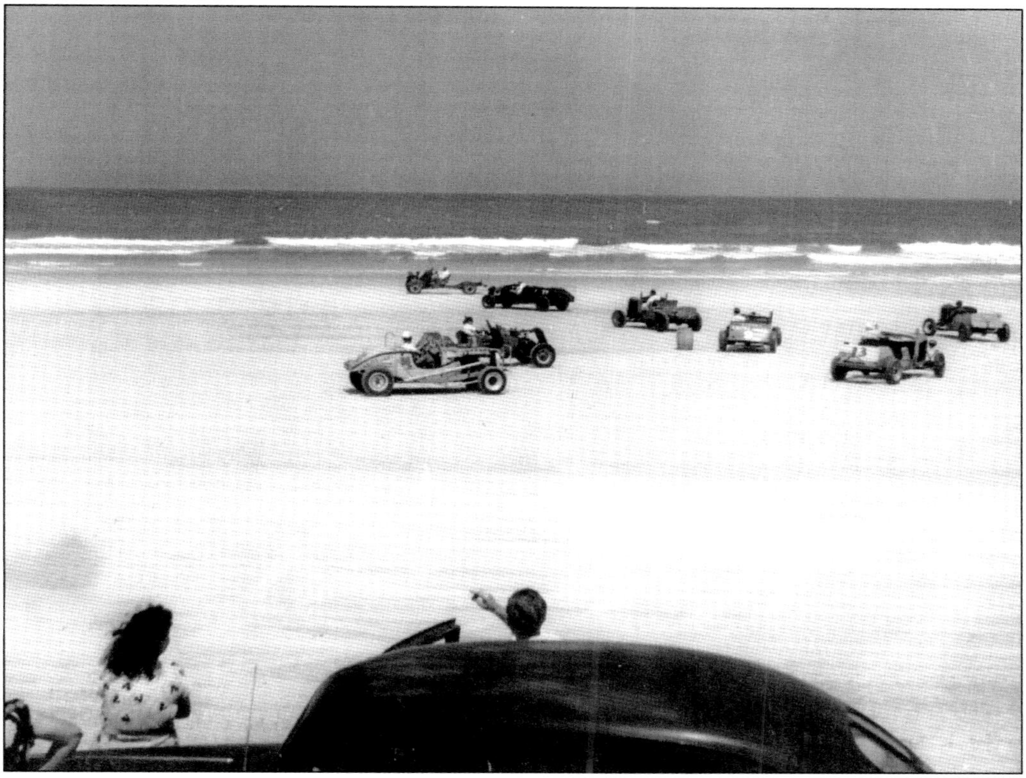

Skeeters raced at low tide, when the beach provided a wide expanse. During the summer, races were held at least once a month. Spectators would gather to cheer on their favorites and enjoy the excitement. The "skeeter" name came about because the cut-down vehicles were said to look like mosquitoes with wheels. (Courtesy of Philip Bernstein.)

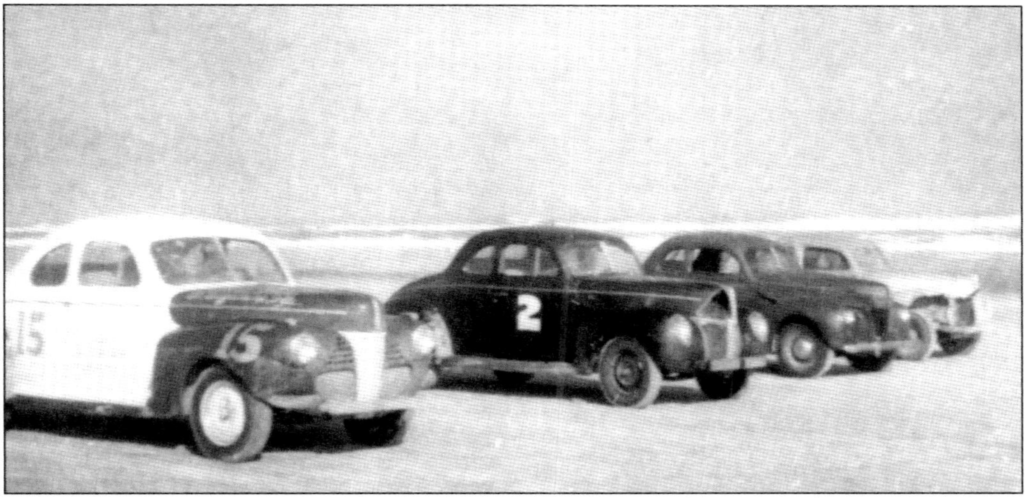

In the early days of skeeter racing, the most popular chassis was that of a Ford; next in popularity was a Chevrolet chassis. Because many of the racers worked during the day, they would practice on the beach in the evenings. The sport continued to be popular through the early 1960s. (Courtesy of Philip Bernstein.)

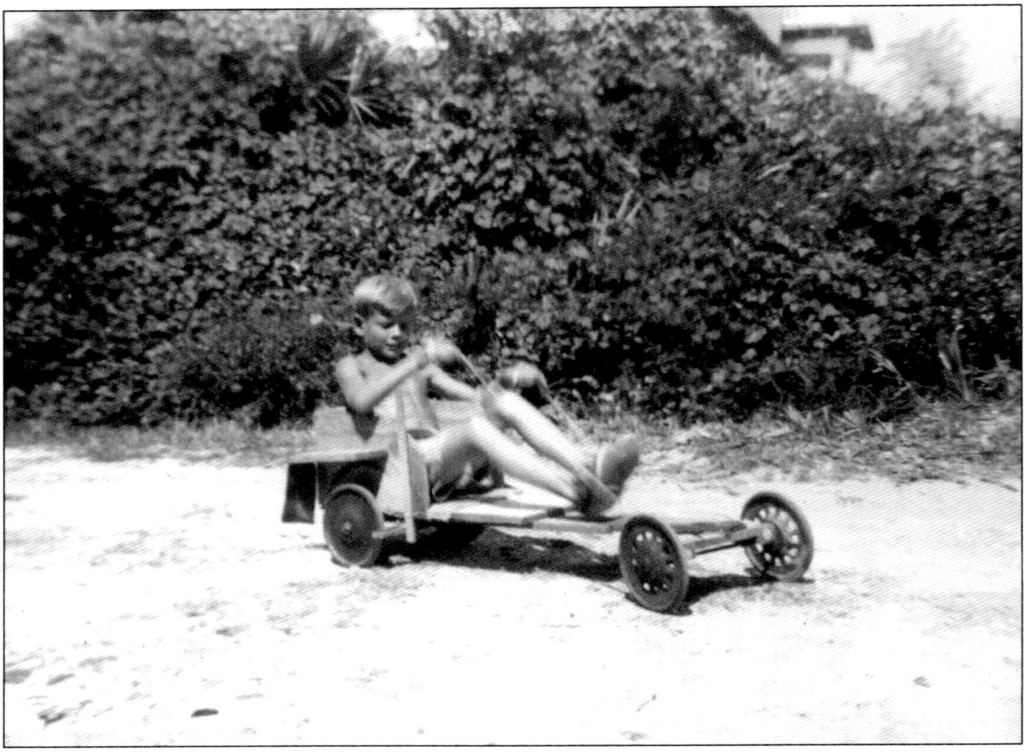

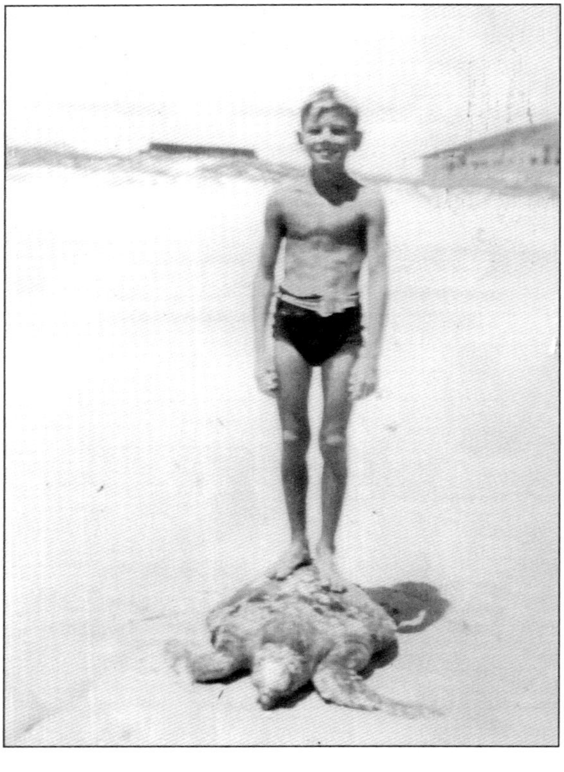

During World War II, people experienced many wartime materials shortages. Youngsters such as this one would build their own go-karts with recycled scraps and a little ingenuity. It was a rewarding project to create one's own vehicle and enjoy hours of recreation with it afterward. (Courtesy of Philip Bernstein.)

Here, an unidentified child stands on an unfortunate female sea turtle that has come ashore to lay her eggs. Sea turtle nesting season is between March and October on the Atlantic Coast. Today, it is against the law to touch or disturb nesting sea turtles, hatchlings, or their nests. Sea turtles are protected by both the federal Endangered Species Act and the Florida Marine Protection Act. Today, this area is a leading turtle-nesting/hatching site in St. Johns County. (Courtesy of Philip Bernstein.)

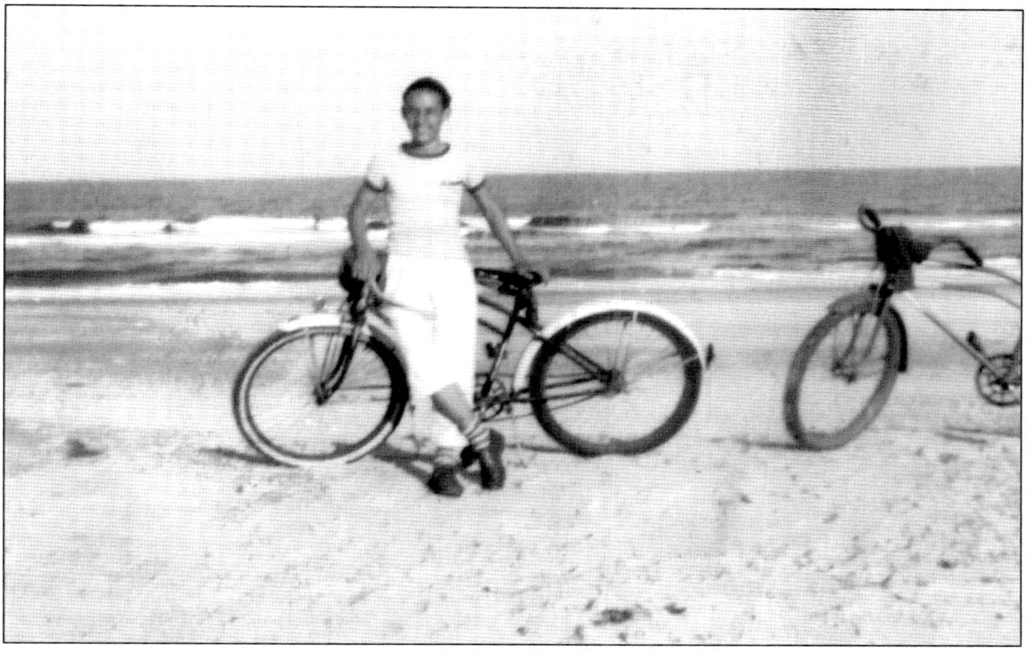

Phil Bernstein pauses during an enjoyable bicycle ride on the beach to have his photograph taken. Bicycle riding continues to be a pleasurable pastime today. State Road A1A was also used for cycling, along with Surfside Avenue around Meadow and Palmetto Roads. The Bernsteins operated the Junior Department Store on St. George Street for a number of years. They spent summers in Vilano Beach. (Courtesy of Philip Bernstein.)

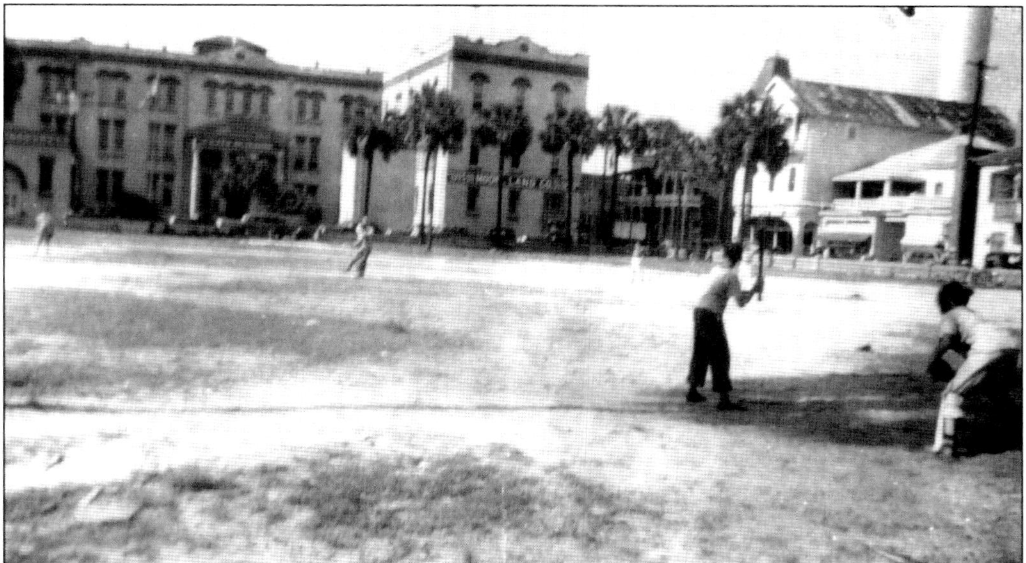

Area students play baseball in the vacant field in front of Ketterlinus High School, now known as Francis Field. The old high school building in the background is now used for the St. Johns County School Board. Children from the Vilano Beach area continue to attend Ketterlinus Elementary School across the street. (Courtesy of Philip Bernstein.)

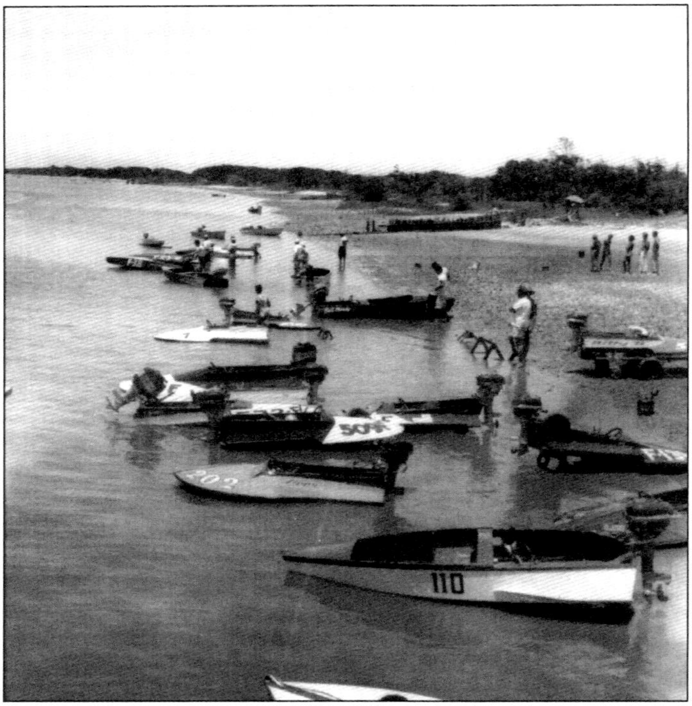

On the banks of the Tolomato River, also known as the Intracoastal Waterway, boaters prepare for a little racing competition during the July holiday season in 1950. The launch site was on the shores near the pavilion at North Beach Campground. This is clearly not a day for leisure fishing, and ladies were not among the participants in those days. (Courtesy of Philip Bernstein.)

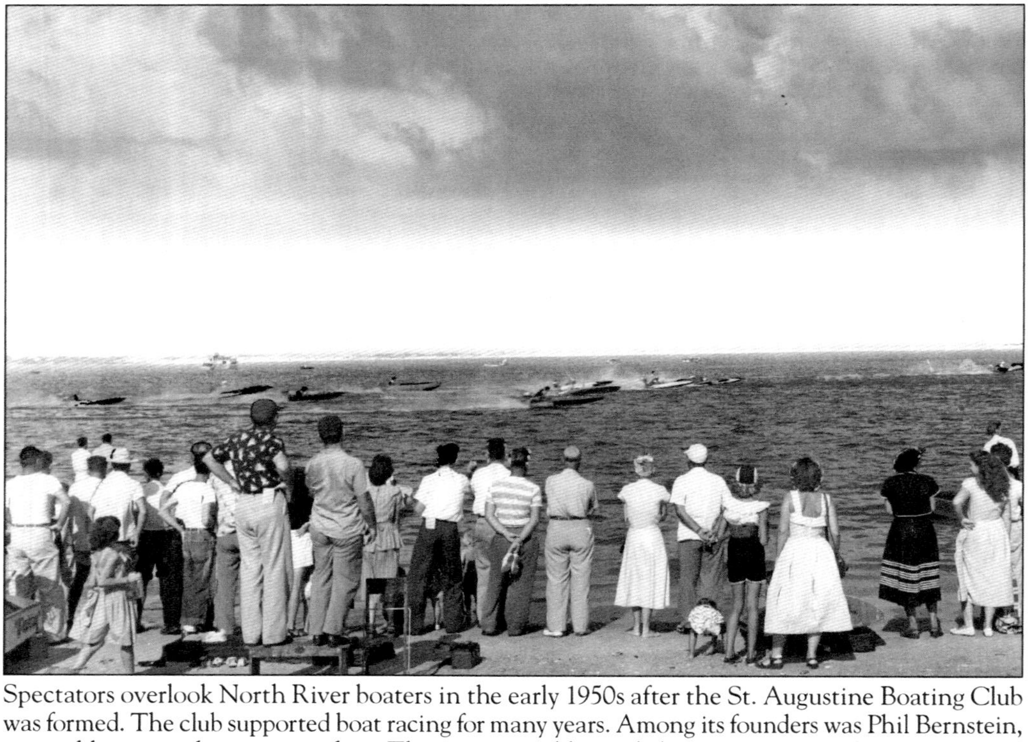

Spectators overlook North River boaters in the early 1950s after the St. Augustine Boating Club was formed. The club supported boat racing for many years. Among its founders was Phil Bernstein, an avid boater in his younger days. The racers would travel the state, racing other clubs. Here, spectators watch tensely as speedboats go screaming past. (Courtesy of Philip Bernstein.)

The St. Augustine Boating Club sponsored national races. This is a photograph of part of a 100-mile marathon race from Jacksonville to Daytona and back. The club received national recognition and was heavily supported by the City of St. Augustine. Competitors came to North River from all over the state. (Courtesy of Philip Bernstein.)

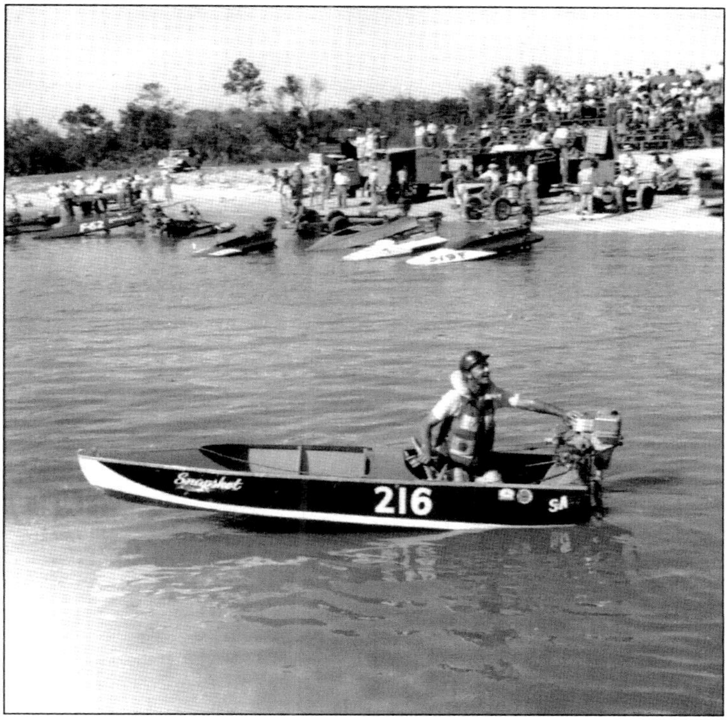

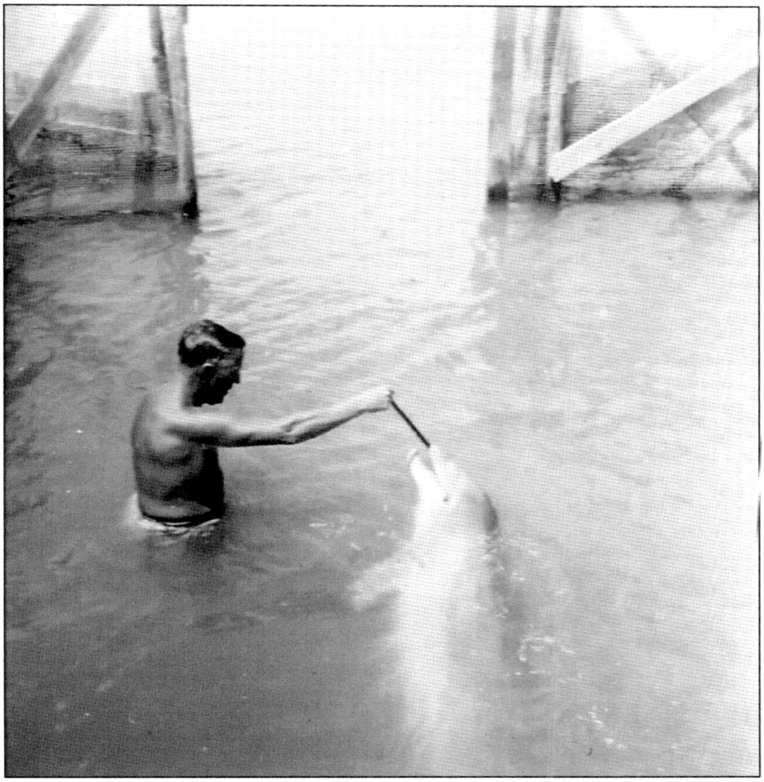

The first dolphin trainer at Marineland, Adolf Frohn, trained Flippy in a sea pen in Vilano Beach around 1950. Dolphins were caught by Ronnie Capo in his boat *Porpoise III*. He was in charge of the collecting crew for Marine Studios, later renamed Marineland. This oceanarium was located south of Vilano, but it relied on expert local fishermen for their catches. (Courtesy of Terran McGinnis.)

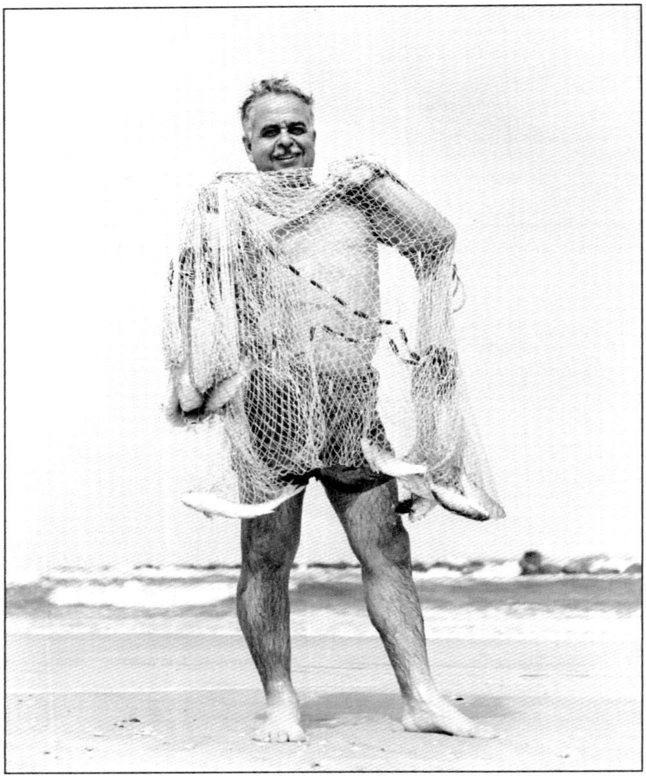

Victor Rahner Sr. proudly holds up his mullet catch in his circular cast net. Mullet fishing was a seasonal tradition among the Minorcans in response to schooling of the fish. When the silvery reflections from their scales through the tops of ocean waves were spotted, a cry of "Mullet on the beach!" would bring fishermen running from other activities to catch this tasty local delicacy. (Courtesy of Tom Rahner.)

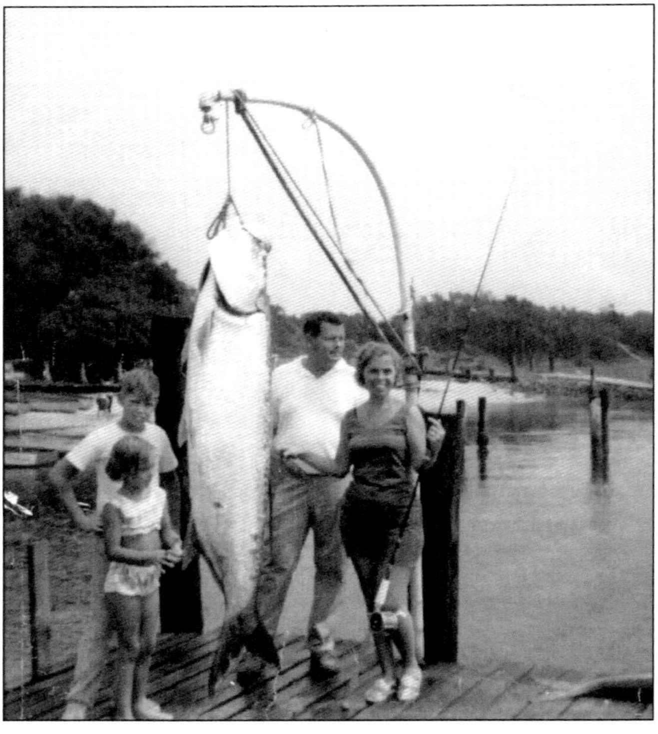

The Moellers are a well-known family living in North Beach and Surfside Beach. Here, family members proudly display a huge fish caught in the waterways nearby. They are standing at the Usina dock at the end of Euclid Avenue, which has seen many a huge fish in its day. (Courtesy of Elizabeth and Frank D. Usina.)

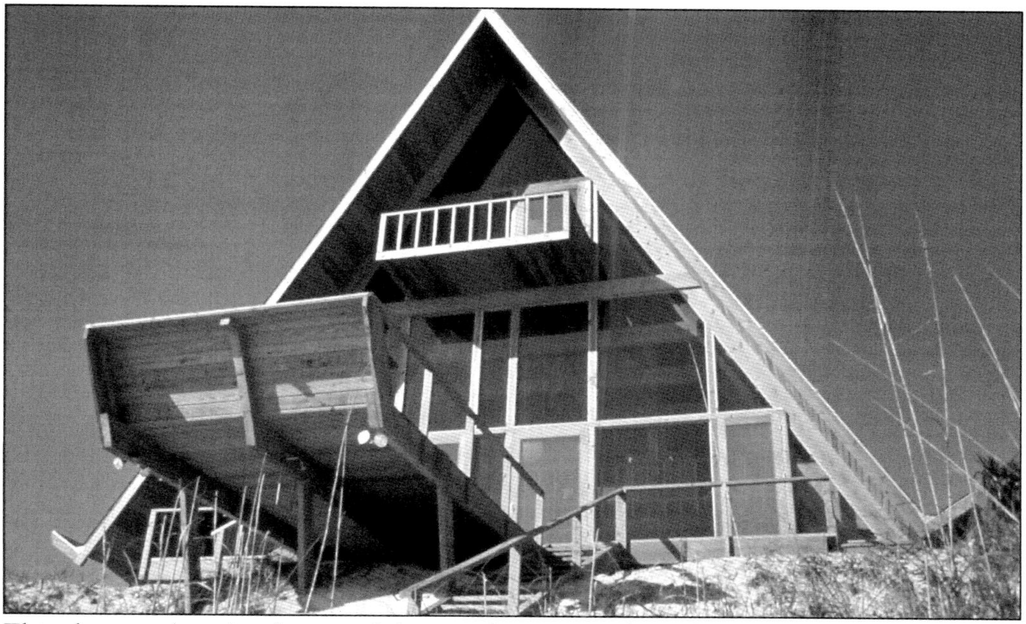

This photograph and architectural drawing depict an A-frame house located at 2541 SRA1A in South Ponte Vedra. Built in the 1960s, this residence had its beginnings in 1947. The house was designed by architect Robert C. "Bob" Broward, who apprenticed with Frank Lloyd Wright. Broward, great-second-cousin of Gov. Napoleon Bonaparte Broward, grew up in Jacksonville and is one of Florida's most renowned architects. The organic design of his buildings reflects his lifelong commitment to environmental stewardship and quality of life. This house was one of the structures that survived the destruction of Hurricane Dora in 1964. It is still standing today. (Both, courtesy of Robert C. Broward Collection.)

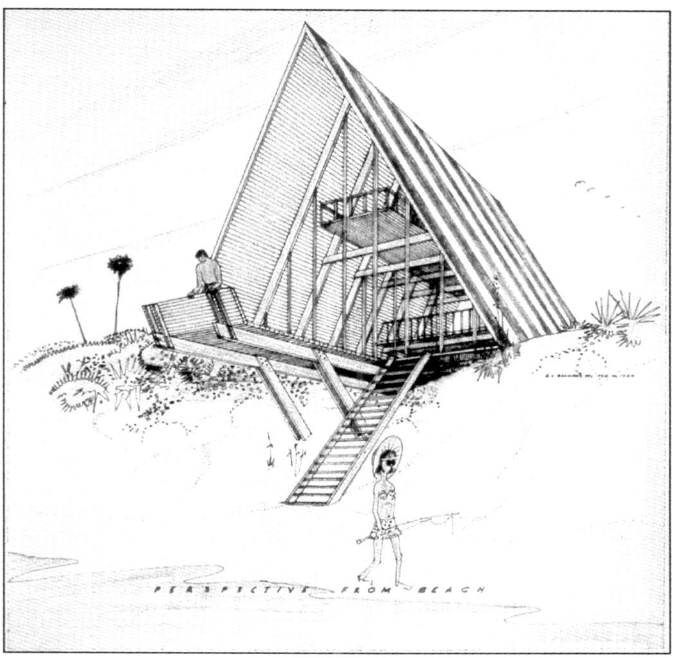

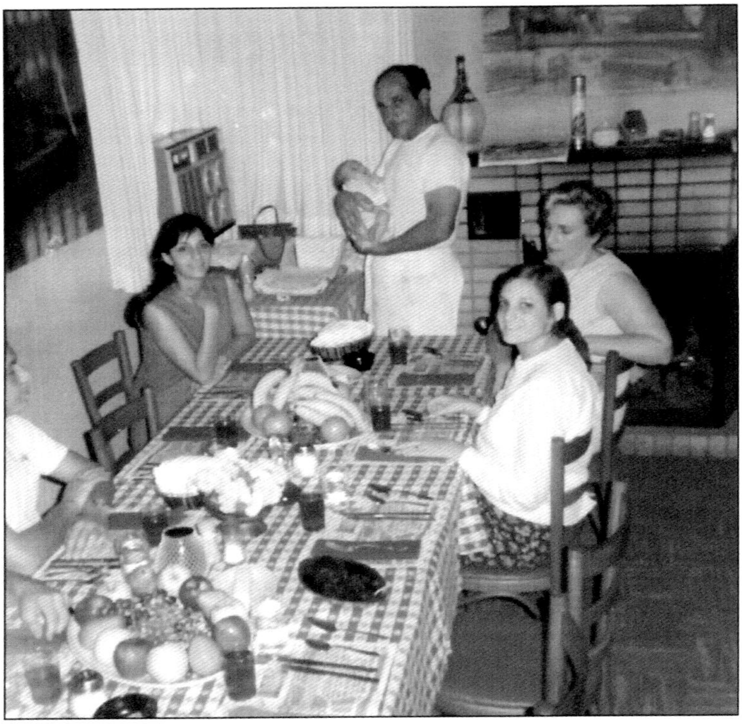

For decades, beginning in the 1960s, Barrancotto's Roma Restaurant was a local institution. People came from miles around to this family-owned restaurant operated by Frances and Sam Barrancotto Sr., and their daughters Cyndi and Charlotte and sons Sam and Jim. The family is seen here on Thanksgiving 1968, on a rare occasion to sit down together in their restaurant to enjoy their own feast. (Courtesy of Cynthia Barrancotto.)

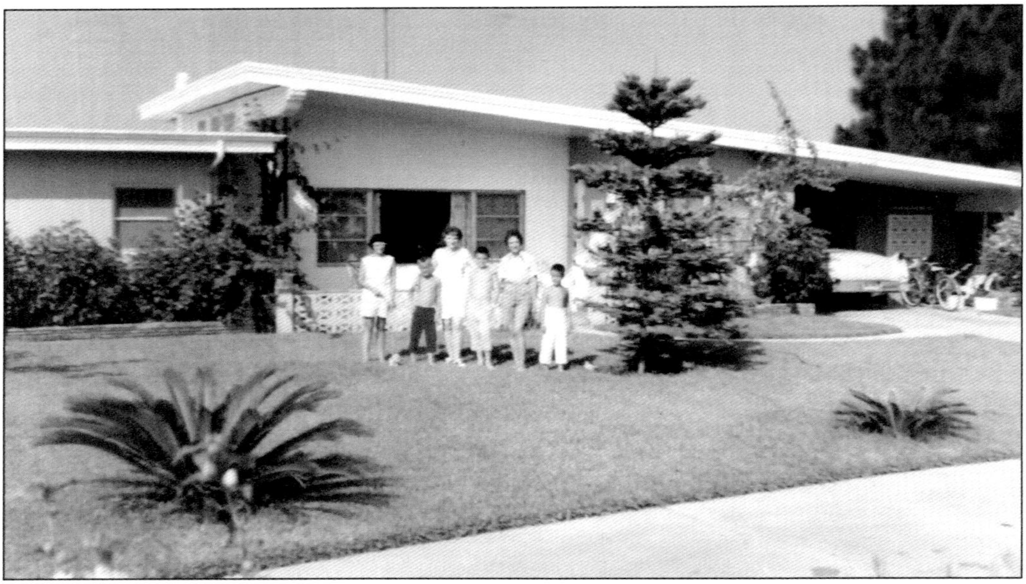

Sam Barrancotto's family home was located on Ferrol Road, behind their restaurant at 165 Vilano Road. In this 1959 photograph are members of the family. They are, from left to right, Cynthia Barrancotto with Bambi, David O'Brocta (cousin), Francis and Jimmy Barrancotto, Mary Lou O'Brocta (aunt), and Sammy Barrancotto. Along Ferrol Road to the south of Vilano Road, the homes were of similar Art Deco styles. (Courtesy of Cynthia Barrancotto.)

For 80 years, Vilano and the North Beaches had little or no local fire protection. In the early 1980s, the community, led by the North Shores Improvement Association, banded together to build this fire station in Surfside. Named in honor of Mary Usina, it was built by William Coleman and Son Construction Company. Today, the former fire station is used as a community center and police substation. (Courtesy of Sacha Martin.)

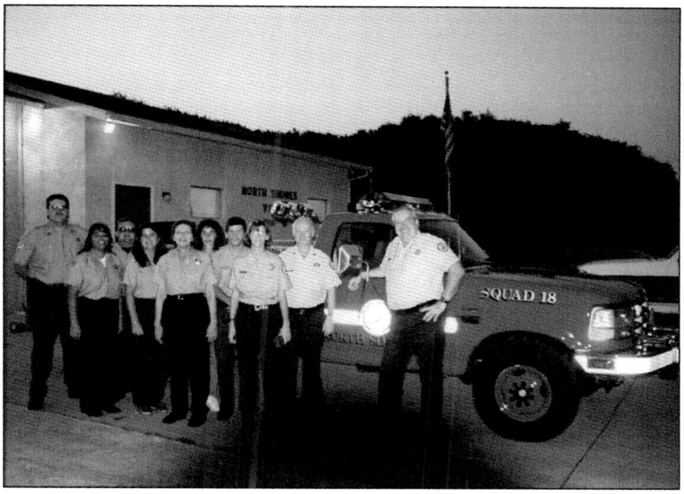

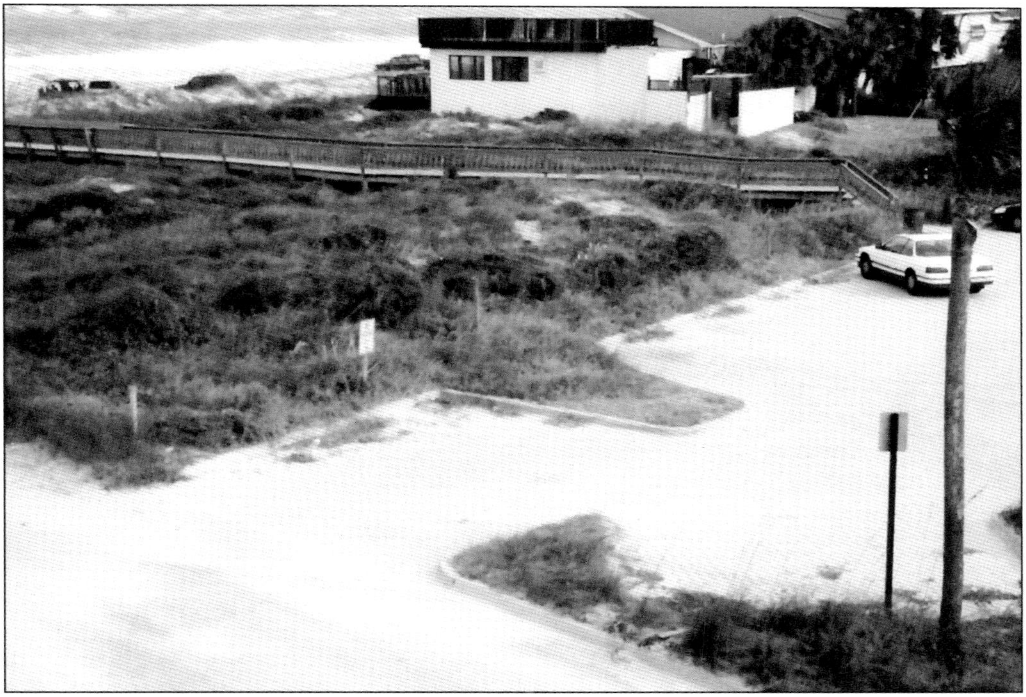

The first restaurant on this oceanfront site at the ramp on Vilano Road was opened as the Seabreeze. It was built at the same location as the Vilano Casino. The building was expanded over the years, eventually becoming the Fiddlers Green under new ownership. In 2007, St. Johns County, with the support of the Vilano Beach Main Street group, received a state grant to create a public park here. (Courtesy of Sacha Martin.)

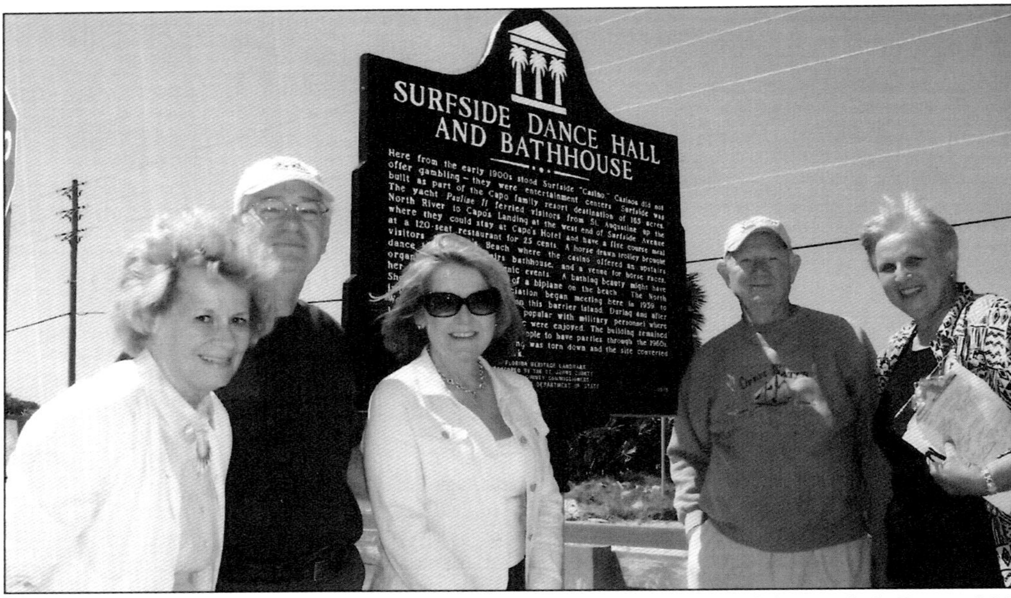

On this day, a historical sign was dedicated commemorating the site of the Surfside Dance Hall and Bathhouse, built in 1922. This was part of the Capo family resort destination at the west end of Surfside Avenue. It included a restaurant, dance hall, bathhouse, and all manner of entertaining activities. Pictured here are, from left to right, Sacha Martin, Keith Willard, Nancy Sikes-Kline, Hal Brackett, and Vivian C. Browning. (Courtesy of Sacha Martin.)

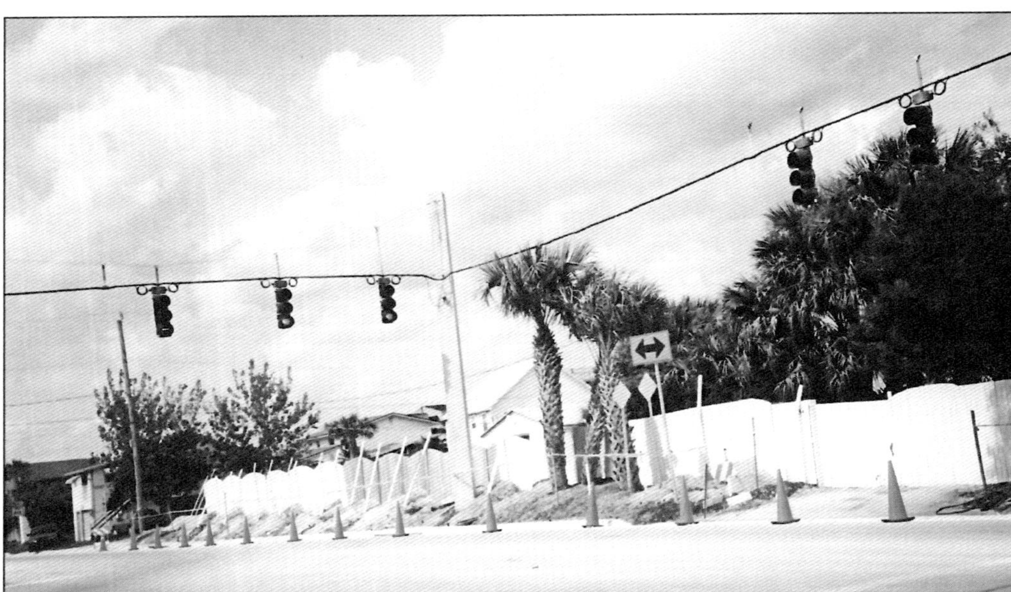

The North Shore Improvement Association encouraged the Florida Department of Transportation to provide landscaping at the base of the Vilano Bridge. A beautification grant was received, with cabbage palms and oleanders chosen for planting. Additional landscaping was added at a later entrance. This location is the only street with a signal on the island. It can be said that this is a one-stoplight town. (Courtesy of Sacha Martin.)

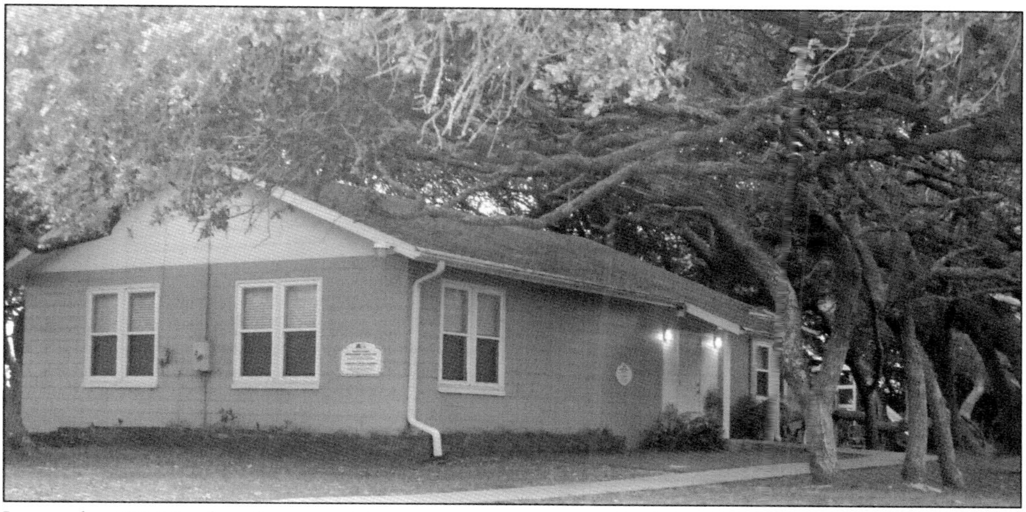

Located at 120 Meadow Avenue, this community center was built by the North Shores Improvement Association as its permanent home. The meetings for planning the Vilano Beach Town Center took place here in the 1990s and early 2000s. It is surrounded by a well-used, open county public park. (Courtesy of John T. Pilecki.)

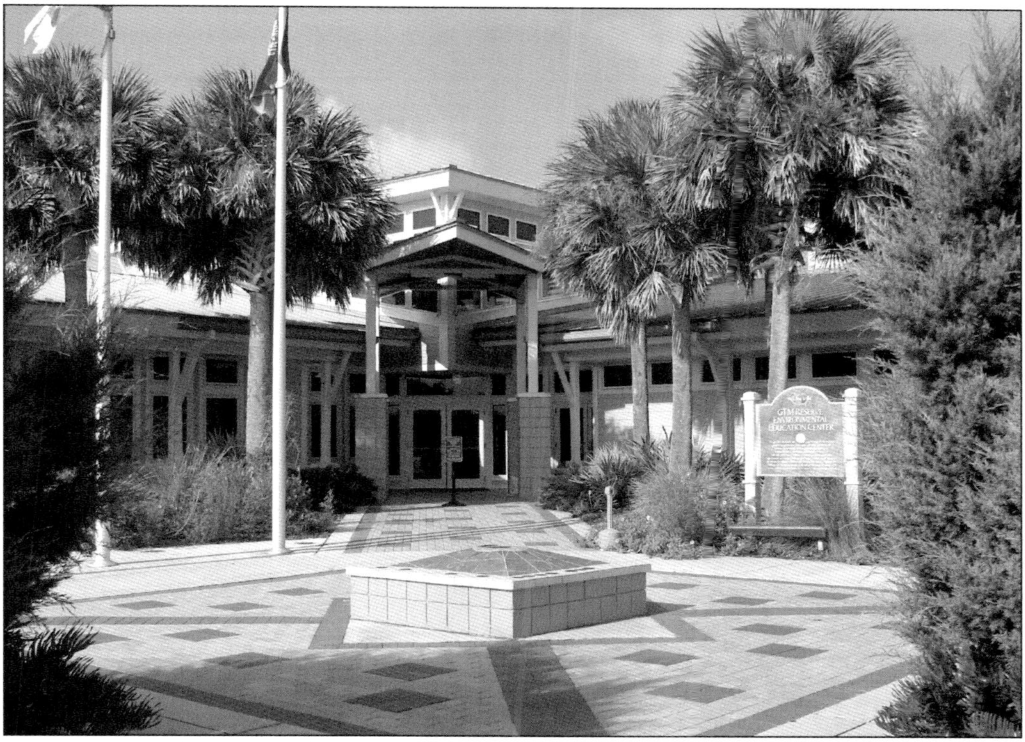

At the northern boundary of Vilano and the North Beaches is the Guana. In recent years, these thousands of acres have been designated as the Guana Tolomato Matanzas National Estuarine Research Reserve. It is included in a network of 26 protected coastal areas along the coasts of the United States. This environmental center is open to the public and includes access to nature trails and waterways. (Courtesy of Sacha Martin.)

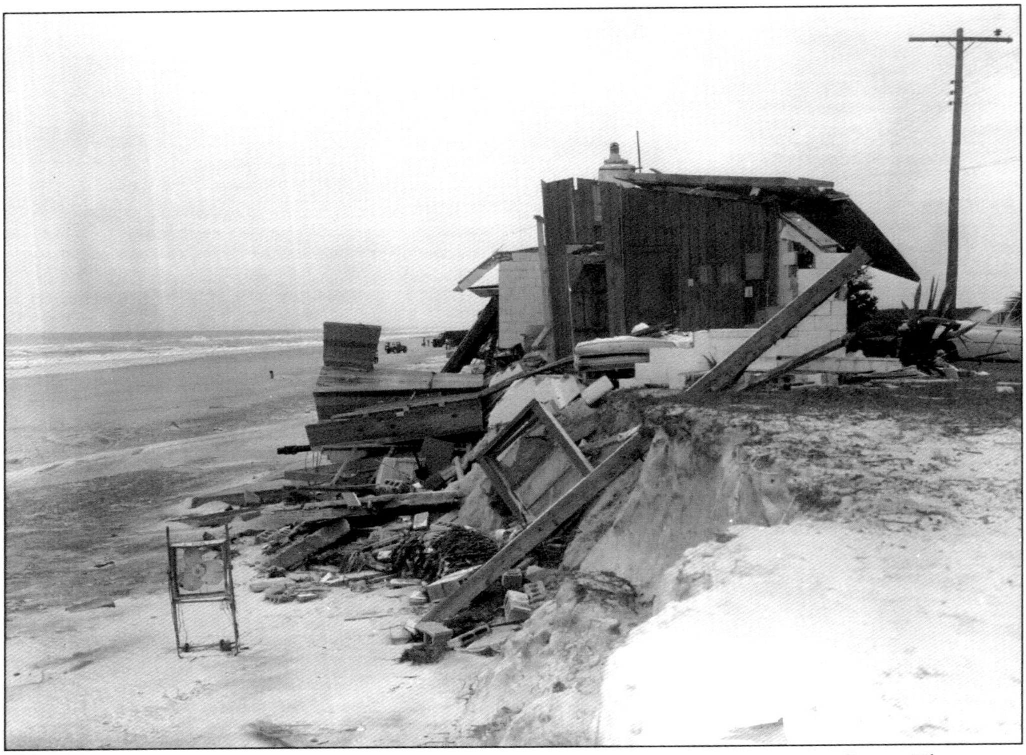

In September 1964, Northeast Florida's coast experienced powerful Hurricane Dora. The storm slammed directly onto South Ponte Vedra's shore, wreaking havoc on nearby Ponte Vedra and Vilano Beaches. Shown here are South Ponte Vedra homes, casualties of extensive destruction. In all, 18 houses in the area were severely damaged, and 12 dropped into the ocean. Law-enforcement officers worked two-hour shifts apprehending people who were stealing items from the damaged homes and keeping back crowds curious to see the destruction. Other areas were affected by the storm, of course, but none as severely as South Ponte Vedra. (Both, courtesy of the St. Augustine Historical Society.)

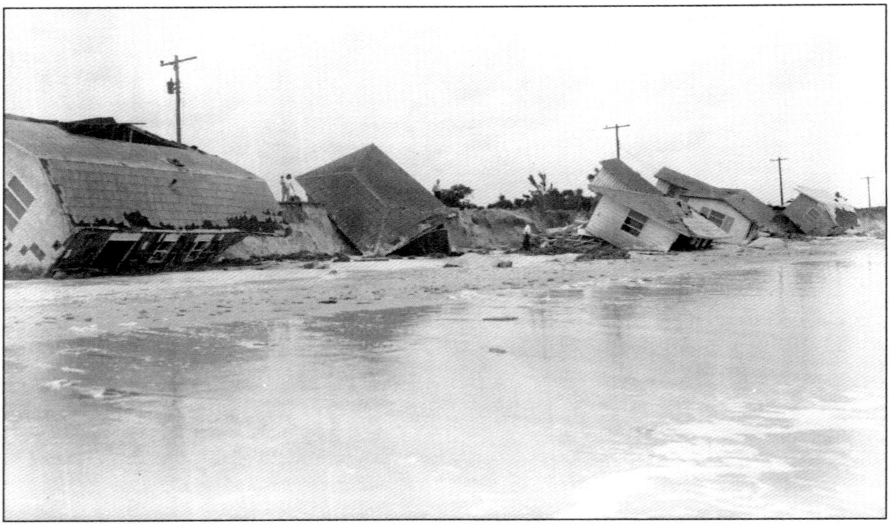

Six

The Sustainable Years

After decades with no significant new development in Vilano and the North Beaches, several new residential neighborhoods were established along A1A beginning in the late 1970s. In the Vilano business district, three oceanfront hotels—the Ocean Blue I (now St. Augustine Beach House), Ocean Blue II (now OceanView Lodge), and the Hampton Inn—were built. During the late 1980s and early 1990s, the drawbridge connecting A1A and St. Augustine was in disrepair and was congested with traffic due to population growth along Vilano and the North Beaches. In 1995, a fixed-span bridge with a pedestrian/bike lane opened. The east end of the old bridge was kept as a public pier for use as a community recreation area.

Since the main business district in Vilano had been bypassed by the new bridge, businesses and residents formed Vilano Beach Town Center Redevelopment Group under the citizen/civic organization North Shores Improvement Association, Inc., in partnership with the government of St. Johns County. The group established tax-increment financing. Through the vision of this organization, citizens identified a need to transition the main business district from a place travelers drove through on their way to other towns, to a destination beachside town under the name Vilano Beach Town Center.

The new infrastructure, including wide sidewalks, angled parking, storm water drains, new water and sewer lines, underground electrical service, and streetscape with more than 300 palms lining the main street, provided the opportunity to bring a full-service grocery store—an Art Deco–style Publix, the community's main goal—plus retail and service shops. Other recreational improvements included a pavilion at the river and the ocean, a boat dock attached to the pier allowing boaters to use the grocery store and restaurants, and a nature boardwalk with tactile artwork under the bridge and over the marsh, connecting the Surfside community and the North Shores Community Center and Park to the town center. Since 2003, the Vilano Beach Main Street group has led the effort to establish this community as a small beach-town and ensure its sustainability for the future.

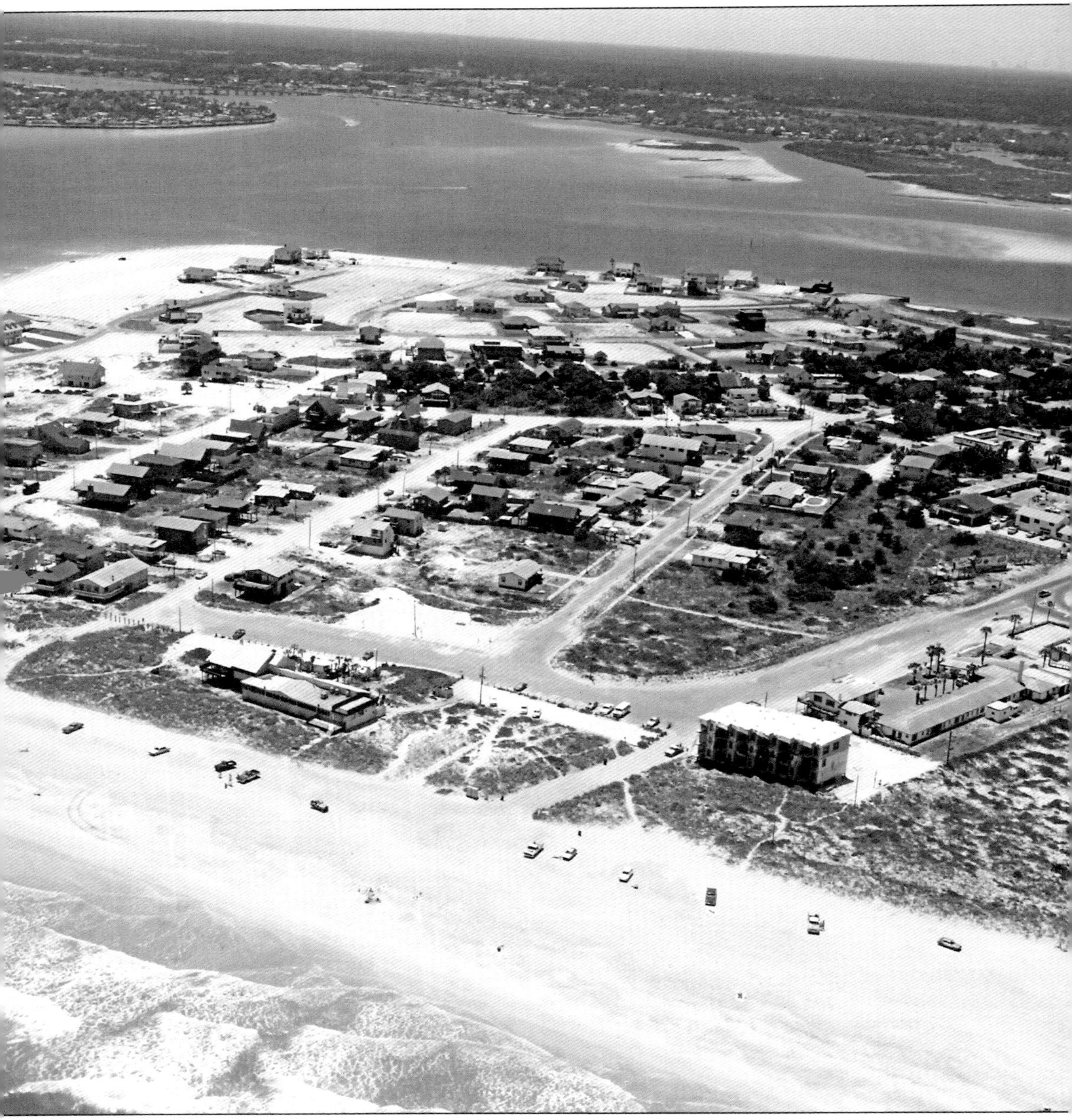

This aerial photograph of the tip of the barrier island at St. Augustine Inlet shows the clear street boundaries of the Vilano commercial and residential sections, including the undeveloped areas of Porpoise Point. The white sandy beaches are a favorite for sports fishermen and surfers. Vilano Beach is home to a growing International Skimboard Tournament because of the natural waterway flows at the inlet. In the northern distance is the Surfside subdivision. The northern section of this photograph shows a number of homes along Poplar Avenue, where the current Publix is located. (Courtesy of Phillip Whitley.)

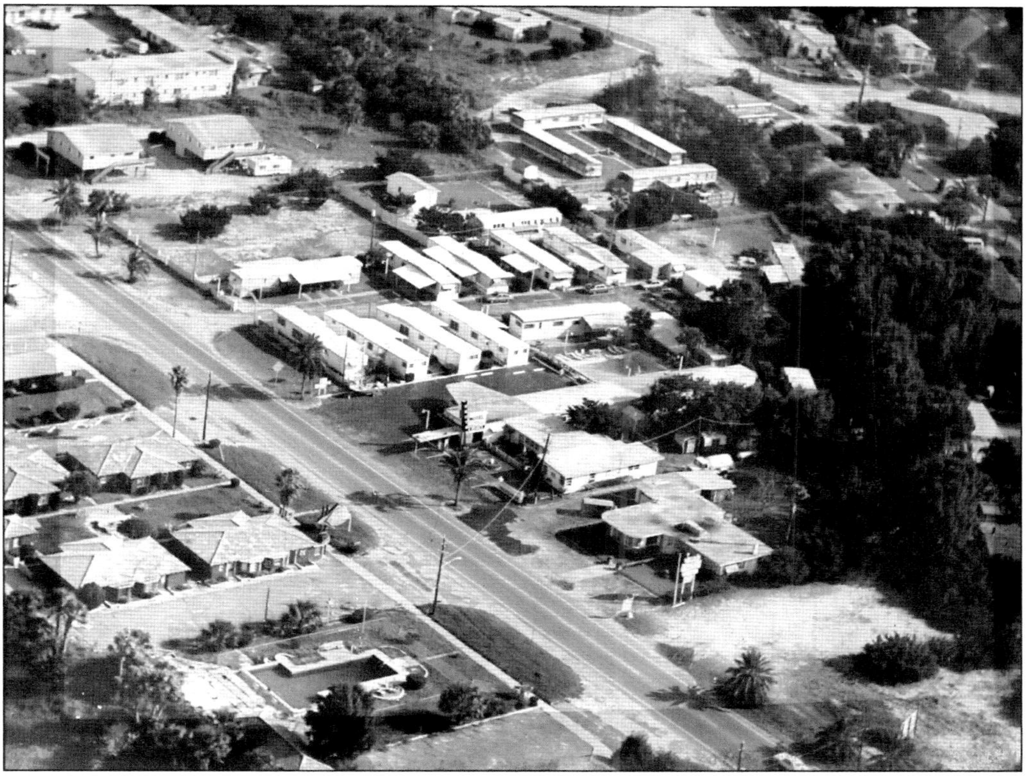

This view of Vilano Road in the late 1960s shows a number of motor courts and residential trailer sites. To travel north, motorists exited downtown over the Vilano causeway and then crossed the drawbridge to get to the first community where visitors could stop and stay overnight. There were a number of trailer parks in the area, used for temporary housing and vacationing. A duplex on the corner of the current Loja Street and Vilano Road is shown. Note that there are a number of hotel pools, no longer visible. Loja Street was formally opened after the streetscape was redesigned and completed in 2006–2008. (Both, courtesy of Bo Pitts.)

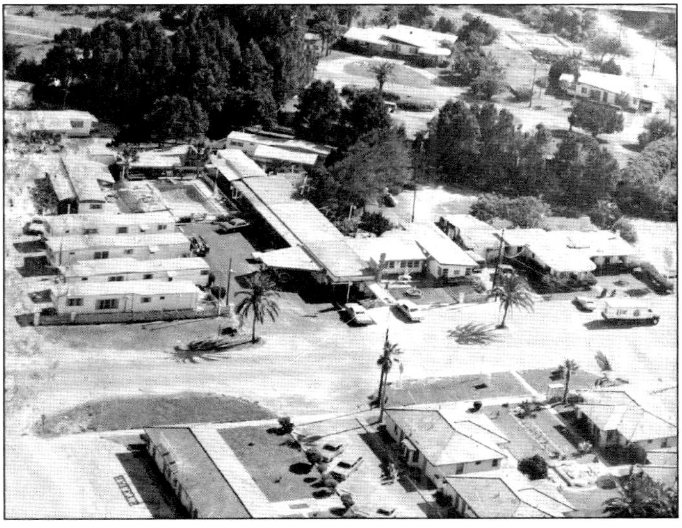

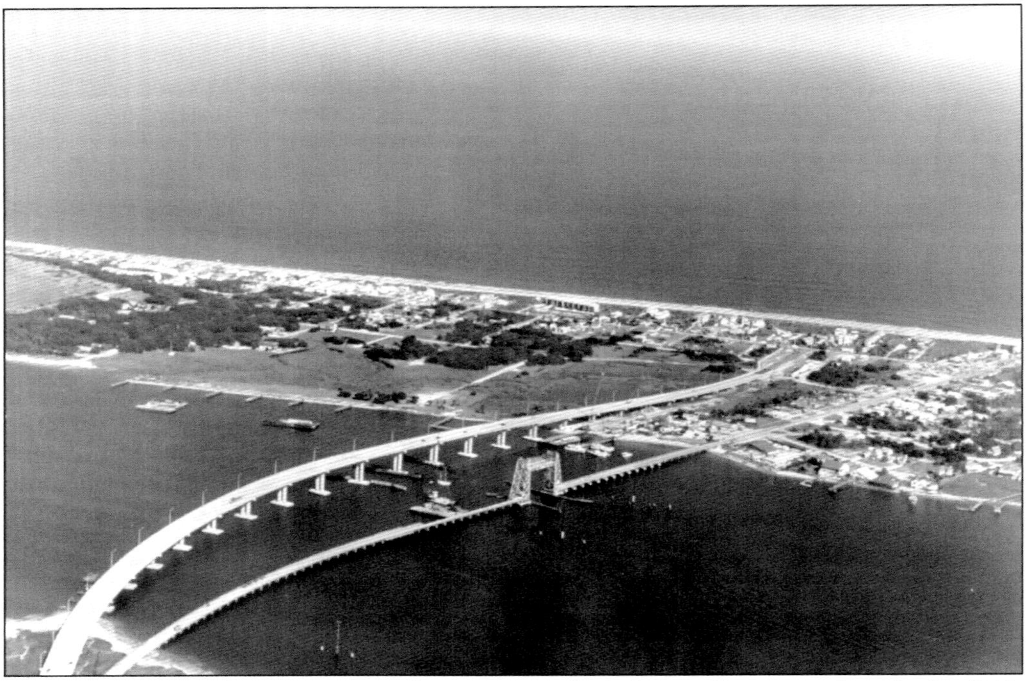

The new Francis and Mary Usina Bridge, spanning the Tolomato River, stands aside the 1940s drawbridge, which was reduced to a 600-foot fishing pier. This aerial photograph, taken by Hamilton Upchurch in 1995, epitomizes the transportation challenges of living on a barrier island. The waterway, with its diverse means of transportation, links the old and new, shaping an ever-robust community. (Courtesy of Elizabeth and Frank D. Usina.)

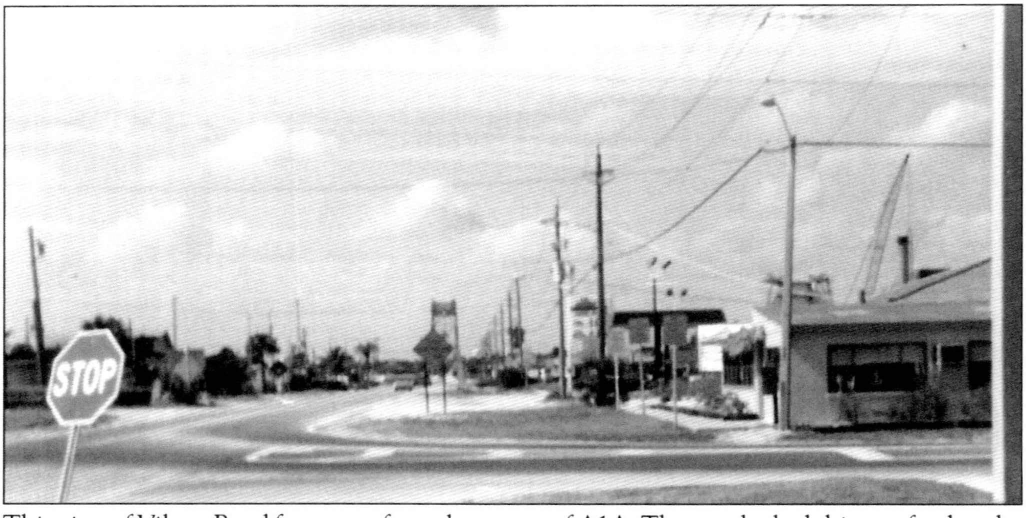

This view of Vilano Road faces west from the corner of A1A. The area looked this way for decades prior to removal of the original bridge and addition of the new streetscape, underground utilities, angled parking, and wide sidewalks. In the right foreground is the Usina Store, and beyond it is the Lil' Champ store and gas station. The Lil' Champ later was used as the Vilano Surf Hut, owned by Steve and Cindy Gianetta. This area now has the Publix Super Market and adjacent retail shops. (Courtesy of Sacha Martin.)

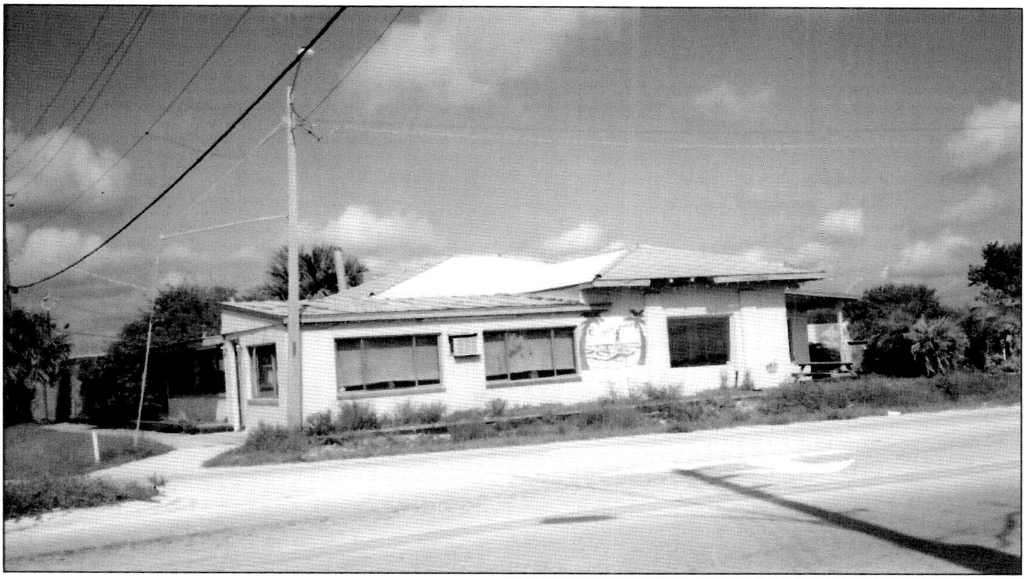

This building was the corner store and gas station, opened by Francis and Mary Usina in 1939. Over the years, it housed several businesses, including the popular Clam Shell seafood restaurant. Here, it is leased by the Pomar family as the Cast Net Restaurant. This building and adjoining land were sold in the early 2000s by the Usina family to make way for the Publix Super Market. (Courtesy of Sacha Martin.)

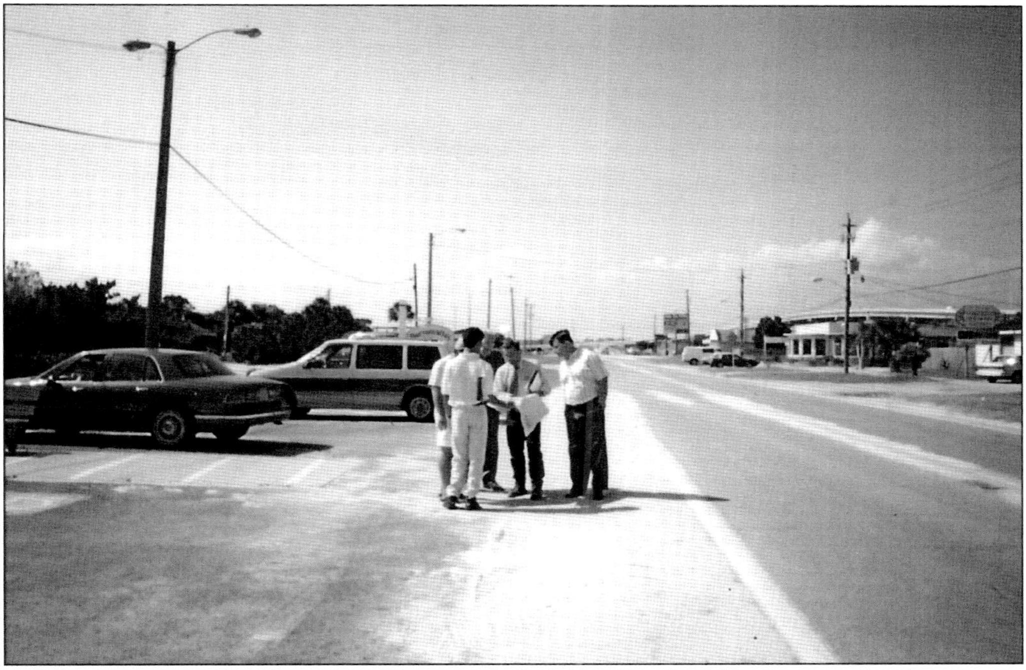

St. Johns County staff and contractors meet on Vilano Road to plan changes to it after the opening of the new bridge. The new Francis and Mary Usina Bridge in the background took the traffic of State Road A1A, approximately 9,000 vehicles a day, away from Vilano Road. The overhead power lines were later removed and placed underground. (Courtesy of Sacha Martin.)

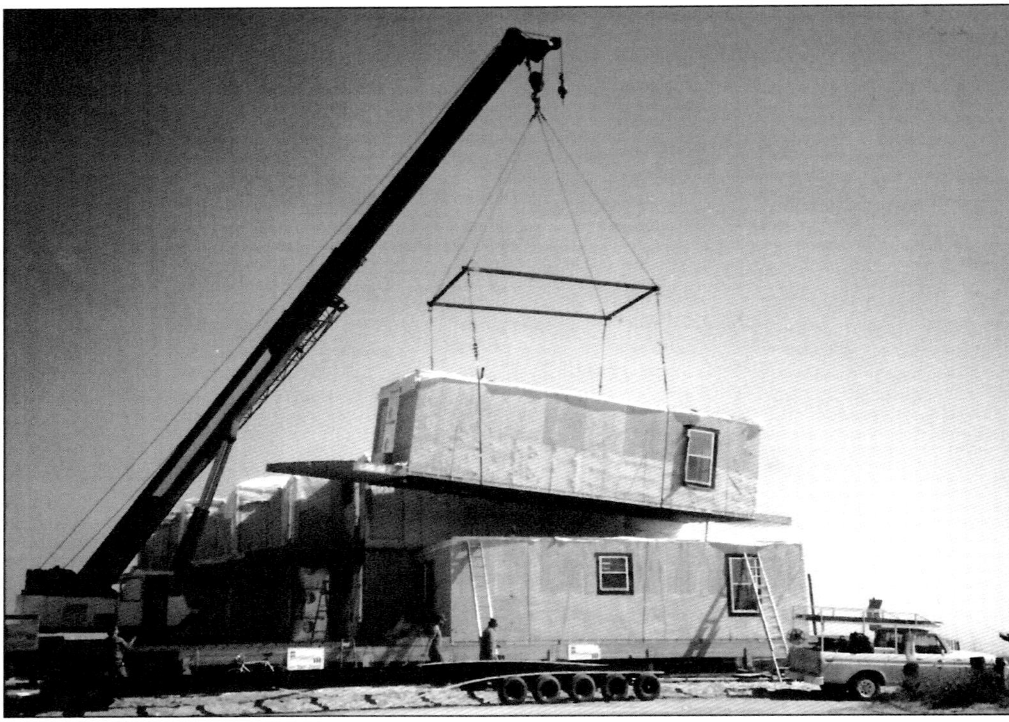

Art McGinnis received permits to build an oceanfront modular hotel on pilings in the late 1980s. He had the hotel rooms built and completed inside off-site. The units were trailered to the site and stacked with a crane, as shown here. The Ocean Blue Motel served tourists for many years. It was purchased and renovated as the St. Augustine Beach House beginning in 2010. (Courtesy of the Art McGinnis family.)

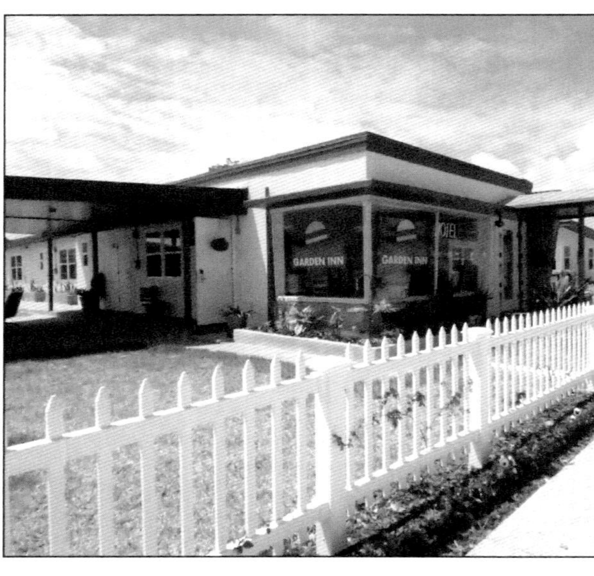

This renovated Garden Inn Motel began life as Newt's Vilano Motel. It was built in 1950 by Newt Haley and operated by him until the early 1990s. Haley built several motels on Vilano Road, all of which have been renovated. For several years, starting in 2004, Vivian Browning's Vilano Beach Town Center Realty and, as of 2006, the Vilano Post Office operated by volunteer Jacqueline Johns were located here. When the building sold, these services moved to the building at 115 Vilano Road owned by Jimma Walters. Dylan Cadwalader handled its renovation and operates the motel today as the Vilano Beach Garden Inn. (Courtesy of Sallie L. O'Hara.)

The Magic Beach Motel was restored to its 1950s glory in 2012 by Earl and Remy Jensen, owners and innkeepers extraordinaire. This Art Deco motel was built in 1958. Admired for its pink-flamingo decor and rooms decorated with murals, the hotel delights visitors with its nostalgic ambience. The WB television show *Safe Harbor* was filmed here in the 1990s. (Courtesy of Sallie L. O'Hara.)

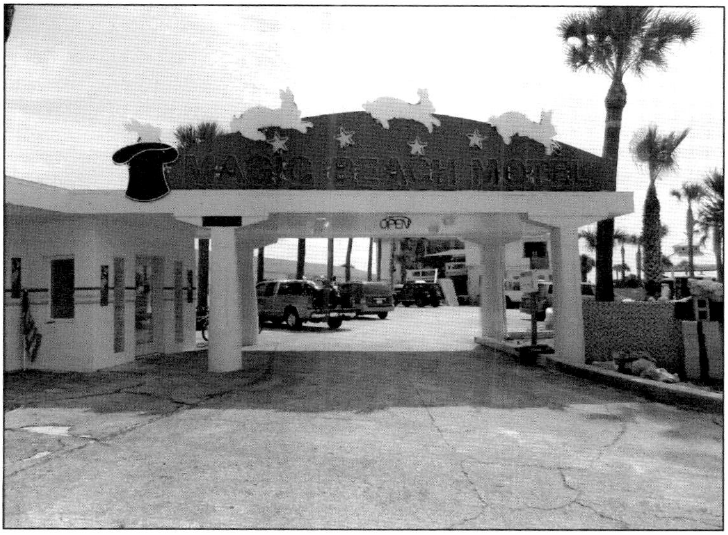

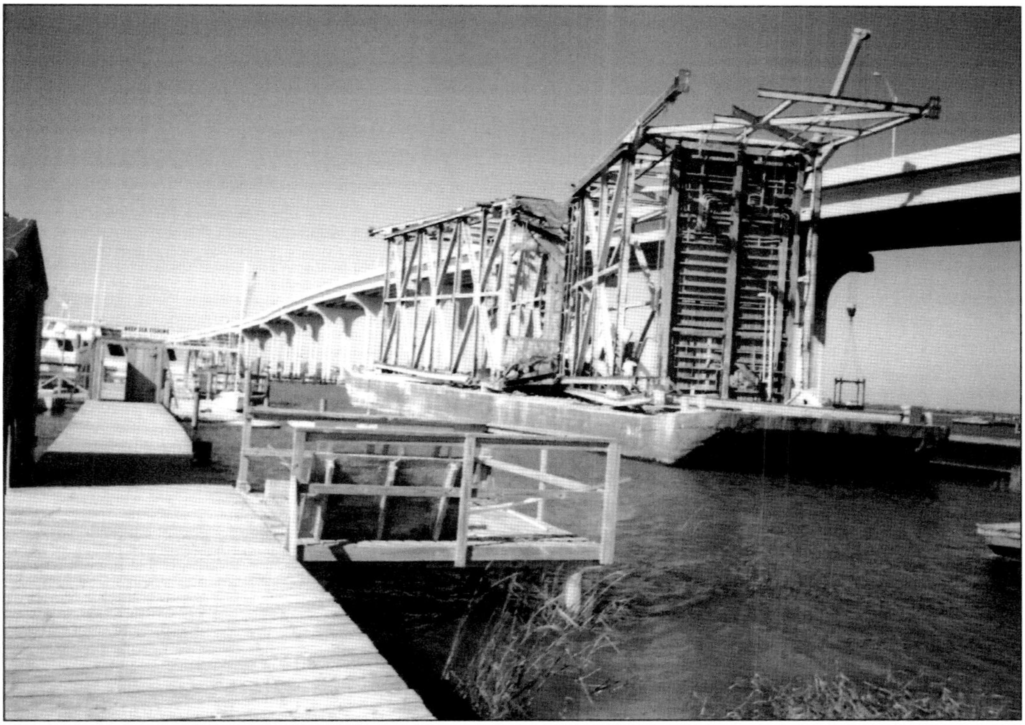

After the Francis E. and Mary Borum Usina Bridge opened in 1995, the old drawbridge was taken down with cranes, placed on barges, and brought onshore to be cut up and recycled. Its service, and that of many bridge tenders, to Vilano and the North Beaches ended. This photograph was taken from the Sea Love Marina dock, operated for many years by Capt. Frank Timmons, his wife, Susan, and their sons. (Courtesy of Sacha Martin.)

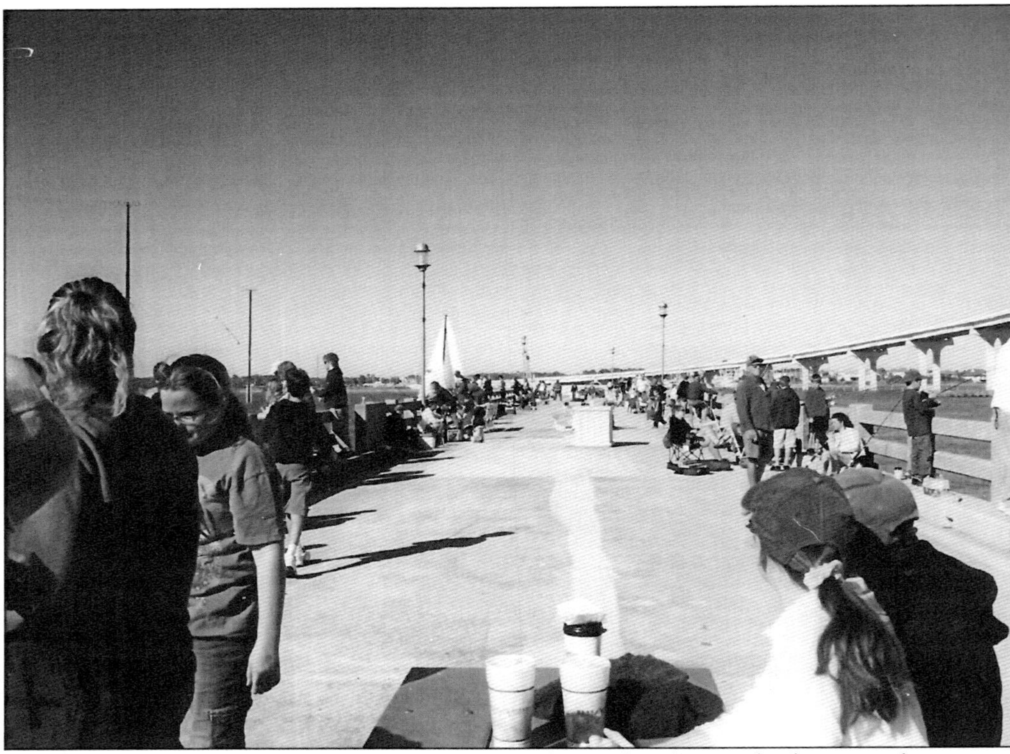

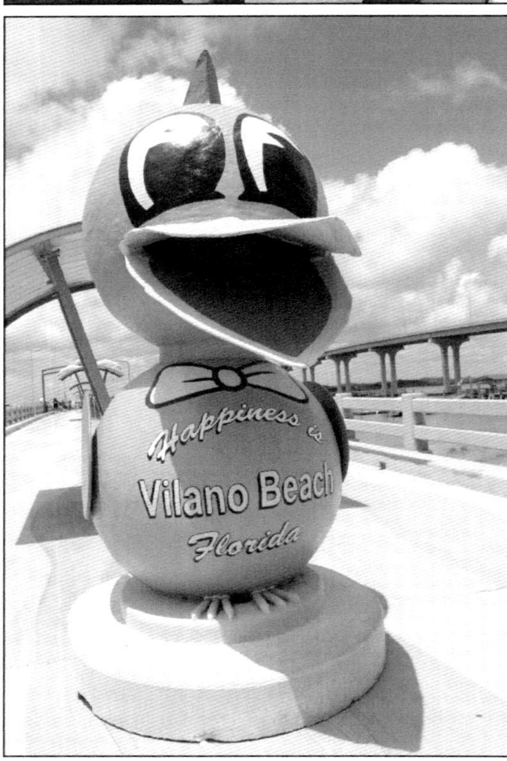

Soon after the new bridge opened, many people began using the east end of the old bridge for fishing and enjoying the view of downtown St. Augustine's skyline across the bay. St. Johns County Recreation Department took over management of the newly named Vilano Beach Public Pier. The pier is now the location of the Vilano Beach Sunset Celebration on the first Saturday of each month. (Courtesy of Sacha Martin.)

This whimsical street art, which was restored in 2013 and named the Bluebird of Happiness, gives visitors to Vilano Beach a fun photo opportunity. Located now at the entrance to the Vilano Pier, this cute bird began life as an orange bird on San Marco Street, beckoning tourists to stop for Florida orange juice. In the 1980s, it welcomed visitors to Newt's Vilano Motel. (Courtesy of Sacha Martin.)

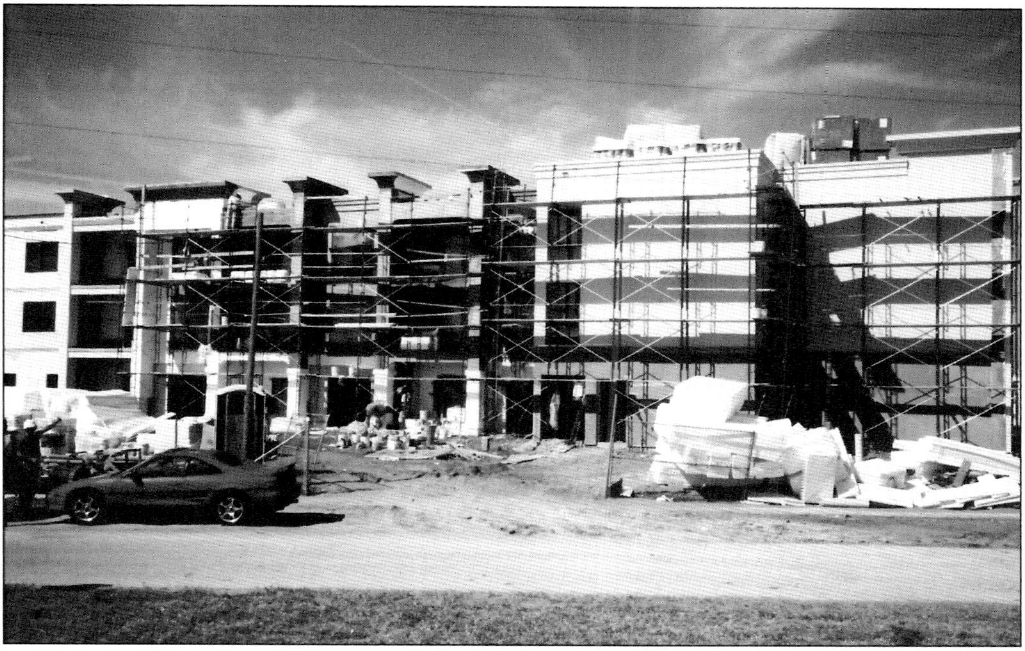

In 2001, the Vilano Beach Hampton Inn opened. Most of the hotel's 94 rooms have an ocean view. Vilano's first franchise hotel, it includes other firsts for area hotels—a two-story lobby, a business center, a meeting room, a fitness center, a bridal suite, and a large pool with hot tub. (Courtesy of Hampton Inn and Suites at Vilano.)

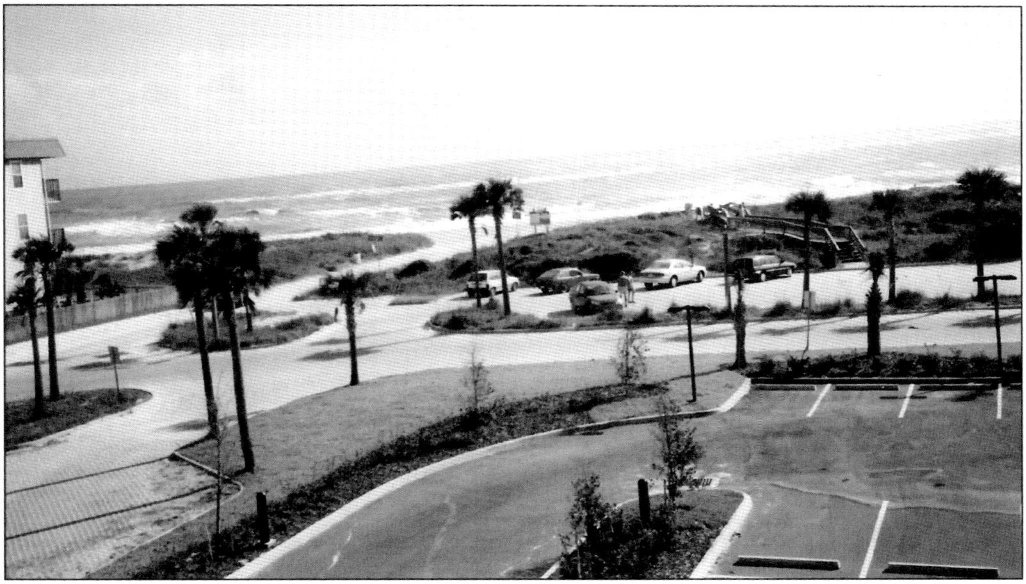

The Vilano Beach Ramp is located at the east end of Vilano Road. This ramp has been used by pedestrians and automobiles for decades. St. Johns County is one of only a few counties in Florida allowing driving on public beaches. The parking lot with cars is now the site of a beach pavilion building providing bathrooms, a water fountain, and outside showers. The beachfront is all public access, with dogs welcomed. (Courtesy of Sacha Martin.)

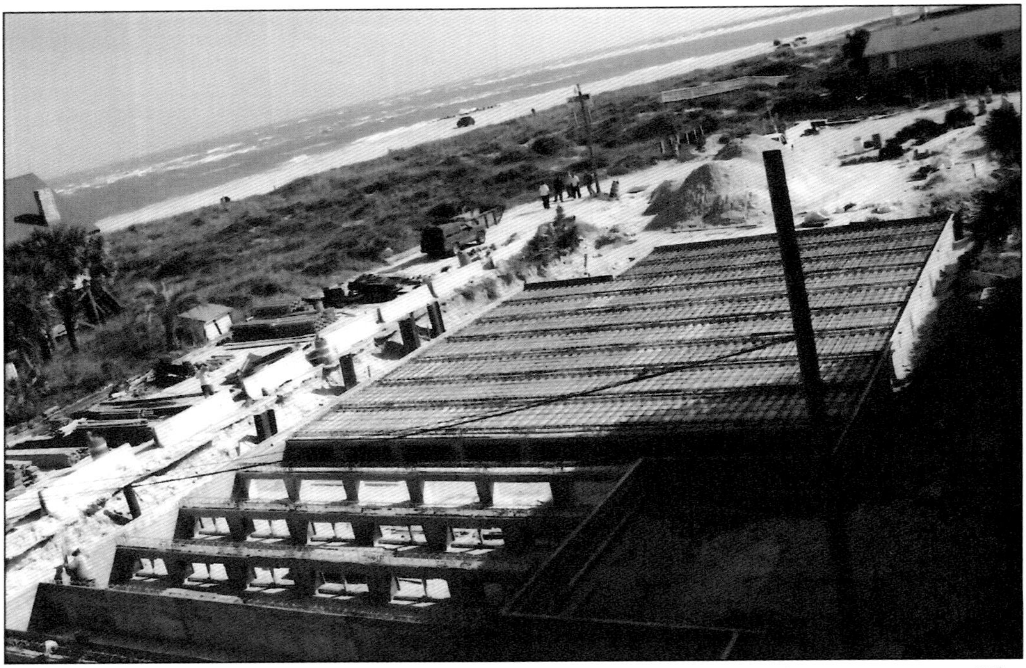

This major infrastructure project in the Vilano Town Center accommodates storm water. The open-bottom caverns allow incoming water to percolate into the soil. The top was paved over for a parking lot. In the distance is the St Augustine Inlet, which allows boats to enter the Intracoastal Waterway. This inlet was cut in the 1930s by the US Army Corps of Engineers. (Courtesy of Sacha Martin.)

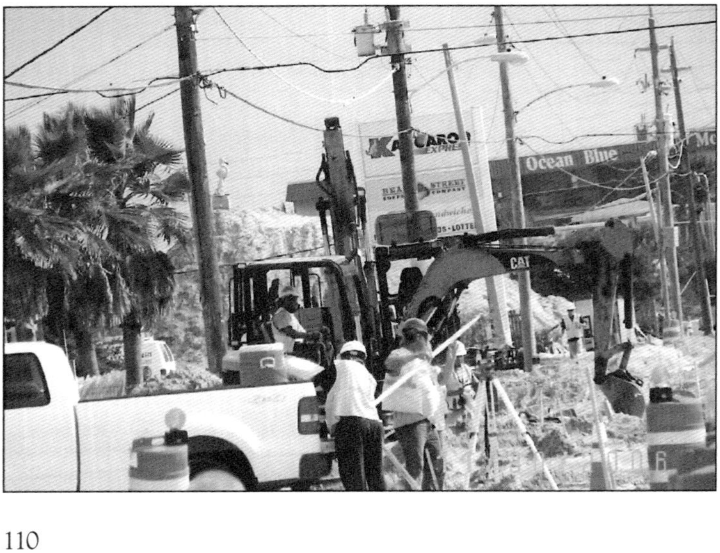

Callaway Contractors' workers are putting the overhead utilities underground, then replacing the surface of Vilano Road. The Kangaroo store is in the distance. It has since been torn down to make way for the top priority in the community, a full-service grocery store. The Ocean Blue Motel in the background is now the St. Augustine Beach House. (Courtesy of Sacha Martin.)

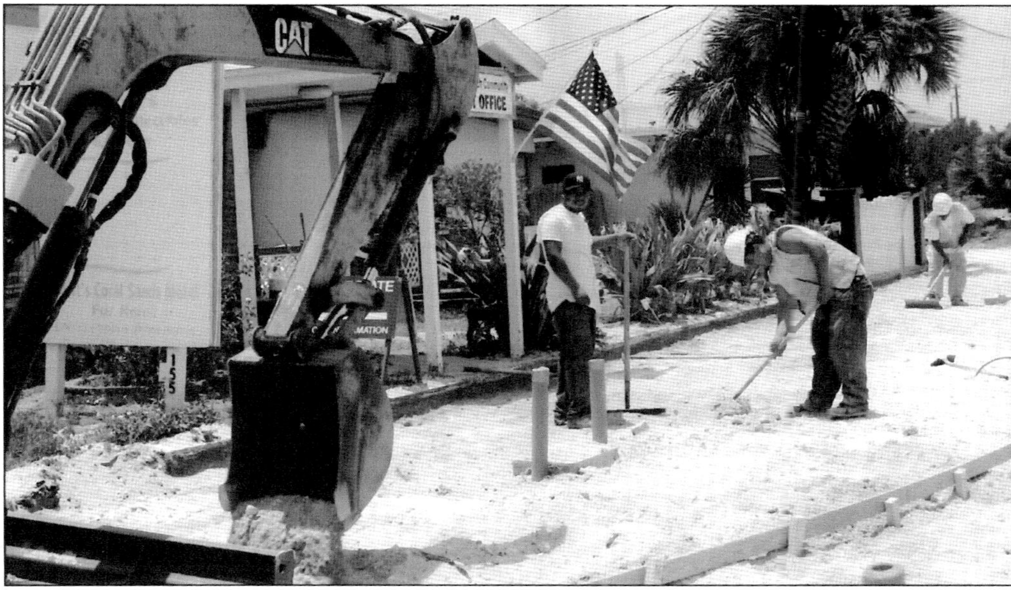

Workers prepare new, wide sidewalks, which will include the blue and green tiles seen today. In the background is the Vilano Beach Post Office, opened in 2006 and run by volunteer Jacqueline Johns. This building at 155 Vilano Road was the last motel built by Newt Haley, who passed away in 1994 in his 90s. The motel is now the Vilano Beach Garden Inn, managed by Dylan Cadwalader. (Courtesy of Sacha Martin.)

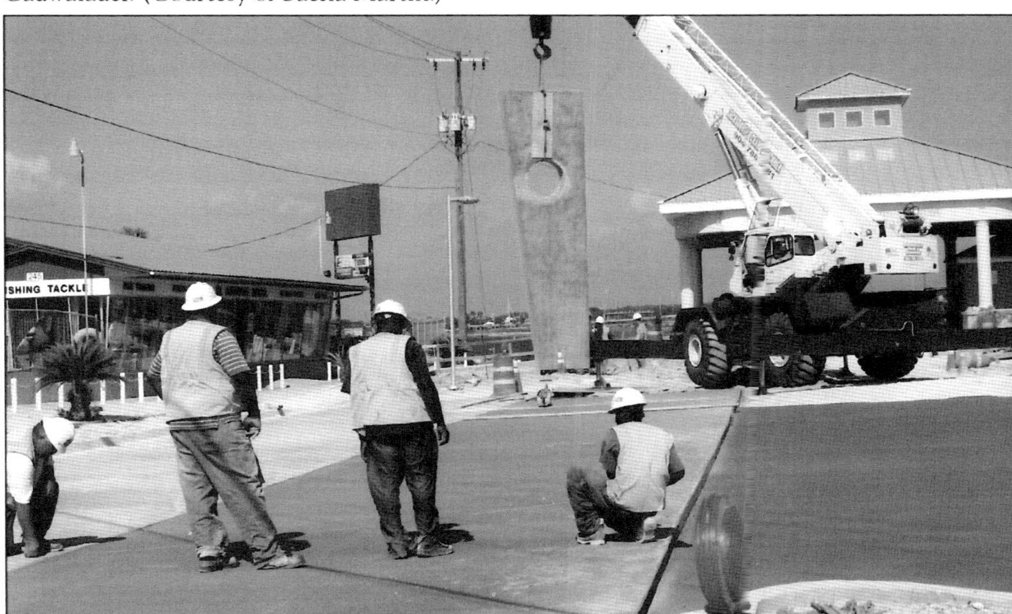

Contractors pave the parking lot at the Vilano Beach Public Pier. This free public parking is for visitors to the pier. The bell tower, shown being set by crane in the distance, has bells that ring on the hour, like courthouse and church bells in other small towns. The Pier Pavilion in the background was built with an earlier grant received by the town center project. (Courtesy of Sacha Martin.)

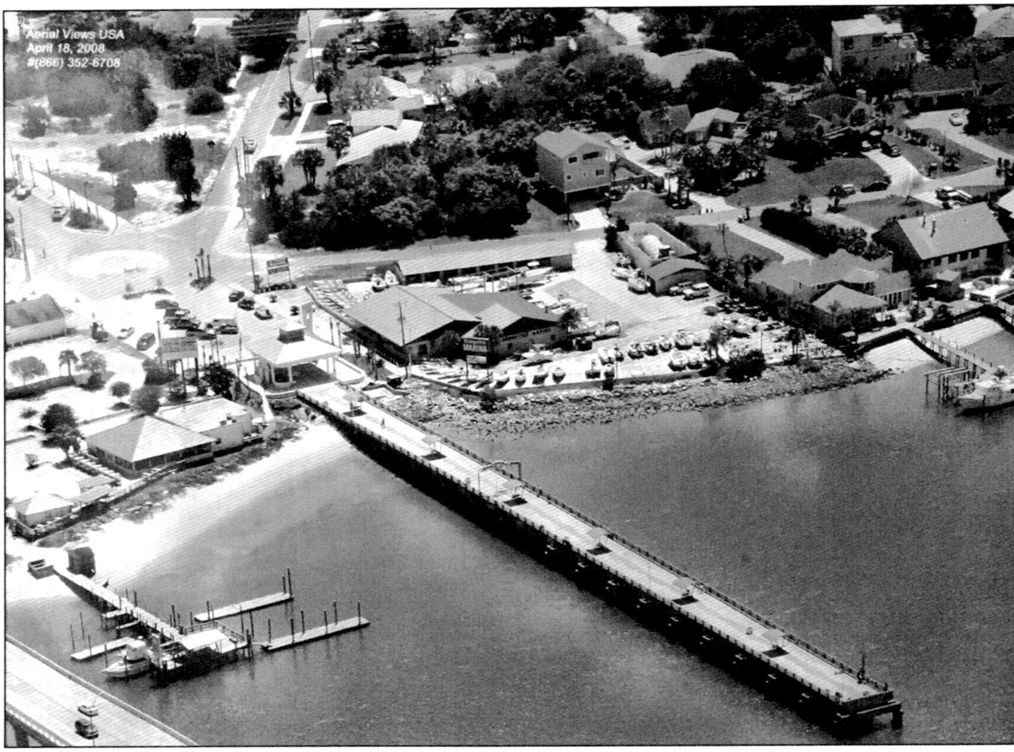

The St Augustine Marina, founded by the Lloyd Small family in the 1950s, remains the oldest continuously operated business in Vilano Beach. The Vilano Bridge was moved north and away from the front of this business in 1995. Now, the Vilano Pier (the east end of the old bridge) brings in customers for the fishing and beach supplies. Local boaters depend on this business to keep their motors running and to purchase new equipment. (Courtesy of Jimmy Beach.)

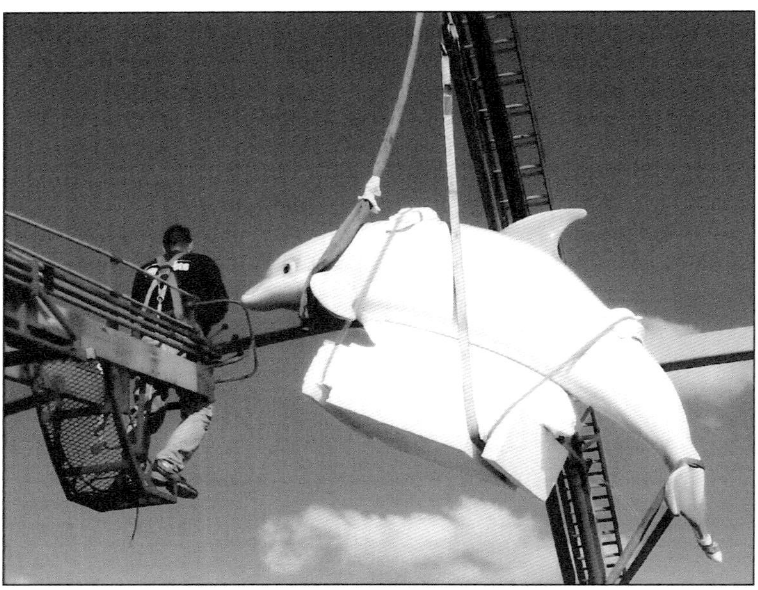

This high-in-the-sky dolphin is being positioned to join two others to form an archway across the Vilano Pier. The pier is the portion of the Vilano drawbridge saved when that 1940s bridge was torn down and replaced by the Vilano Usina Bridge in 1995. This artwork delights all visitors to the pier, who come for events or to stroll on or fish from the pier. (Courtesy of Sacha Martin.)

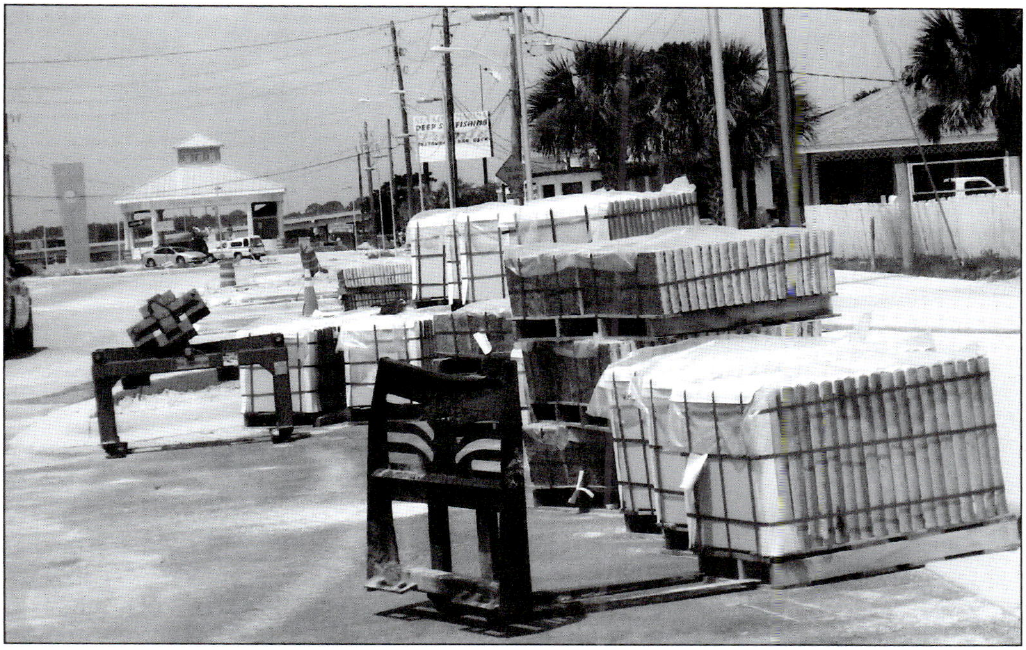

The tiles are delivered for the sidewalks, built to beautify Vilano Main Street. The streetscape's sidewalks are unique in that they are made of blue and green recycled glass that sparkles in the sunlight and enhances the Art Deco town center. The wide sidewalks allow for outdoor seating at restaurants and room for benches for strollers. (Courtesy of Sacha Martin.)

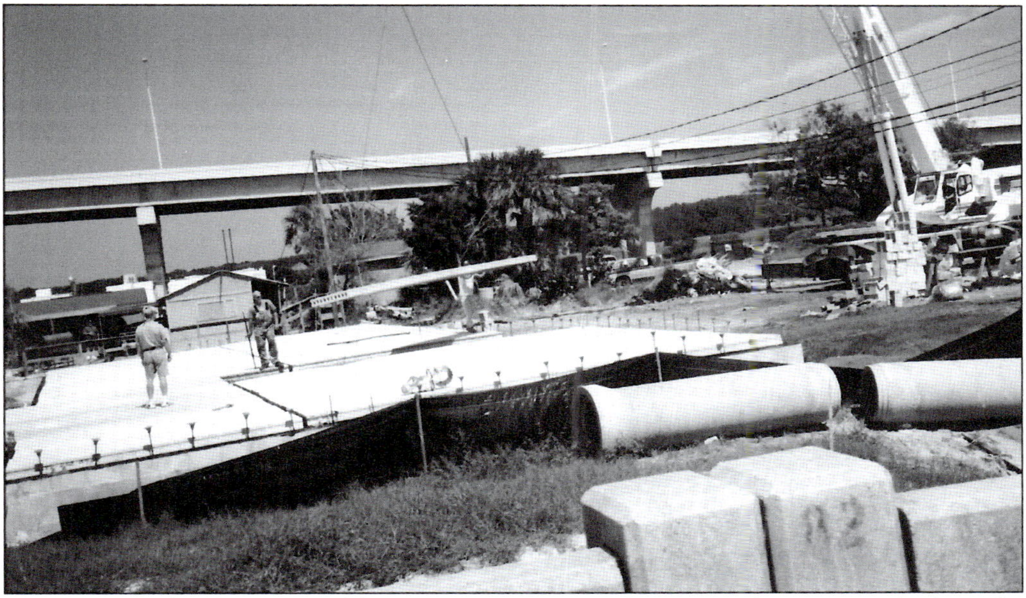

The Timmons family, owners of the Sea Love Marina on the river, had a restaurant built on the property. The tenants who occupied the building over the years brought many hopes with them. It is now Beaches at Vilano. From the riverfront location, customers can enjoy perfect sunsets over the North River. This Vilano Beach Town Center property has approximately 50 dock slips yet to be built. (Courtesy of Sacha Martin.)

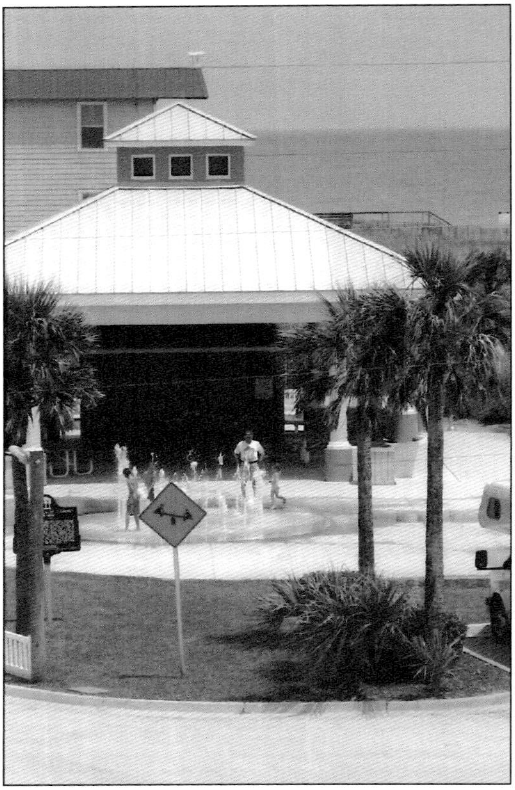

The Vilano Beach Pavilion is the centerpiece of the oceanfront end of the area's main street, Vilano Road. Built to accommodate events, this public venue features an outdoor shower, bathrooms, an interactive fountain, and a covered gathering space. The architecture is a blend of Art Deco and Florida vernacular. Dave Mancino designed this structure and its bookend pavilion at the pier. (Courtesy of Sacha Martin.)

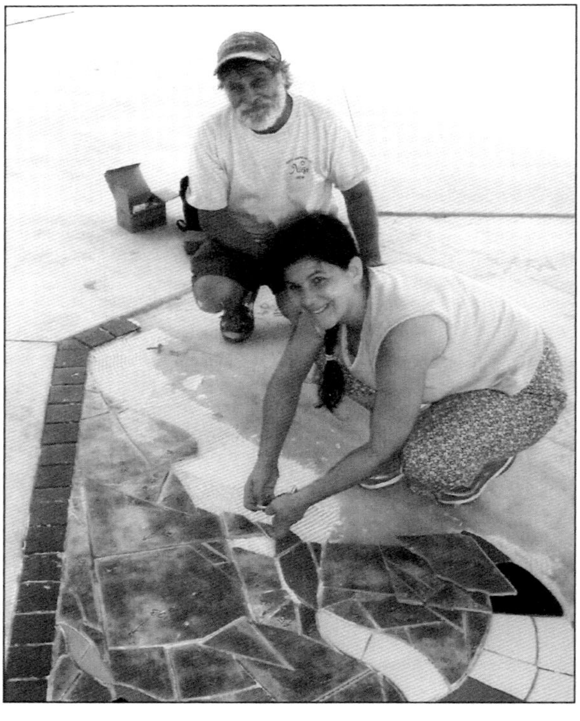

A beautiful tile mosaic is the centerpiece of the oceanfront beach pavilion. Local artists Bob and Theda Bonner created this original artwork depicting recreation and nature at the beach. Its beauty enhances picnics, weddings, and community gatherings, as does the tile mosaic by the Bonners located in the pier pavilion at the west end of Vilano Road, the town's main street. (Courtesy of Sacha Martin.)

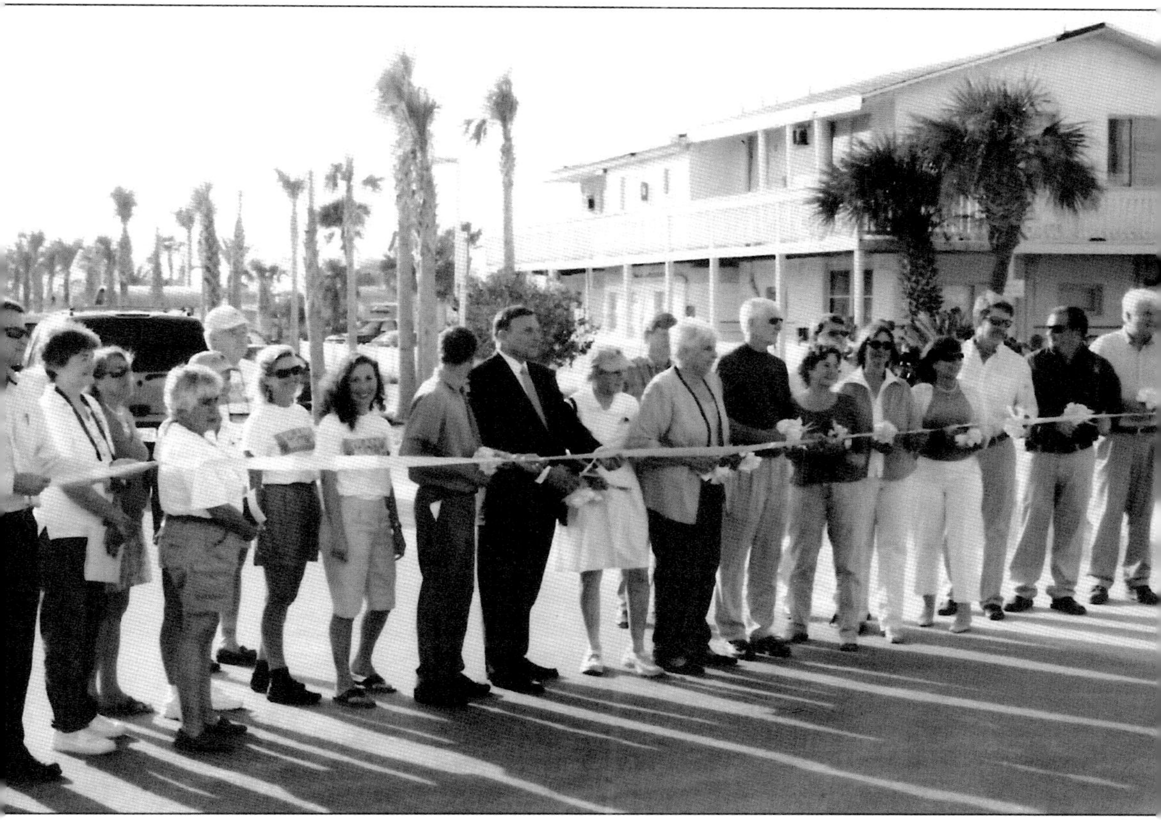

During October 2008, several elected officials, community leaders, county staff members, and contractors met to officially open the Vilano Town Center Streetscape Project. This infrastructure project was planned and designed with years of input by the community. It was funded by a tax-increment financing project by the St. Johns County government that allowed the Publix grocery store and retail to be built. Pictured are (center in suit) Congressman John Mica; (from center to right) Sacha Martin, president of NSIA; Vivian Browning, community leader for the Vilano Beach Town Center Project; Jim Bryant, St. Johns County commissioner; Catalina Usina-Morse, great-granddaughter of the founders of North Beach; Cyndi Stevenson, St. Johns County commissioner; Georgia Katz, St. Johns County planner; Brett Goddard, streetscape architect; Greg Caldwell, St. Johns County project manager for the Town Center Project; Patrick Callaway, Callaway Contracting, builders of the Town Center Project; (from far left to center) Wil Smith, St. Johns County director of recreation and parks; Sallie L. O'Hara, Vilano Beach Main Street Program manager, and other attendees. (Courtesy of Sacha Martin.)

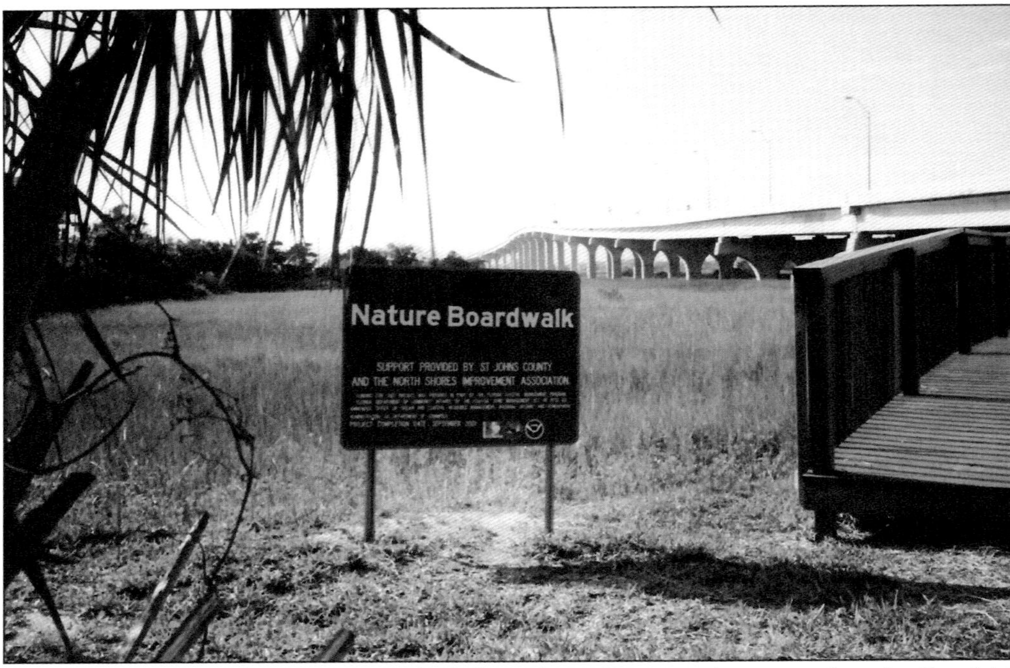

One of the earliest enhancements in the Vilano Town Center is this nature boardwalk, which meanders under the bridge over the marsh. It provides close-up views of nature for walkers and bikers and is enhanced by tactile artwork by Florida School for the Deaf and Blind students. Community, county, and civic contributions, as well as grants, funded the boardwalk, which connects the Surfside neighborhood to the town center. (Courtesy of Sacha Martin.)

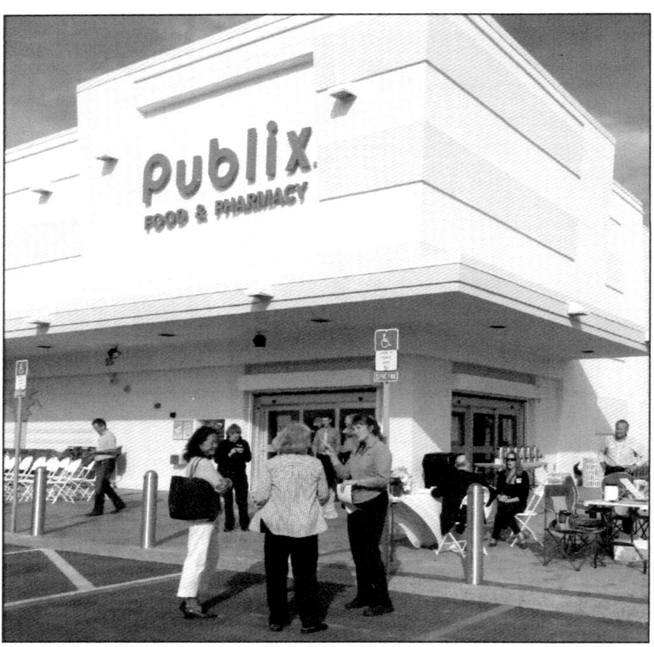

The Vilano Publix opened in January 2012. This grocery store, with pharmacy, was the top priority of the community. This freestanding Art Deco–style building is reminiscent of the original Publix supermarkets. Most of the land was assembled and owned by Kelly and Victoria Smith. Atlantic Land Corporation bought the land and built and owns the development; its principals are Joe Lelonek and Bob Bentz. (Courtesy of Sallie L. O'Hara.)

Seven

NOTABLES

History really emerges through a community's people, whose lives and contributions shape civic and commercial developments.

Who has not heard of Ponce de León and his landing in Florida in 1513? Yet his citing of longitude 30 degrees, 8 minutes north is not well known as being in South Ponte Vedra, only a few miles north of North Beach. Later, Pedro Menendez established a permanent settlement at St. Augustine in 1565; the community celebrates the 450th anniversary in 2015. The Spanish continued to govern Florida until 1764, when a treaty exchanged it for British Cuba.

The British Crown made James Grant governor of St. Augustine, and he was given 1,440 acres where the North and Guana Rivers meet. Grant's Villa Plantation began planting indigo with the use of African slaves. When Governor Grant left in 1771, the villa continued hiring Minorcans to farm it.

Development came in the late 1800s, when Henry Flagler changed St. Augustine with grand hotels and churches. He changed North Beach by promoting the hospitality of the Usina family. He and his wealthy friends patronized Frank Andreu and Kate Usina's oyster shack, which helped finance their businesses. Another wealthy man, August Heckscher, founded Vilano Beach in 1920 and built a famous casino.

Some individuals who had a part to play in World War II affected the coastal community. Victor Rahner Sr. became an air-raid warden. Shorty Rees was a pilot in World War I and operated an airport afterward. Newt Haley, a vacationing soldier, saw the need for tourist accommodations and built motels on the beach, as did Art McGinnis.

Minorcans are known for family unity, and this was displayed in the Usina family, along with their community service, which each generation continues to perpetuate. Another family, the Capos, had similar business ventures and was influential in establishing the character of the neighborhood.

Many communities can point to a celebrity who lived in their area. For Vilano and the North Beaches, it was the author Sinclair Lewis, winner of the 1930 Nobel Prize in Literature. He rented a home at Surfside and found inspiration there writing his novels

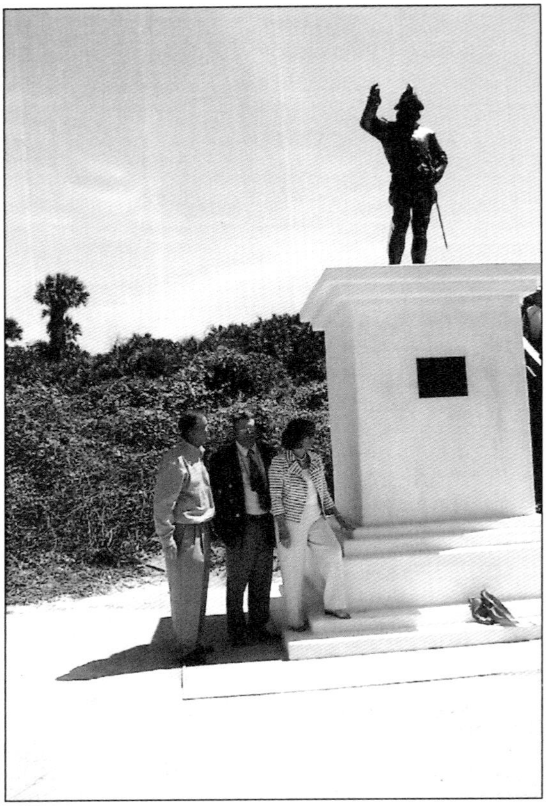

Explorer Juan Ponce de León claimed La Florida for Spain on April 2, 1513. This statue stands where he first landed, at latitude 30 degrees, 8 minutes north, as noted by his navigator in the ship's log. His landing site has been in its original state of natural habitat since that time, now on the northern boundary of the current GTM Research Reserve. (Courtesy of Tom Rahner.)

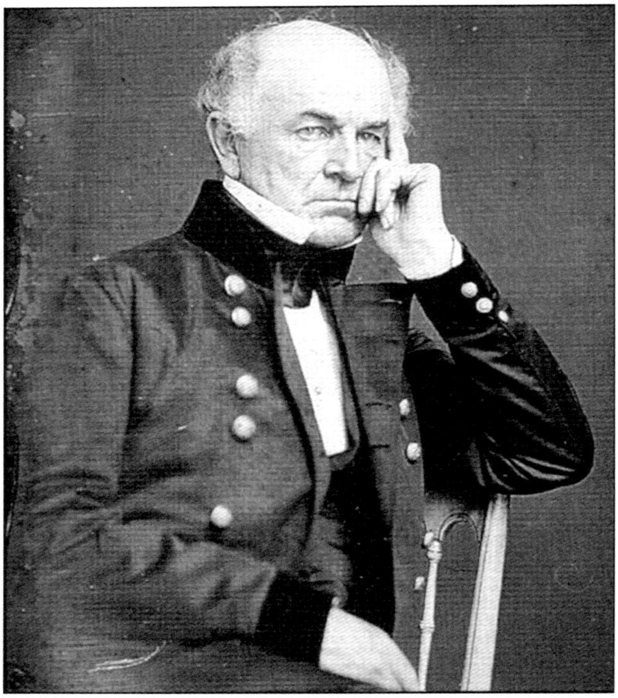

James Grant was the first civil governor of East Florida during the British period, serving from 1764 to 1771. Prior to being assigned as governor, he was an experienced military leader in the colonies. His holdings included acreage northeast of St. Augustine along the Tolomato and Guana Rivers. He was responsible for instigating indigo and rice plantings in Florida with the use of slave and indentured laborers. (Courtesy of Tom Barry.)

Henry Flagler came to St Augustine for his wife's health and was impressed by its history and weather. He built a magnificent hotel for his wealthy New England friends, then a railroad for access. He also built the Memorial Presbyterian Church, which has a mausoleum containing the remains of his wife, daughter, her child, and Flagler himself. Flagler had a plan to change Florida by railroads. (Courtesy of Florida Memory.)

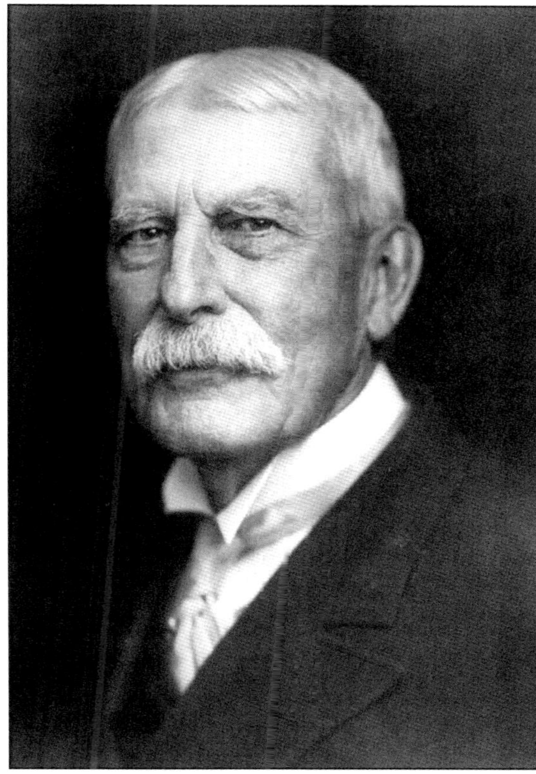

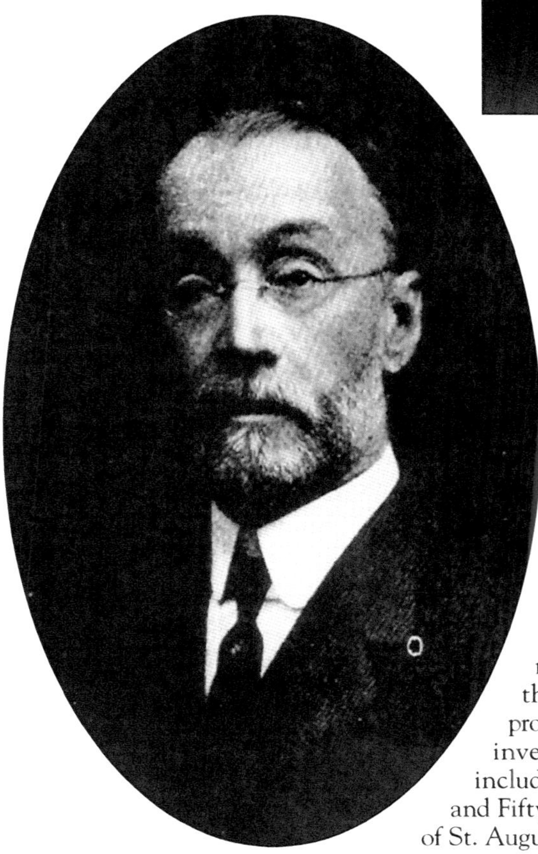

Vilano Beach was developed by the St. Augustine & Atlantic Corporation, headed by August Heckscher. He was the director of many large corporations in America, including the Anahma Realty Corp. As one of the largest property owners in Florida in the 1920s, Heckscher invested in large office buildings in America, including the Hecksher Building at Fifth Avenue and Fifty-seventh Street in New York City. (Courtesy of St. Augustine Historical Society.)

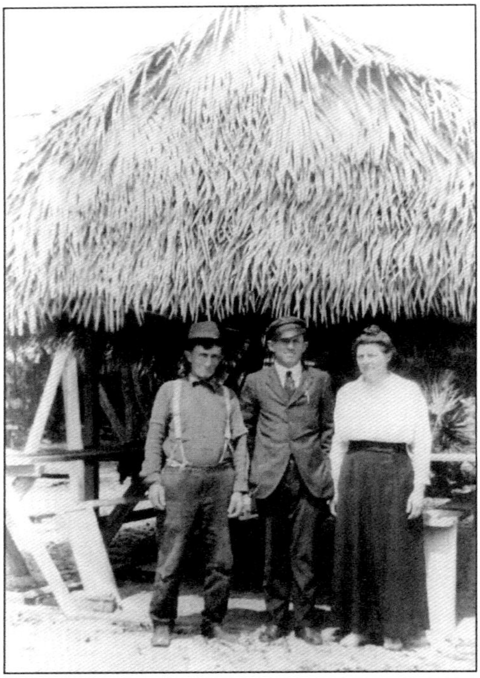

Frank Andreu (left), Francis E. (center), and Catherine Usina settled in North Beach in 1900. In 1909, Frank began running excursions from downtown St. Augustine to North Beach on their boat, *Victory I*. Frank and Kate cooked many an oyster under their palmetto-thatched pavilion at Usina's Beach Oyster Shed while entertaining visitors. Henry Flagler loved to bring his guests there during sailing outings to enjoy the oyster roasts. (Courtesy of Elizabeth and Frank D. Usina.)

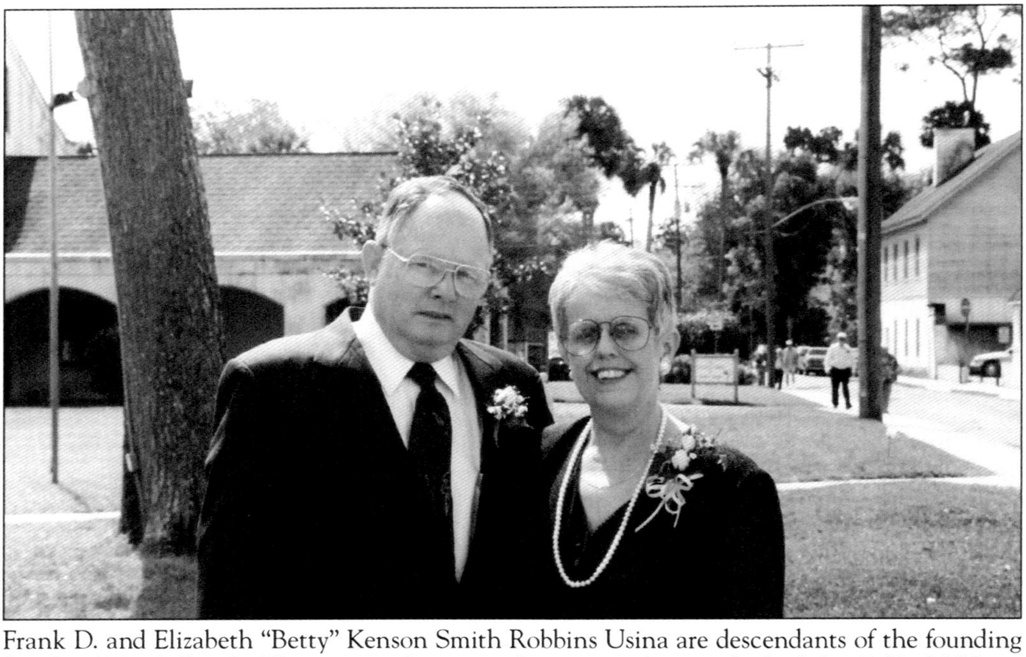

Frank D. and Elizabeth "Betty" Kenson Smith Robbins Usina are descendants of the founding family of North Beach. They currently own and manage, along with the John F. "Jack" Usina family, the North Beach Camp Resort, North Beach Utilities, the *Victory III* tour boat, Aunt Kate's Restaurant, and the Reef Restaurant. Frank and Elizabeth were inducted into the Florida Tourism Hall of Fame in 2003. They have long advocated the importance of nature-based tourism in Florida and have been extremely active in promoting not only this area but the entire state as a tourist destination. (Courtesy of Elizabeth and Frank D. Usina.)

Mary Borum Usina helped her husband, Francis E., develop and improve the Usina enterprises, which had grown with the increasing population. After Francis passed away in 1973, Mary continued her civic work, devoting her time and talents to improving life along the coast. In 1939, she had assisted in starting the North Shores Improvement Association and was a key player responsible for establishment of the neighborhood firehouse and community center in later years. In 1995, the Florida Department of Transportation named the new bridge after Francis E. and Mary Borum Usina. Just as the bridge spans the North River to connect the St. Augustine mainland with Vilano and North Beach, so, too, the Usinas were strong links between the communities. For half a century, Captain Usina skippered the sightseeing vessel *Victory II*. (Both, courtesy of Elizabeth and Frank D. Usina.)

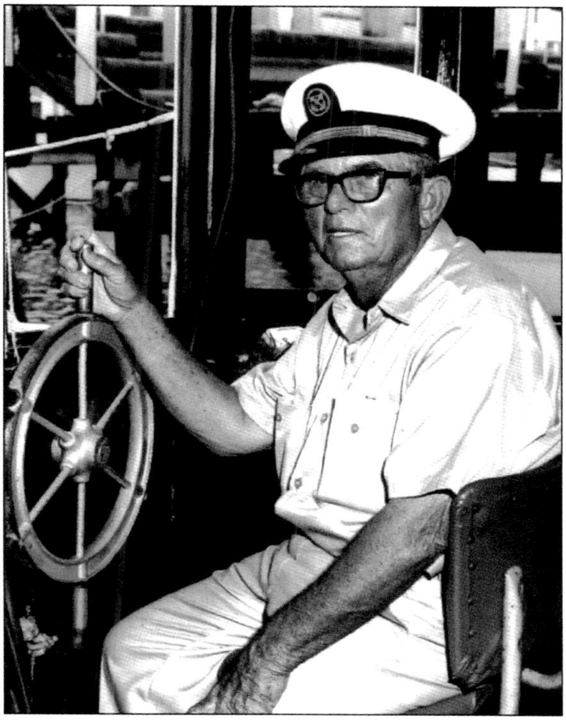

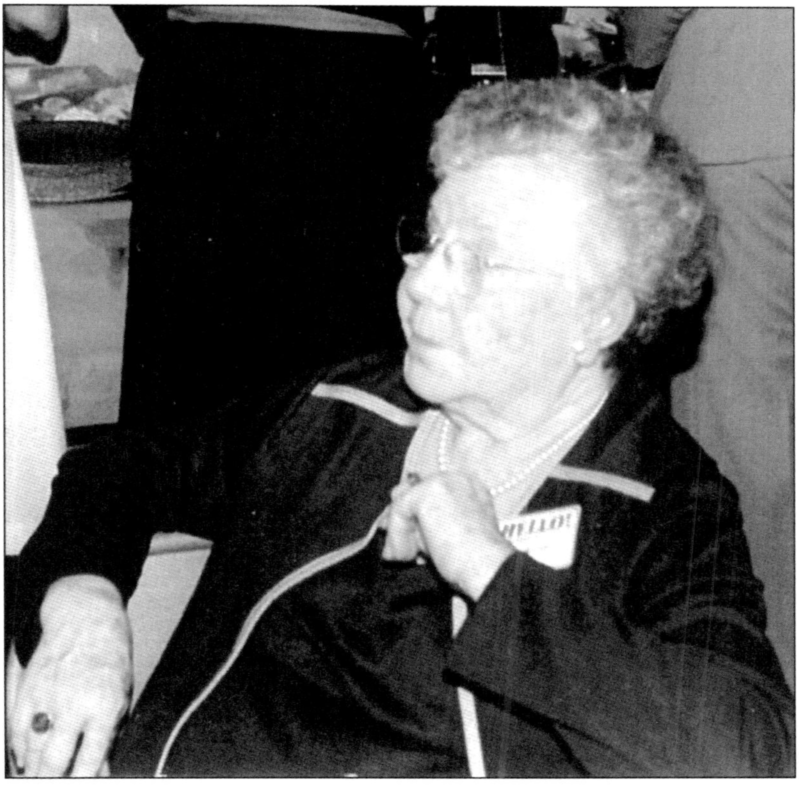

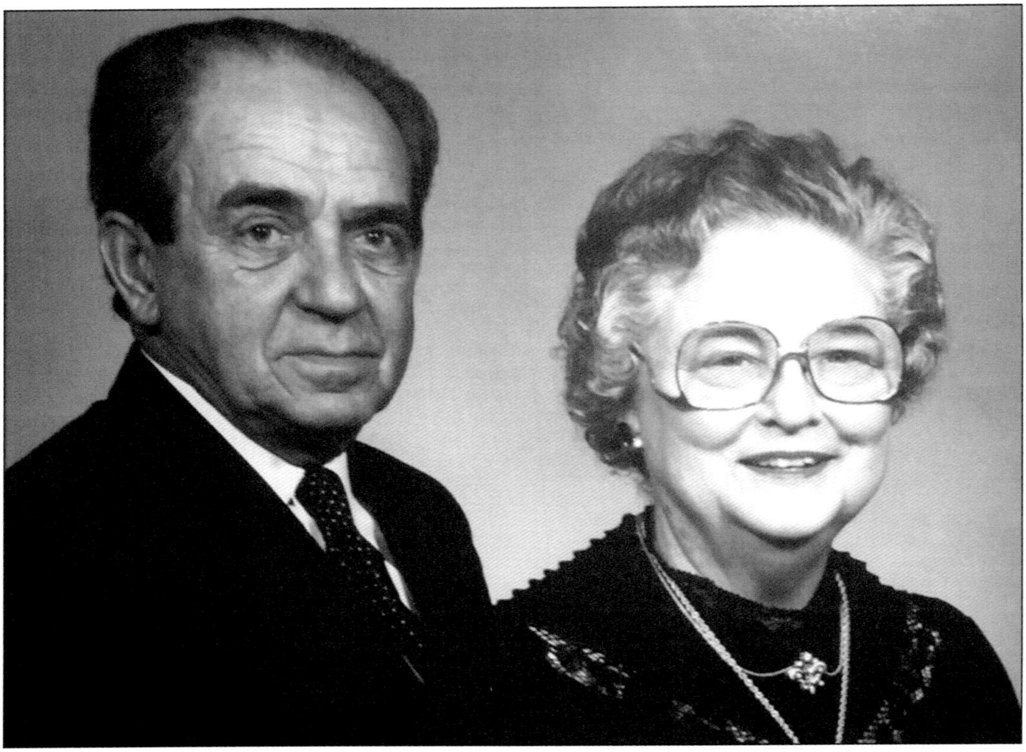

Lloyd Small and his wife, Kate, opened a small family business, the St. Augustine Marina, in the 1950s. It remains the oldest continuously operated business in Vilano Beach. It is now run by son-in-law Jimmy Beach and his wife, Marilyn Small Beach, and their son Brian. Pier visitors enjoy buying fishing equipment from the marina because of its proximity to the pier. (Courtesy of Jimmy Beach.)

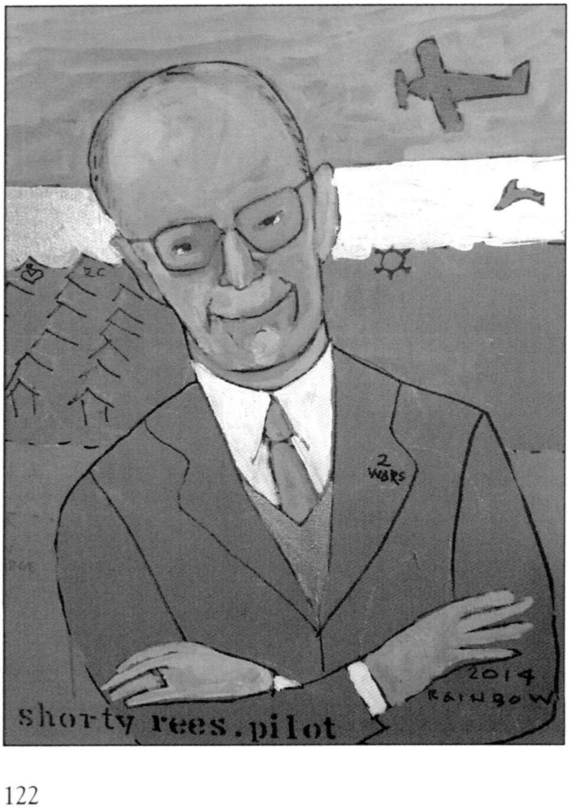

Lucius Gibson "Shorty" Rees learned to fly during World War I and later did barnstorming out west with Charles Lindbergh as a parachute jumper. In the 1920s, he actively promoted the need for an airport. In 1928, Rees and his partner J.W. Richbourg set up St. Augustine Flying Enterprises, Inc., to operate the airport. Rees later developed property in Surfside. (Courtesy of Sue "Rainbow" Williams.)

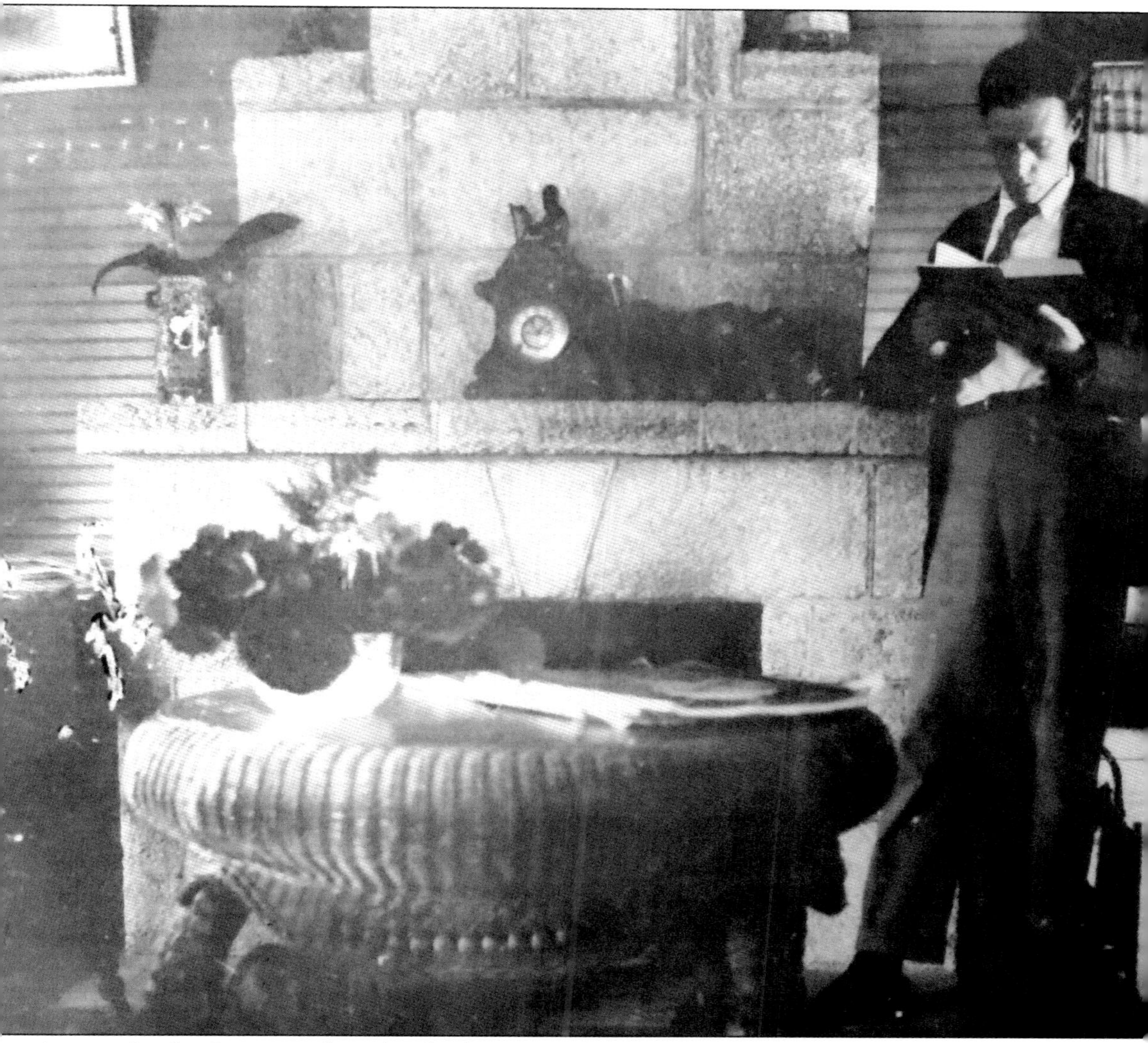

A young Sinclair Lewis stands reading by the coquina fireplace inside the cottage in Surfside Beach. His novel *Main Street*, published a few years afterward, made him a millionaire; however, success was hard on his marriage. He turned down the 1926 Pulitzer Prize (Novel) for *Arrowsmith*. In 1930, he became the first American writer to win the Nobel Prize in Literature, after the publication of his novel *Dodsworth*. In the early 1920s, he and his first wife, Grace, spent a good amount of time at 177 Surfside Avenue. The house was actually built in 1885, according to Florida Master File records, and the current occupants have preserved its 1920s appearance. The porch affords a view across the bay to the city. Fame, fortune, and divorce gradually separated Lewis from his intermittent stays in Florida. He died in Italy in 1951 after a notable career as an accomplished author. (Courtesy of Dawn Jones.)

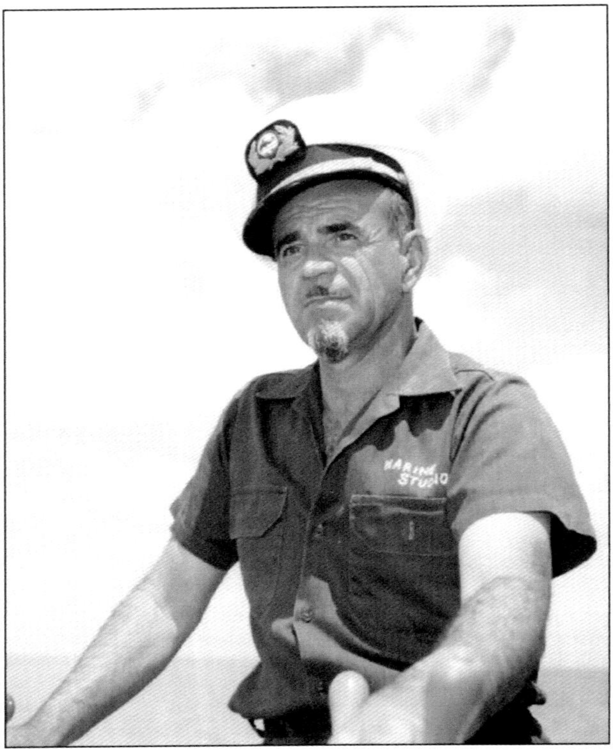

Ronnie Capo, the captain of *Porpoise III*, worked at Marine Studios and later Marineland of Florida. He lived in Surfside and was related to the founder of the Surfside community. An avid fisherman, Capo gained so much respect that an artificial environmental reef was named in his honor. (Courtesy of the St. Augustine Historical Society.)

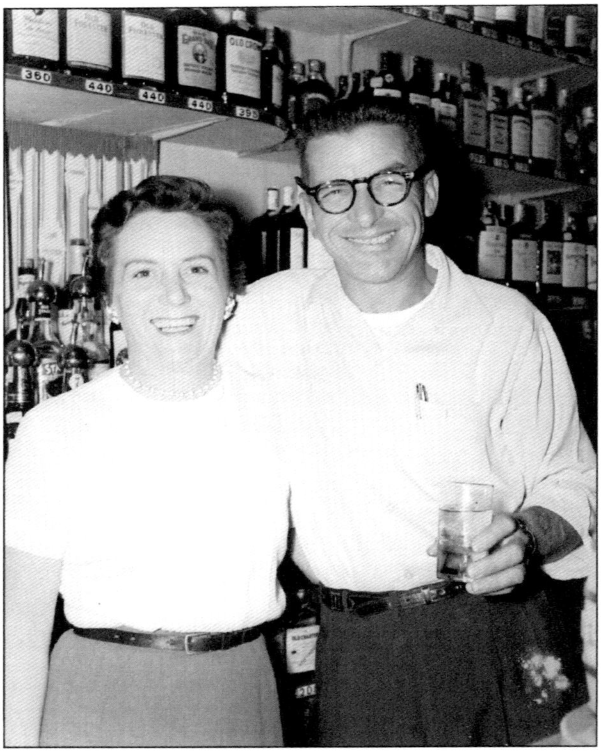

Mr. and Mrs. Heckendorf were longtime residents and business owners operating the Lazy Sands on Vilano Road. It was a small building with a bar and grill. A most important feature was the drive-thru for purchasing bottles. Lazy Sands changed hands several times, as did its featured menus. (Courtesy of Bo Pitts.)

Art McGinnis was a businessman who moved to Vilano Beach and bought the Vilano Beach Motel, now the Magic Beach Motel. He opened a fried chicken restaurant at 80 Vilano Road and, on the same property, built the Ocean Blue I Motel—now the Saint Augustine Beach House—closer to the oceanfront. He built his motels with a modular design. An additional Ocean Blue II, later built nearby, is now the OceanView Lodge. (Courtesy of Susan Burke.)

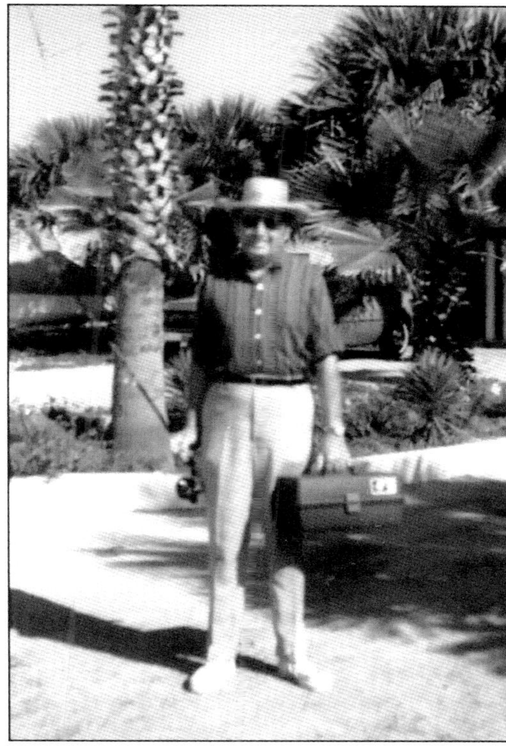

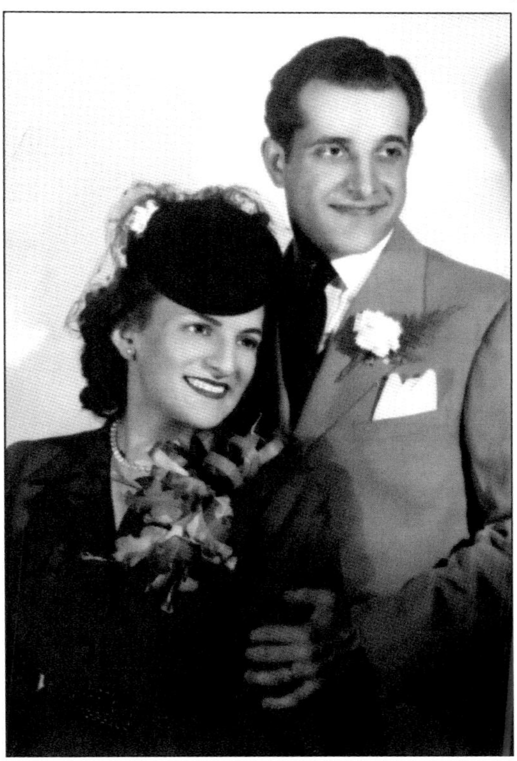

For decades, beginning in 1958, Frances and Sam Barrancotto Sr. owned and operated Barrancotto's Roma Restaurant on Vilano Road. Locals loved it, and others came from far and wide to enjoy their delicious Italian meals. It was truly run by the family, including all four of the Barrancotto children. Several restaurants followed at this location, but the Barrancotto family still owns the Art Deco building. (Courtesy of Cynthia Barrancotto.)

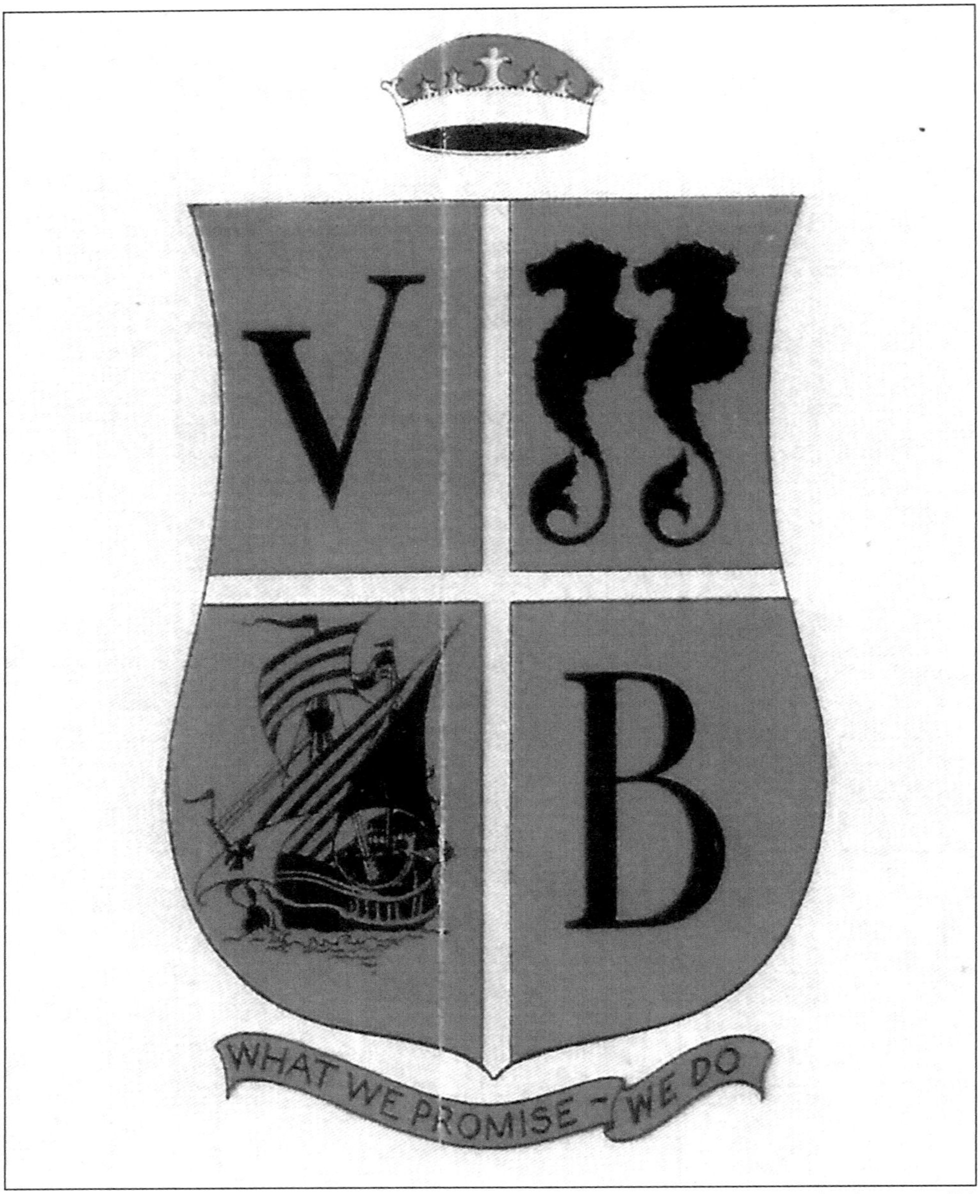

The motto on the back cover of the 1927 sales brochure used by August Heckscher to sell land in the new Vilano Beach development epitomizes the spirit of the notables who developed the communities along the coastal barrier island near historic St. Augustine: "What we promise, we do." The resulting efforts over decades created a sustainable, mixed-use town center in Vilano Beach surrounded by residential developments supporting its viability. The 23-acre town center design remains historically intact as originally platted. Heckscher's dream did not materialize as planned, but it did not deter subsequent community-builders in shaping a quality of life envied by others, replete with culture, heritage, nature, recreation, and scenery in a small beach-town community. The fourth and most modern bridge to Vilano, completed in 1995, bypassed the town center and created challenges for remaining businesses. The coastal communities found ways to rebound, demonstrating their resiliency. (Courtesy of the St. Augustine Historical Society.)

Index

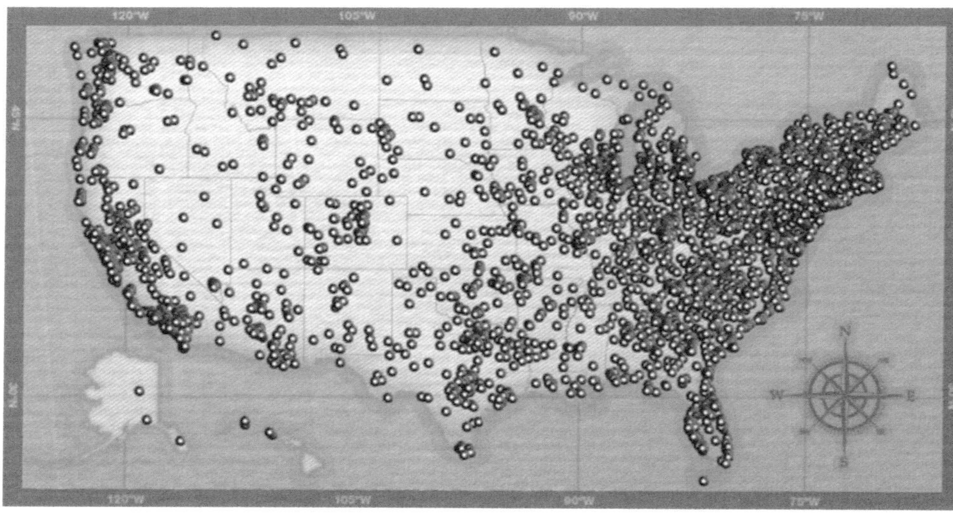